----- A FAMILIAR WILDERNESS -----

A FAMILIAR WILDERNESS

Searching for Home on Daniel Boone's Road

S. J. DAHLMAN

THE UNIVERSITY OF TENNESSEE PRESS ⫶ KNOXVILLE

Excerpts from "Notes on 'The Natural Man'" from A COMPANION
FOR OWLS by Maurice Manning. Copyright © 2004 by Maurice Manning.
Reprinted by permission of Houghton Mifflin Harcourt
Publishing Company. All rights reserved.

Library of Congress Cataloging-in-Publication Data
Names: Dahlman, S. J. (Simon James), author.
Title: A familiar wilderness: searching for home on
Daniel Boone's road / S.J. Dahlman.
Description: First edition. | Knoxville: The University of
Tennessee Press, [2019] | Includes bibliographical references and index. |
Identifiers: LCCN 2018034890 (print) | LCCN 2018050924 (ebook) |
ISBN 9781621904793 (Kindle) | ISBN 9781621904809 (pdf) |
ISBN 9781621904786 (pbk.)
Subjects: LCSH: Wilderness Road—Description and travel. |
Boone, Daniel, 1734–1820. | Pioneers—Kentucky—Biography. |
Dahlman, S. J. (Simon James)—Travel—Wilderness Road. | Wilderness Road—
History. | Appalachian Region, Southern—Description and travel. |
Appalachian Region, Southern—History, Local.
Classification: LCC F454 (ebook) | LCC F454 .D34 2019 (print) | DDC 917.504—dc23
LC record available at https://lccn.loc.gov/2018034890

To Stacy, Sarah, and Rachael
And in memory of Melissa

Contents

Illustrations

Author's Note

This book is work of nonfiction—a snapshot of people and places found along a particular route through southern Appalachia. Most of the meetings happened randomly, usually the result of providence or good timing.

Everyone described in this book is a real person; there are no composite or invented characters. Actual names appear whenever possible. First names alone are occasionally used to guard an individual's privacy or at the person's request. A few individuals were given pseudonyms when particularly sensitive personal details were involved. Pseudonyms are indicated in the endnotes.

To document my hike, I carried a digital voice recorder, several notebooks, a camera, and a journal. Besides taking notes during most interviews, I used the voice recorder to recount conversations, capture descriptions of places and people, make ongoing observations, and immediately record my reflections on every conversation. Each evening during the journey I wrote a summary of the day's events and conversations and transcribed my voice recordings.

After finishing the trip, I collated and typed my notes, arranged them chronologically, and added relevant historical accounts, current data, and additional interviews. Those digital documents formed the initial draft of the manuscript. All the materials from the hike—voice recordings, notebooks, and journals—have been saved for reference and verification.

While this work has benefited from numerous people and sources, I am responsible for its content. I regret any factual errors. Observations and opinions not otherwise attributed are mine alone and do not reflect the views of any institution or organization.

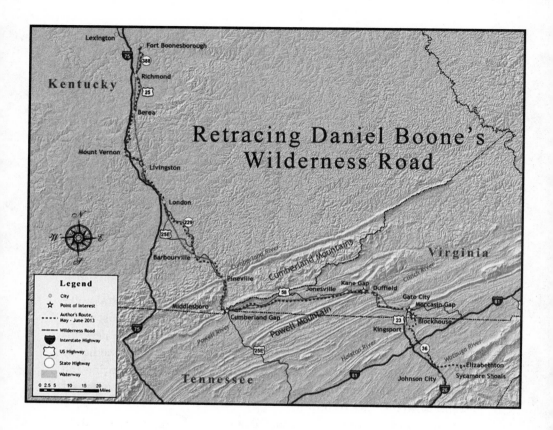

PROLOGUE

On a warm and humid day in June 2012, I decided to meet Daniel
Boone.

At the time I thought I was only stretching my legs during a long
drive back from Ohio to my adopted home in East Tennessee. I
stopped to take a short hike at the Cumberland Gap, that iconic notch
in the long green wall of the Appalachian Mountains where Virginia,
Tennessee, and Kentucky meet. But when I paused for a moment in the
lowest part of the gap, the "saddle," the ground seemed almost electric.
On the edge of the broad, dusty trail stood one of those wooden National
Park signposts: *Wilderness Road.* Without warning, my memory flew
back to the 1960s—to third-grade history lessons in New York City's
P.S. 116, to the televised hokum of "Daniel Boone" with clean-cut Fess
Parker, his coonskin cap, and a bouncy theme song: *Daniel Boone was a
man, yes, a biiggg man....* Then my mind ricocheted to another image
of Boone, this one from a vaguely familiar nineteenth-century painting,
with the man dressed in buckskin and a broad-brim hat, looking every
inch a man of nobility. Moses-like, he was leading a group of settlers over
the very piece of ground where I stood.

After more than two centuries, someone believed that this piece of
ground and the road crossing it were still worth signposting, and I wondered why.

The Wilderness Road was America's first major migratory route to
the West, a rough path traced from nascent settlements in what is now

1

northeastern Tennessee, through the Cumberland Gap, and into the "wilderness" of central Kentucky. It thus extended a network of roads from Pennsylvania, Virginia, and North Carolina, where white settlers lapped up tales of plentiful and fertile lands in the West, just beyond the Allegheny Mountains. A group of land speculators, wanting to take advantage of this growing thirst, purchased millions of acres from Native Americans and commissioned a road that would enable settlers to travel to these newly acquired backcountry lands. The plan worked: More than a quarter-million men, women, and children walked—*walked*—the route in less than thirty years. They, in turn, planted new settlements that became springboards for further expansion. Before Kansas, Colorado, and California, there was Kentucky. Before the Oregon Trail, the National Road, the Erie Canal, or the railroads—before the United States, for that matter—there was the Wilderness Road.

The route crossed the Cumberland Gap simply because it was the most sensible path through the mountains. Hardy explorers and hunters, including Boone, had traversed the green, undulating Appalachian wall at various points for years, but settlers migrating in large groups and hauling their worldly possessions could not follow suit. The gap offered a natural break in the mountains, a pass used for centuries by the Cherokee and Shawnee, who themselves had followed the buffalo and elk.

Before Lewis and Clark, Davy Crockett, or Kit Carson, there was Daniel Boone. Hired by those land speculators, Boone led a crew of thirty "ax-men" and two women (including one of his daughters) to carve a "trace" in 1775. In less than a month, they crossed almost three hundred miles of forests, rivers, canebrakes, and mountains, marking a thin trail that formed the basis of what came to be known as the Wilderness Road. Thus, it was obvious that if I were to explore this route, then Boone—whose legend sprang up in his lifetime as quick as dandelions—would somehow surely be my companion.

He and the other explorers and settlers came west seeking new homes, better lives, and bigger fortunes. They set out with few grandiose plans and even fewer ideals. Thanks to their journals and stories handed down through generations, we know that many of these travelers were spurred to venture into the wilderness because things were missing or amiss where they were, or because life had grown too crowded, messy, or predictable. So, they decided to shake off old dust—or flee from old debts—in hopes that different ground would prove more bountiful. They left their settled and sure places to start fresh in the then-wilderness of Kentucky, propelled by a desire to create new homelands on their own terms. Few of these pioneers thought about making history, but they were doing just that, forming the first massive migration over the mountains, opening up the West, and anticipating the later push to the Pacific. They formed the first wave of commoners in history who could stake a piece of land and call it their own.

Some settlers stopped along the way. Maybe they found a plot of land they liked, or maybe they got tired of traveling, or maybe tragedy halted them in their tracks. (Attacks by Native Americans were common and often devastating.) Supply stations grew into settlements, and settlements grew into towns. Within a generation, the old hunting grounds were transformed into farms and timberland, the buffalo were gone, the Native Americans were scattered, and the next frontier was already opening. Another generation after that, railroads and coal would alter the landscape again, figuratively *and* literally.

The Wilderness Road comprises a bundle of routes that flowed from the east, funneling through the Cumberland Gap into southeastern Kentucky. Boone's 1775 trace skewed north to the Bluegrass region, bound for Fort Boonesborough. Two decades after he blazed that trail, the newborn commonwealth of Kentucky commissioned improvements to accommodate the growing waves of westbound migrants. Officially dubbed the Wilderness Road, that route took a more westerly course, terminating at the Falls of the Ohio, to meet the increasing river traffic at what is now Louisville.

Today, the Wilderness Road is not a single identifiable road, not uniformly labeled like the National Road or Route 66. The early routes have been overwritten, rendered redundant, or simply bypassed by federal and state highways, county roads, and country lanes, and the early route's parts are identified only intermittently. Local historical groups are still working to piece together long-abandoned portions of Boone's trace. The road's dismemberment was due, ironically, to its own usefulness. It was once so well traveled that it served as the basis of a road network that eventually linked parts of Tennessee, Virginia, Kentucky, North Carolina, Ohio, Indiana, Illinois, and Missouri. In the subsequent two hundred forty years, pioneers and politicians widened it, paved it, flattened it, added spurs to it, sectioned it, straightened it, and occasionally rerouted it. For decades, US Highway 25 ran through the Cumberland Gap.

A handful of small museums and parks pay homage to the early road, and local historical associations do what they can to draw attention to it and to Boone's earlier trace. Sections are indicated approximately and sporadically by informational signs and historical markers, which some drivers just might notice as they barrel past farms, towns, stores, abandoned coal mines, colleges, offices, and other components of modern rural America.

I was often one of those drivers. But contemplating the Wilderness Road on that June day, I wondered if it not only was an artifact of America's past but also a lens for viewing the present. If the Wilderness Road was foundational to the nation's growth and identity—and it was—then it was no stretch to think that its development might reveal something about the whole country. For better or for worse, the decisions and deeds of the early settlers were repeated elsewhere, often on a larger scale. The familiar litanies of American expansion—of putting down roots, of creating commerce, of cooperating and competing, of caring for the land and wrecking it, of occasionally dealing decently with Native Americans and often dealing terribly with them, of exploring and exploiting—all had antecedents on this early route into the West. The pioneers' choices and actions revealed their priorities, values, and hopes, all of which have trickled down through two-and-a-half centuries of American expansion. The Wilderness Road was a harbinger for the America to come. There was more to the old road than a national park sign.

Sweating, I climbed back into my black Suzuki station wagon and headed for home.

Home. The word can seem like a moving target among people who grow up with several addresses or bounce from place to place in adulthood. Even after living in East Tennessee for thirteen years—I had lived nowhere else as long—I still felt a subcutaneous detachment and a nagging restlessness. I blamed the feeling on something akin to a midlife crisis, but leaving the Cumberland Gap on that day in 2012, I wondered if there might be a connection between my sense of rootlessness and the attraction I felt to the story of the Wilderness Road. Other than geography, I did not share much in common with the people who traveled it—except perhaps a vague yearning for home. Their story of moving to unknown territory for the very purpose of creating new homes resonated with me. I wondered if the Wilderness Road might teach me about my adopted home and offer a few lessons in simply settling down.

When my family and I moved to East Tennessee in 1999 so I could teach journalism at the small university where my wife, Melissa, and I had graduated almost twenty years earlier, I hoped to find a home there. My childhood was split between New York City and Tampa, with about a dozen scattered addresses in less than nine years and a few brief sojourns elsewhere. After we married in 1980, Melissa and I lived in other far-flung places including England, Ohio, and Colorado. I carried few regrets—we and our two daughters, Sarah and Rachael, had lived in beautiful places—but by the time we moved to Tennessee I was nursing an ache for home. "I want to point to a spot on a map and call it home, once and for all," I remember saying. I hoped this change would finally let me do that.

I loved the land—the green, smoky, stone-strewn mountains with their streams and hollers and grassy balds. I loved the music with hints of Ireland and Scotland singing in dulcimers and fiddles and mandolins. I loved the tangy dialect that regularly blurs the difference between one- and two-syllable words, sometimes hints at Elizabethan English, and occasionally needs a translator. ("There's a fire on the hill" can come out "Thar's a far on the he-uhl.") Most of the time, I loved the people and their easygoing ways of friendship and kinship and hospitality, how they take matters of faith seriously, and how they aim to balance a certain amount of slow going with a strong work ethic.

And, indeed, this was home; we had put down roots. Even so, I had never been sure how deep they sank. Despite our community, our friends, and our mortgage, I still felt like an outsider and wondered if I always would in you're-not-from-around-here-are-you Appalachia. Occasionally I wasn't even sure I cared, especially in those fleeting moments when any affection I felt for the place boiled away as I encountered folks who fueled the stereotypes of superstitious, poorly educated, clannish, bloody-minded people. I caught myself occasionally thinking that I would always be a Yankee and a big-city guy at heart and that I didn't belong here. In those spells I wanted to move far, far away. *Go north, middle-aged man*, I would tell myself.

In my more objective moments, however, I knew that I myself was guilty of holding the place at arm's length, unable or unwilling to embrace my would-be home. And that ambivalence, I decided, was a second good reason to walk the old Wilderness Road: Not just as a matter of journalistic curiosity, but out of a desire to know the place and the people in a way I hadn't before. This trip might offer a chance not only to grasp this place but to embrace it. Maybe presence would make my heart grow fonder.

So, I decided to explore the route, or what remained of it, to see for myself how and why it had grown up from a wilderness in the way that it had and to meet the people who lived there. In short, I wanted to get to know the place, and the best way to accomplish that was to travel it as the earliest travelers had, on foot.

At the same time, my family and I were facing another, more critical journey: Melissa was dying from Huntington's disease, an incurable neurological disorder caused by a genetic glitch that had gradually incapacitated her. (Probably the most famous HD casualty was Woody Guthrie.) For about fifteen years, starting in her late thirties, our family had watched and cared for Melissa as her cognition, memory, emotional affect, and motor control faded. By 2012 we sensed that she was closer to the end than to the beginning.

Melissa died peacefully the day after Thanksgiving in 2012, and her memorial service took place the following Monday. It was standing room only in our old church building, which seated just over two hundred people. Every positive word that might fit such an occasion applied: uplifting, poignant, celebratory, respectful, life affirming, comforting, loving, and hopeful with St. Paul's promise about "the redemption of our bodies" and creation being set free from "its bondage to decay." And it was wrenching—not because of the grief we felt, but because of the collision of grief and liberation. Melissa was free from her disease, thankfully at rest—but so was I, a thought that filled me with relief and shame for feeling so eager for what lay ahead. Sitting in the front pew, flanked by my two adult daughters and surrounded by family and friends, I let sadness have its day, expecting it not to last long. We had grieved much in advance.

The next afternoon—a chilly, gray, damp Tuesday—I felt the urge to be on my own, and so I made the easy forty-five-minute drive to a quiet, narrow valley in southwestern Virginia, to the historical starting point of the Wilderness Road.

Thousands of people had begun their journeys here, the site of a small defensive wooden blockhouse built in 1774 or 1775, where pioneers and would-be settlers gathered to start their westward migration to "Kentucke." The blockhouse was long gone, but a stone-clad marker now stood in its place.

On the way I stopped at the funeral home to drop off the small casket that would hold Melissa's ashes. A group of men in our church had crafted the breadbox-sized container from ceramic tile and wood three years earlier, and it had sat empty in a corner of my home office ever since, waiting for this moment.

Then the drive took me through Kingsport and across the state line to Carter's Valley Road, a two-lane blacktop threaded between forested ridges and dotted with old farmhouses, barns, and incongruous split-levels. Where a narrow gravel lane met Carter's Valley Road, a sign pointed to the Wilderness Road Shooting and Conservation Club. A hundred yards up the lane stood the squat, gray monument, just over four feet tall. I parked in the narrow lay-by next to the monument, which was separated from a cow pasture by a barbed-wire fence.

A car occasionally announced itself with a hiss of tires on wet blacktop, but otherwise the only sounds were the cattle's random mooing, birds chirping in the distance, and the faint gurgle of a creek hidden beyond the pasture.

I had stood there about fifteen minutes, taking photos and making notes, when my phone rang. (*Cell phone service out here? Impressive.*) It was David, the funeral-home director. He wanted to know how the memorial service went (very well), whether I thought the obituary turned out all right in Sunday's paper (it did), and to let me know that I could pick up my wife's ashes later that afternoon or tomorrow but there was no hurry.

"And who made the box?" he asked. "It's beautiful."

I told him church friends had done it for us.

"Well, it's really nice. Really well made, and I love the details."

I thanked him and said I'd pass on the compliment.

"By the way," he then asked, "did you ever work at First Christian Church in Erwin?"

I had, as one in a series of college and seminary students who worked part-time as youth ministers at the church in the small Tennessee railroad town. I was there for a couple of years, I told David, from 1979 to 1981.

"Then I knew you," he said. "That was my home church. You lived in that old house next to the church, right?"

I had. That drafty parsonage. Melissa's and my first home. A slideshow flashed through my brain: Tall ceilings and dull, off-white paneling. Our fretting at burst water pipes and then laughing when we realized the water ran harmlessly through gaps in the floorboards to the dirt-floor basement. Sitting around the huge dining room table with college friends who were glad to escape the dining hall. Lounging in the living room for Bible studies and pizza with high school kids, some only a few years younger than we were. Melissa's early-morning newspaper route. Melissa and I, married a matter of months, lying in bed as trains boomed and crashed as they coupled in the railroad yard behind our house.

David's voice brought me back to Carter's Valley. "I was in your youth group. I graduated from high school in 1985."

I tried to picture him as he might have looked thirty-plus years ago but drew only blanks.

"I'm sorry," I told him, feeling awkward. "I can't remember you. I guess I wasn't a very good minister."

"Nah, that's not it," he said brightly. "I knew I'd seen you somewhere before, but I couldn't place you until my mother said something to me about your wife. I didn't really remember you either."

After we finished talking, I stared at the phone in my hand and laughed. I seemed to be more connected to this place than I realized. Melissa and I started our marriage in Erwin, where I was her future funeral director's youth minister. And here he was, calling me as I stood at the start of the Wilderness Road, on the brink of a different kind of wilderness.

Six months later, almost to the day, I started tracing Daniel Boone's path. This is the story of that twenty-four-day, nearly-three-hundred-mile journey.

----1----

FALSE START

From pioneer trails to the latest car commercial, the "open road"
has continually been perceived as a mythic space of possibility.
In the vast United States, and in our vaster imaginations,
the road offers new horizons to an individual liberated from the
confines of home and society. . . . [But] mobility is not a method
of freeing oneself from space, society, or identity but
instead the opposite—a mode of engagement.

—ANN BRIGHAM

T he sky was hung with gray scalloped clouds tinged with old-copper green, and rain lashed the pavement on Bristol Highway. It was almost six o'clock on a Wednesday afternoon in May. I watched the storm from inside a small fire station perched on the edge of a park in northern Johnson City: sheltered, filled with chicken and rice, waiting for my older daughter to arrive, and wondering if, at the end of my first day of walking, I had already failed.

Sarah was coming to take me home for the night. After more than seven hours and almost thirteen miles on foot, I was still in my adopted hometown in northeast Tennessee. That fact alone wasn't a surprise. My original plan for that night was to camp in a friend's backyard, just two miles from where I had stopped to sit out the day's latest, largest, and longest thunderstorm. The two firefighters on duty had invited me inside and even fed me dinner. By then it became obvious that to walk those last couple of miles on a narrow, curving road with dusk falling on the storm-darkened day would be something like playing Russian roulette. (*Would the first car come around a bend a bit too fast and send me to eternity, or might it be the sixth pickup truck?*) By the time I thought to

9

ask the firemen, Jeff and Michael, if I could just pitch my little tent behind their station for the night, I was already sitting in my own kitchen, as I had that morning, except now my feet were soaking in an Epsom salt bath and I was second-guessing myself.

The day had begun brightly. The midmorning air on May 22, 2013, already felt warm when Sarah and I arrived at Sycamore Shoals State Historical Park in her silver Honda Civic, with my pack and trekking poles tucked in its small trunk. The park, located on the western edge of Elizabethton (pronounced with the stress on "beth"), was a familiar place, only six miles from our front door and the site of many casual walks and a few picnics when my daughters were teenagers. More recently, I had come to run the two-mile gravel path that loops along the Watauga River. Under the shade of mature maple, oak, and sycamore trees, locals come to exercise their dogs and push babies in strollers.

A publicist from the college where I teach arrived a few minutes after Sarah and me, soon joined by a photographer from the town's newspaper. I pulled on my pack and my beige wide-brim hat and followed their directions: *pose on the concrete deck behind the visitor center . . . walk toward the photographer . . . let's go out to the historical markers by the road.* The attention pleased me for a few minutes, but soon impatience tugged me toward the road. (*Let's get moving.*) Finally, the photos were finished, and a few minutes past ten, I hitched on my pack for real.

Sarah walked with me past the picnic tables and out the park entrance, passing the markers where I'd posed minutes earlier. Treading in the grass shoulder a few feet from the humming four-lane traffic of the US Highway 321 bypass, her thin leather sandals looked flimsy next to my black-and-blue hiking shoes. She and I had already covered the logistical bases, so we just chatted, occasionally dropping in some version of "It'll be great" or "I'm proud of you" for each other's benefit. It was true, though: I could see by the glint in her blue eyes that she understood this wasn't how most fifty-four-year-old dads spent their summers, and she appreciated what she saw as her father's audacity. My pride in her welled up as we walked because she had so obviously grown into a mature, responsible young woman. I felt comfortable leaving the things of my life in her hands for three or four weeks—or longer if things went badly.

After a quarter-mile we stopped in front of an Applebee's restaurant, hugged, and said goodbye, both of us holding back tears. My vision blurred for a moment as I started walking east and she turned back toward the park. I felt ridiculous, knowing that I would never be isolated or in true wilderness, never more than three hours' drive from either her or her sister, Rachael, who lived in Lexington, Kentucky. Even so, the weight of sudden solitude felt heavy.

A local chain of drive-through restaurants, Pal's, is known for its teeth-achingly sweet iced tea, "frenchie fries," small, turquoise buildings topped by statues of giant hot dogs, and bite-sized slices of advice on the marquees. "Dare to dream," the Elizabethton restaurant urged passersby. It seemed fitting. "Okay, I will," I said aloud. Wisps of cirrus clouds floated directly overhead. Mounds of cumulus clouds were rising in the southern sky.

Geographically speaking, Sycamore Shoals is not on the Wilderness Road, but in a more historical sense it is precisely where the route began, a piece in the frame of a historical jigsaw puzzle. An interpretive marker at the park recalls that this was where the Watauga Association was formed in 1772, where three hundred Cherokee warriors put Fort Watauga under siege in 1776—partly as a fight for their lands and partly as an aid to the British—and where nine hundred settlers mustered in 1780 to hike to South Carolina and fight the British.

It is also, as the marker states, where the Transylvania Purchase was signed in 1775, the largest private real estate deal in American history and the impetus for Daniel Boone's mission and the road that followed: "Judge Richard Henderson, a North Carolinian, formed a stock company in 1774 to found a new colony, Transylvania. Henderson persuaded the Cherokee chiefs, led by Little Carpenter, to sell his company 20,000,000 acres" between the Kentucky and Cumberland rivers, land that today makes up enormous chunks of present-day Kentucky and Tennessee.

Someone had scratched the Plexiglas cover of the marker, trying to obliterate the word "persuaded." Apparently not everyone appreciates euphemism.

Sycamore Shoals is a small state park: seventy-five acres fronting the Watauga River, which winds sixty miles down from the Blue Ridge

Mountains in North Carolina into Tennessee before emptying into the
Holston River, which flows to the Tennessee River, which in turn meanders across the state to join the great Mississippi. The park, opened
in 1975 to mark the bicentennial of Henderson's big land deal, includes
a visitor center with a high-tech interactive historical exhibit and gift
shop, a replica of a stockade fort, and an amphitheater where the state's
official outdoor drama, *Liberty!*, is performed each summer with an enthusiasm that only amateurs can bring. A life-sized bronze statue of a
man in frontier garb stands in front of the visitor center, aiming a long
rifle skyward, ready to bring down either a fleeing bird or a levitating
redcoat. The re-created frontier fort stands behind the visitor center,
across a field laced with curving paved paths. Its timber stockade walls,
enclosing almost an acre, are laid out in an irregular shape, its corners
marked with two-story blockhouses. The fort serves as the focal point
and all-around headquarters for a variety of events throughout the year,
from historic reenactments and cultural festivals to cross-country races.

Beyond the facsimile fort runs the Watauga River, which is less than
a quarter-mile wide at that point and relatively shallow, though not as
shallow as it was before the Tennessee Valley Authority's (TVA) Watauga
Dam went online in 1949. The Cherokee forded the river here for centuries before white settlers arrived in the late 1700s. The sandbars that
appeared when the water was low were the "Watauga breaks," just upstream from the shoals that gave the place its name. After heavy rains
or when the TVA releases water from the dam, those shoals boil into
impressive rapids. Hills rise almost immediately from the opposite bank.

From the park, the town of Elizabethton gradually builds eastward
toward the old town center. A city pool is next-door neighbor to the park,
then a small hospital and a medical office building. Beyond that, a massive derelict factory molders in a grassy field, the dark remains of the
twentieth-century rayon industry, visible from the main road. The highway has evolved into a typical rural Southern bypass: short strip malls;
chain restaurants including Fatz, Taco Bell, Burger King, Subway, and
Applebee's; Wal-Mart; Lowe's; a discount grocery store; and the high
school, an enormous, almost–windowless brick box with a parking lot
that could contain a dozen frontier forts. Churches point heavenward
every two or three blocks. In the heart of the old town, incorporated
1790, two miles from Sycamore Shoals, at least a half-dozen antique
stores and a few locally owned eateries stand at the ready, including a

tiny, authentic, and entirely unexpected Korean restaurant. The brick façade and high cupola of the Carter County Courthouse dominate one end of the town, standing next to a three-story-tall white obelisk war memorial. Nearby, the town's most famous landmark—a wooden covered bridge, painted white and now limited to walkers—spans the Doe River. The far end of downtown is defined by another four-lane highway and a wall of mountains.

A state parks brochure claims that Sycamore Shoals is "perhaps the most historically significant site in Tennessee"—an audacious claim in a state that stretches from the Blue Ridge Mountains to the Mississippi River and boasts dozens of Civil War battle sites, the homes of three presidents, the official birthplace of country music (Bristol, that is—not Nashville), the Oak Ridge National Laboratory complex, and Memphis. Even so, it's hard to argue with a sign at the Elizabethton city limit that bluntly claims that this is "Where Tennessee Began." It might also claim, with only minor exaggeration, that this was where the American West began.

The place can certainly boast a fine historical pedigree. The Cherokee nation, which at its height embraced more than 120,000 square miles in eight present-day southern states, valued this location long before any white man laid eyes on it. Sycamore Shoals was a popular rendezvous for these wide-ranging people, who would come to its relatively flat ground and set up a temporary town to trade and talk for weeks or months.

By 1772 about ninety white families had settled around the region, scattered between the Blue Ridge Mountains to the south and east and the Holston River to the north. "The Wataugans" were barred from owning any land by the monumental treaty signed in 1763 that concluded the Seven Years' War, a provision that helped pacify the Native Americans with a promise of limited incursion by the English, and, conveniently, let the British Crown forbid people from making side deals with the Indians. But the treaty said nothing about settlers leasing land, and in 1772 they met the Cherokee at Sycamore Shoals to sign a ten-year agreement. At the same time, they voted to create their own local government, the Watauga Association, even though the region was a part of North Carolina. Predating the American Declaration of Independence by four years, this association was the first independent, democratically elected government in America. According to that parks brochure, it was "Where Liberty Began!" According to the British Crown, it was illegal.

By 1775, a few farms and one or two mills dotted the area within a two- or three-mile radius. By 1776, one farm was integrated into a small stockade as a defense against Cherokee raids. In 1780, almost a thousand colonial militiamen mustered at Sycamore Shoals to march into the Carolinas and meet the British army. The so-called Overmountain Men, settlers who lived on the frontier "over the mountains," walked east over the Blue Ridge Mountains, traveled more than two hundred miles in twelve days, and won a decisive battle at Kings Mountain in South Carolina. (Teddy Roosevelt later called the fight "among the decisive battles of the Revolution . . . the turning-point in the southern campaign" because it forced Lord Cornwallis to change his plans and retreat from Charleston, opening a door to the final American victory the following year.)

That dubious 1775 land deal, however, may rank as most historically significant of all, because the agreement triggered the avalanche of settlers that rolled along the Wilderness Road and opened up the West.

The transaction was a land grab, a get-rich-quick scheme by nine North Carolina land speculators who knew an opportunity when they saw one. Styling themselves "The Transylvania Land Company," in 1774 they hatched a plan to secure as many acres as possible of virgin, verdant land in what was then the wilderness on the far side of the Appalachian Mountains and recruit people to buy or rent shareholds to settle and cultivate it. Then, fait accompli, the entrepreneurs would appeal to the government to name Transylvania as the fourteenth colony. Along the way, they would make a killing.

The mastermind behind the Transylvania Land Company was Richard Henderson: North Carolina plantation owner, lawyer, Superior Court judge, and, according to an interpreter at Sycamore Shoals, the eighteenth-century equivalent of a used-car salesman. One problem with Henderson's speculation, however, was that several parties already claimed the land. The colonies of North Carolina and Virginia both thought they had dibs. The Cherokee, Shawnee, and Iroquois nations regarded the area as their hunting grounds, although virtually none had lived there for decades. Furthermore, that 1763 treaty intended to keep out free-ranging white settlers.

But the British Crown was far away, the colonial governments were occupied with a growing rebellion in the East that would soon erupt into the American Revolution, and Henderson was a good lawyer. He "studied the legal questions concerning the disputed territory west of the mountains, weighed the claims of the English crown, analyzed the charter rights of Virginia and North Carolina and became conversant with the claims of the Cherokee as recognized by the treaties," according to Robert Kincaid, who wrote a classic history of the Wilderness Road. Henderson "decided the Cherokee were the rightful owners of the Kentucky land reaching from their nation to the Ohio River and could deal directly with private individuals if they desired."

But the shareholders of the Transylvania Land Company were not regarded as hardy pioneers or daring entrepreneurs. The colonial Virginia governor called them "Land pyrates."

At the time, approximately one hundred white settlers lived in the vast area between the Ohio and Cumberland rivers, scattered over hundreds of miles among a handful of settlements, small forts, and "stations." The Indian nations—Shawnee to the north, Cherokee to the south— generally left them alone because their numbers were so small and because treaties with the British had thus far kept the Europeans at bay. That restraint would not last long.

High taxes in North Carolina and the building tensions of an impending revolution prodded settlers to look westward, and soon a few new settlements were planted just over the mountains. Hunters, trappers, and other explorers returned from "Kentucke" with tales of rolling hills, grand forests, plentiful rivers and streams, fertile soil, and abundant game, including massive herds of buffalo. (The name, Kentucky, is derived from an Iroquois word meaning "meadow lands.") Entrepreneurs and plantation owners who wanted to extend their holdings, such as Henderson, saw great prospects. So, in the fall of 1774, Henderson traveled to the Cherokee town of Chota in the Great Smoky Mountains to ask the head-men (i.e., chiefs) if the Indians thought they owned the land and would be interested in selling. They said yes, and Henderson invited them to negotiate a treaty for a sizable swath. They would meet at Sycamore Shoals.

The Cherokees started arriving in late December. More than twelve hundred Native Americans had arrived by the time final negotiations began in February. Fewer than two hundred white settlers were present. Henderson arrived, accompanied by a respected long hunter he had hired from North Carolina's Yadkin Valley: forty-year-old Daniel Boone. They brought the payment in a wagon train laden with goods worth ten thousand British pounds, from shirts to rifles, which they stored in cabins until the time came to complete the exchange. Henderson wanted twenty million acres, "the block of land west of the mountains between the Cumberland and Kentucky Rivers," according to Kincaid's description in *The Wilderness Road*. This parcel encompassed half the present-day state of Kentucky and a chunk of north-central Tennessee as far west and south as present-day Nashville. At the last minute, Henderson also pushed for a "path deed," the equivalent of a right-of-way, to build a road that would link the existing Wataugan settlements with the new purchase.

Most of the Cherokee headmen agreed, including the two most senior, Attakullaculla and Oconostota, perhaps hoping to make the best deal they could in the face of inevitable white encroachment. The British had dubbed Attakullaculla "Little Carpenter" because of his skill in piecing together agreements. But Attakullaculla's son Tsi'yuTsi'yu-gunsini, known as "Dragging Canoe," opposed the bargain. He was infuriated that the headmen, including his father, were willing to deal the land away at any price. According to a translator's paraphrase, Dragging Canoe gave an impassioned, prescient speech:

> Whole nations have melted away in our presence like balls of snow before the sun, and have scarcely left their names behind, except as imperfectly recorded by their enemies and destroyers. It was once hoped that your people would not be willing to travel beyond the mountains, so far from the ocean, on which your commerce was carried and your connections maintained with the nations of Europe. But now that fallacious hope has vanished; you have passed the mountains and settled upon the Tsalagi [Cherokee] lands, and wish to have your usurpations sanctioned by the confirmation of a treaty. When that should be obtained, the same encroaching spirit will lead you upon other lands of the Tsalagis. New cessions will be applied for, and finally the country which the Tsalagis and our forefathers have so long occupied will be called for; and a small remnant of this nation, once so great and formidable, will be compelled to seek a retreat in some far distant wilderness. There we will all dwell but a short space of time before we will again behold the

advancing banners of the same greedy host; who, not being able to point out any farther retreat for the miserable Tsalagis, would then proclaim the extinction of the whole race.

The speech "threw the council into an uproar," according to Kincaid, and the headmen withdrew to reconsider while Henderson fretted. The older chiefs persuaded almost all the younger ones to accept the deal, and the meeting continued. The final papers were prepared, translated, read aloud, and signed on March 17, 1775. Only Dragging Canoe held out, and he and a small band of followers departed in rage, eventually joining with the Chickamauga to the south and turning into a regular thorn in the side of white settlers.

But even before the treaties were signed, Henderson dispatched Boone to start the job for which he had been hired: to lead a crew of thirty to thirty-five trailblazers to hack out a corridor into the Kentucky wilderness. On March 10, Boone and his team, including one of his daughters, set out from Anderson's blockhouse, a small, isolated stockade forty miles north, near Long Island on the Holston River, the site of present-day Kingsport, Tennessee.

--- --- --- --- --- --- --- ---

A mile east of Sycamore Shoals, I walked across a wide concrete bridge spanning the Watauga River. (Daniel Boone would have waded across. He likely never set foot on a bridge in his life.) On the other side, the road looped west again, back toward the shoals.

Starting at such a familiar place as Sycamore Shoals appealed to my sense of irony. The road was cut for the very purpose of transporting people into the unfamiliar and the unknown—but now the whole way was familiar, just another set of highways I had been driving long before I realized its significance. But once I decided to walk the route, I paid greater attention each time I drove it, gauging every hill and each narrow shoulder—perilous places for a man on foot—and noting the spots where I might refill water bottles, restock food supplies, or pitch a tent. In the months leading up to the walk, I knew how different the trip would be on foot—purposeful, solitary, unpredictable, and slow.

I had never thought of myself as a man in a hurry, at least not like one of the office drones who scurry in packs on New York sidewalks, nor even like local teenagers who rev their muscle-car engines at red lights and squeal their tires at green. (I live in a NASCAR-rich environment.) But whenever I contemplated the rate at which I would travel from Tennessee to Virginia to Kentucky, I felt my skin itching to go faster. In detached moments of curiosity, I wondered what the effect of viewing the land at such an unhurried pace would be. I liked the concept, but in more instinctive moments I was surprised to discover that inside I felt like a racehorse straining at the bit.

And like a horse I needed gear. So, starting about seven months before departure, every few days I would duck into Mahoney's, a local outfitting store where my daughter worked, to gawk and ask questions and jot down prices. It had been almost twenty years since I bought any camping gear, and that was for the relatively cushy world of "family camping" with its four-person tents, four-burner camp stoves, and four-pole tarps that could fit into a minivan but not a backpack. A spending spree was in order. As I wrote my first shopping list, Henry David Thoreau's desire to live "deliberately" by Walden Pond came to mind. "To front only the essentials of life" appealed to me in an abstract way, but really there was no comparison. Thoreau took an almost perverse pleasure in his frugality, the one-upmanship of the simple life. I did not want to be extravagant, but I would be no Thoreau.

Intending to gradually accumulate supplies and clothing, I occasionally visited the store to talk with some of Sarah's coworkers. Dave, a big, grizzled veteran of the outdoors, eagerly coached me. He once spent an hour explaining in his calm, soft Appalachian Highland twang the finer points of choosing a backpack: how it should feel on the shoulders when loaded, how and where the hip belt should fasten, which features are important and which are window dressing. Dave was the one to whom the younger salesclerks deferred. Rob, a compact twenty-something with rust-colored hair, introduced me to the latest technology in tents and sleeping bags. On another day, a tall blond fellow named Rieppe guided me around the crowded aisles for almost two hours, describing in his laid-back tones the pros and cons of various pieces of equipment. He seemed so familiar with the countless models of sleeping bags and boots that I wondered if he had owned every item in the store at one time or another. And if someone had told me a year before that I would spend an hour in earnest conversation about camp stoves, I would have said he or she was crazy.

As it turned out, I bought my first piece of gear less than two months before departing—but then the purchases quickly accumulated. I piled the equipment in my spare bedroom until I could try them out and begin familiarizing myself with their workings. One warm Sunday afternoon, I shoved thirty-five pounds of books in the pack and walked a three-mile circuit around my neighborhood. By the time I returned, my back was soaked with sweat, my knotted shoulders ached, and my right thigh registered a slight tingling. My toes, stuffed into old shoes, felt like they were going to explode out the front.

At first, I blithely estimated that I could outfit my trip for about a thousand dollars. By the time I bought a tent, backpack, sleeping bag, and shoes, it was obvious that my total investment would likely end up being twice that amount. With less than a month to go before the trip, I had purchased:

Aether backpack (60 liters, blue)	191.99
Tarptent Double Rainbow two-person ultralight tent, with liner	305.00
Mountain Hardware UltraLamina 32 sleeping bag	188.79
MSR Whisperlite camp stove	79.96
Salomon XA3D Ultra 2 hiking boots	99.99
Darn Tough wool socks (3 pairs)	40.77
Sony NEX-F3 digital shutter camera, with case, on eBay	349.95
Total (plus tax):	$1,256.45

More was to come: Leki trekking poles, two sturdy water bottles, water purifying tablets, a small blinking light to wear for visibility, a wide-brim hat, and more. Then there was food: fifteen pouches of freeze-dried meals, granola bars, instant oatmeal, thin bagels, and peanut butter. I made my own trail mix.

About a month before leaving, I ate lunch with a friend, a professional photographer named Joel who had once traveled from Thailand to Turkey. During a lull in our conversation, he asked if I planned to carry a gun.

No, I had ruled out that option long ago. If I ever faced a situation that called for a gun, it would probably be when I couldn't reach it fast enough or, more likely, when I'd be so flustered that I'd shoot my own foot. I'd fired guns before, but not often enough to feel confident handling one in an emergency.

I would carry some protection, however. My telescoping trekking poles, with pepper spray for reinforcement, could fend off animals that came too close. Then there was the wooden club fashioned by the Maasai in Kenya, a gift from a friend who used to live there. The club was about two feet long, with a solid, baseball-sized knob on one end and a handle tapering to the diameter of my thumb. The club was wonderfully balanced and felt almost magically light. I figured a good swing could brain a dog or a man and seriously discourage a curious bear. (I later realized that it was nearly identical to a Cherokee war club.)

Joel asked if I had thought about dogs. No question about it: Of all the potential hazards I might meet, dogs had weighed most heavily on my mind. I had noticed them as I scouted the route, particularly the ones loping around untethered on isolated, narrow roads. I didn't even need to leave home to understand the threat. Several close calls while running had taught me firsthand how diligently dogs will guard their territory—which often extends well beyond their owners' property—and how they are completely undiscriminating as to the actual threat an intruder poses. A semitruck can rumble by or a motorcycle buzz within a few feet of a dog, and he will not budge. Let a runner quietly pad along on the opposite side of the street, and the same dog will go berserk. *A man on foot these days must be a strange and threatening sight . . .*

That fact alone reinforces the obvious point that we Americans have almost completely oriented ourselves away from walking and toward driving. This is not a new or profound thought, but it is, in this case, particularly paradoxical. The Wilderness Road, after all, began essentially as a bridle path. Not even wagons could travel this so-called highway in its first twenty years. But after decades of development, walking it has become almost inconceivable. When I told a ranger at Cumberland Gap National Historical Park about my plan to do exactly that, she first reacted with excitement. "That'll be a great adventure," she said. But then she squinted at me. "Wait—are you *sure*?"

Apparently, for a while, I wasn't. About two months before the trip, on three mornings in a row I woke up long before dawn, damp with sweat and tinged with anxiety, my mind locked in a recurring scene: I'd be walking along the edge of a narrow, winding road with only a steep

drop-off where a shoulder should be, when a truck or SUV came careen-
ing around a blind curve. I'd feel myself brace for impact.

When I told my friend Joel about my dreams, he smiled in sympa-
thy more than amusement. "The first people on that road worried about
Cherokee Indians," he said. "You've got to worry about Jeep Cherokees."

- - - - - - - - - - - - - -

Sycamore Shoals Park, now on the opposite bank of the Watauga, briefly
came into view through the trees, just before the road started up a long
hill. I panted as I climbed. The faint hiss of the river was fading when
I saw a sign announcing Turkeytown, a name worth noting for its own
sake. By noon—less than two hours into the trip—I already felt hot, tired,
and jittery. The first twinge of *what-was-I-thinking* hit as I stopped at
the crest of a hill to rest in the shade of a small tree. After eating some
beef jerky and gulping water from my green Nalgene canteen, I set off
again, feeling revived and suddenly more confident. I was rediscovering
the close connection between the belly and the spirit.

Next came the Range School, which merited its own historical marker.
The original schoolhouse was built in 1843, named for Jonathan Range,
who donated the land. The marker noted that the current single-story
brick building "still serves the community." Two months earlier, however,
the Carter County Board of Education had voted to close the school in a
round of budget cuts.

After another mile and a half of undulating road came the tiny village
of Watauga, a proverbial wide spot in the road. There, in front of the
single-story brick box of a town hall, squatted one of the dozens of monuments marking the path of Daniel Boone's 1769 explorations: simple
bronze plaques bolted to rectangular stone blocks, about four feet tall
and erected in 1915 by the Daughters of the American Revolution (DAR).

Just down the road stood the Country Diner. I was eager to eat a real
meal and sit for more than a few minutes. Dropping my pack and poles
on the restaurant's covered front deck, I stepped inside, where a couple of booths and three tables filled the small dining room. A woman
in glasses was bustling behind the high Formica counter. Two women
chatting in a booth made a matched set: Both a little pudgy and both
wearing glasses and brightly colored tops—one paisley, the other floral.
Maybe dentist office receptionists?

"I see your pack," one said. "Are you hiking?"

Yep, I replied. When I told them my plan, one of the women whistled softly, but that was the end of our chat. They returned to their conversation, and I sat at a window table opposite them, a full three feet away, thankful that the vinyl upholstery wouldn't absorb my sweat and hoping my stink did not spoil the women's appetites. I pulled out the gallon-size Ziploc bag that held my notebook, pen, and map, and studied the route ahead. I had walked about five miles in about two and a half hours. I planned another eight miles today in the rising humidity, about another four hours of walking at my current rate.

Between bites of a thick, excellent cheeseburger and a pile of french fries, I occasionally glanced at the two women. Suddenly one of them turned and asked where I lived. Johnson City, I said—just a few miles away—and that seemed to signal that I was safe for conversation. They introduced themselves as Janice and Sharon, who worked not for a dentist but for the nearby Kennametal factory, a manufacturer for heavy-duty industries such as construction and mining. Business was good; orders were starting to pick up after several years of decline. In fact, demand was growing so quickly that the management had been caught flat-footed, creating backlogs in production. "That's the problem we're dealing with," Sharon concluded, "but it's better than not having orders at all."

Janice asked if I was packing a gun. When I told her no, she shook her head, apparently baffled, and I felt compelled to add that I had protection: a whistle, a can of dog Mace spray, and a club. Sharon said it was sad that it had to come to that. They wished me luck as they got up to leave. "Watch out for dogs," one of them said.

Beyond the village, a concrete bridge spanned the Watauga River. Just after the bridge, I turned onto the aptly named Riverside Road, which soon forked. The left prong brought me over a rise, where the quiet blacktop rolled past suburban houses clumped between farms. About a half-hour after I left the diner, thunder rumbled in the distance. To the south, cumulus clouds were rapidly building into a looming gray-to-black column. I dug out my rain jacket, put the waterproof cover on my pack, and kept walking.

Rain and lightning caught up with me in less than two miles. I hunkered down in a line of trees and honeysuckle as the storm rolled in hard and horizontal. When I tried to tighten my brand-new pack cover, its elastic cord snapped, opening gaps to the thrashing rain. I improvised a knot to keep the cover taut, anxious about my suddenly vulnerable pack and its contents. Under my breath (*why under my breath?*) I cursed my shoddy equipment. And then I laughed.

On several days leading up to the hike, I woke early and lay in the darkness, expectant and eager and nervous. I had read enough travel accounts to know that taking to the road can change a person, and I found myself keenly anticipating the changes to come. I might come out wiser, or more spiritual, or more confident. Maybe with a new sense of independence! A different life! The possibilities thrilled me, and I decided to prepare accordingly, to be ready for any eventuality.

But one morning, I woke with a mild sense of dread, vaguely aware that I had grown so primed for *something* to happen that I would miss any real surprises. I was at serious risk of spoiling the journey by overthinking it. Lying there a few mornings before departure, I vowed to allow room for the unexpected, unsure exactly of what I even meant by that.

Apparently, part of what I meant was riding out a mighty thunderstorm with a leaking pack cover after just five hours of journeying.

The storm passed after twenty minutes, and I resumed walking, ascending a hill as water ran down the road in rivulets under my feet. The sun emerged, steaming the asphalt and the air as two-lane roads meandered past houses and farms and churches, leading to a narrow bridge crossing high over the river. I was approaching the four-lane Bristol Highway, officially known as US Highway 11E/19W.

The sky straight ahead had turned eerily dark. Two storms—one to the west, the other to the southeast—looked like they would surely collide almost directly over my head. My intended destination for the night—a friend's backyard—was still several miles away, and most of that distance was along Carroll Creek Road, a twisting two-lane blacktop with long, shoulderless stretches. In the last two decades, it had evolved from a quiet country lane into a busy thoroughfare serving strings of subdivisions and minimansions. But while the traffic had increased exponentially, the road itself had barely changed. Hiking that crowded stretch during a storm at rush hour seemed almost suicidal.

The storms hurtled toward each other like two fleets sailing into battle. I scurried across the four lanes, my trek poles click-clacking on the concrete, to take shelter under a narrow overhang in front of a fire station perched on the edge of a city park. Seeing no one through the locked glass door, I shed my pack and my wet shoes, fished my canteen and a granola bar from the top of my backpack, and hunched down as the storms crashed in front of me.

Then a muscular, dark-haired man in a blue firefighter's T-shirt opened the door.

"Can I help you?" he asked.

"I'm just hiking through and thought I'd wait out the storm," I said.

"Sure. In fact, you can come in if you want," the fireman offered. I hauled my gear into the brightly lit office, which featured a desk with a computer and a couple of padded chairs for visitors. I peeled off my soggy socks and draped them over my shoes on the floor.

The firefighter's name was Jeff Margeson. As we chatted, I learned he had moved to Johnson City, his wife's hometown, from Seattle, and had been working with the fire department for two years. His partner that day, Michael Britt, was a local guy who had been with the department nine years. Both looked like they were in their early thirties. They took turns behind the desk as we talked about their work, their families, and their off-duty lives. (Michael owned a mowing and landscaping business on the side.) Every fifteen or twenty minutes they would switch. One would talk with me while the other went to another part of the station to do heaven-knows-what.

Almost an hour had passed when Michael invited me out to the truck bay, where a telescope was aimed out the back door toward hills a half-mile away. An overstuffed recliner sat next to it.

"Have you ever seen an eagle's nest?" he asked. The telescope was trained on a small brown bundle near the top of a tree in the hills. I couldn't see any birds, but that was not surprising in this weather. I was keeping my head down, too.

Jeff was cooking a skillet full of chicken and rice. Maybe he heard my stomach growl at the aroma, because he invited me to join them for dinner. I sat at the counter and had shoveled in a few bites when I noticed they were standing. I stopped, feeling awkward. They were standing out of habit, they assured me. . . . I could relax.

The storm teased us for almost two hours, pounding down rain and lightning for a while and then growing calm just long enough to catch its breath for another ferocious blast. When dark started to fall, Michael offered to take me to my friend's house. "It might be your only chance to get chauffeured in a fire truck," he said with a grin.

Thanks, but no, I said. One of my self-imposed rules was to walk the entire route. I had not thought much about setting guidelines for the trip, but this one felt instinctual.

Still, here I was, stuck about a dozen miles from where I started and about a dozen miles from my house. Then I recalled that Sarah would soon get off work. I called her, and we formed a plan: She would pick me up (and bring a new pack cover) and then take me home for the night. In the morning she would return me to the fire station, where I would resume my trip.

It felt a little like cheating, but I rationalized. This was practical and less of an imposition than getting a ride to my intended stop and a ride back in the morning. Michael and Jeff agreed.

So, I was back at my own house less than ten hours after leaving. I laundered my hiking clothes, rearranged my pack, and soaked my feet. Sarah and I sat at the kitchen table while I told her about the people I'd met and the events of the day, and then I started explaining again—as much to myself as to her—why coming home was a good idea and well within my still-amorphous rules. The forecast predicted rain, rain, and more rain for the next five days, and we pondered the pros and cons of delaying the whole trip. It wasn't the weather itself, I said, but meeting people was a major goal. How likely was that to happen in almost-constant rain? I went to bed undecided.

Long before sunrise, I woke to the sound of rain gurgling through downspouts. I lay there, contemplating my options. But mostly I wondered if I was just kidding myself. I felt like I'd already blown the trip.

----- **2** -----

FIGHTING MEN

*[I]t doesn't take long before your
conscience gets sticky, as if someone poured molasses
in your powder horn; and now, however far west I go,
I've got three dead Indians on my soul: What kind
of civilization is that?*

—MAURICE MANNING,
"Notes on 'The Natural Man'"

Rain was still falling when I rose at half past six. Sarah and I checked and re-checked the extended forecast—rain for the next seven to ten days—and I debated with myself, Hamlet-like: *To go now or not to go now? Maybe if I wait a week . . .*

A few shards of blue sky piercing the leaden clouds finally settled the matter, and by quarter past nine Sarah and I stood in the fire station parking lot for a brief second round of goodbyes. Neither of us wept this time.

I headed west on Carroll Creek Road. Within a half-hour the rain had stopped spitting, and the sun had come out. My shirt was sweat soaked by the time I reached the first in a series of generic subdivisions composed of large homes rising behind iron fences, tidy shrubs, and mounds of fresh brown mulch. These could have been the suburbs of any American city.

Carroll Creek Road intersects the Kingsport Highway about three miles from the fire station, and there I would turn north. The built-up area around that junction—stores, billboards, a brick school—were in view as I walked in front of a ranch-style house where a man with gray hair, a down-swooping mustache, and the inevitable trucker's cap was walking in the yard with a small white dog. We waved to each other, and he called out, "Where you going?"

John Wayne Boone

"Boonesborough, Kentucky," I said as I stopped at the edge of his yard.
"Why do they call it Boonesborough?" he asked.

Is he really that clueless? I wondered.

"That's where Daniel Boone went and ended up for a while," I said.

"Well," he drawled, "my name is John Wayne Boone, and I'm descended from him, the seventh generation."

He'd set me up.

John Wayne Boone possessed a double-decker iconic American name and the birthday to go with it: born on the Fourth of July in 1940-something, in a four-room log house that once stood across the road from his current home; only a fire hydrant stood there now. His father was a tenant farmer who worked the land, a few hundred acres belonging to "old man John Glaze." Their family of six raised dairy cows, tobacco, corn, and "whatever we could grow."

We stood talking in his yard, which was dotted with a half-dozen pear and dogwood trees. As a boy, John attended the brick school we could see from his yard, which is still in use as a middle school. Carroll Creek

Road, which now buzzed with cars, was so quiet in his day that he and his friends could play hopscotch in the middle of the road for hours without interruption. His sister, John claimed, was the only girl who had lived on the entire stretch of road I'd just walked.

Maybe the place started to change when a new development started going up across the road from Glaze's farm. John's father saved up and bought the first model home in 1959 for $9,300, a small brick rancher on a corner lot—the house where John still lived. Eventually, old man Glaze sold his farm as well, and now only a small field and a barn remain. The rest of Glaze's land was turned into a cookie-cutter subdivision, with rooftops sprouting like mushrooms a quarter-mile behind me. Altogether, the picture of the past he painted made it clear that today this corner of Appalachia—his corner—bore only a passing resemblance to what he had known as a child.

John left it behind for a while when he followed a common career path for Appalachian men coming of age in the 1960s: He joined the army.

Appalachian men made good soldiers. While they made up 8 percent of the fighting forces in Vietnam, they were awarded 13 percent of the Medals of Honor. A Veterans Administration psychologist heard from officers that because Appalachian men knew how to handle rifles and deal with rough terrain, the officers regularly put them "on point," leading platoons into unknown territory. Some historians credit this reputation to the region's long patriotic warrior tradition, going back to those Overmountain Men who beat the British at Kings Mountain. Others suggest that the military offered an escape from the nation's most perennially impoverished region. In 1970, near the height of the Vietnam War, 18.1 percent of people in Appalachia lived below the poverty line, compared to 13.7 percent nationwide. The Appalachian parts of Kentucky, Tennessee, and Virginia were especially hard hit, with 28.5 percent of people living below the poverty line.

What is certain is that more soldiers from Appalachia were killed than from any other region. West Virginians, for example, died in Vietnam combat at a rate of 84.1 for every 100,000 of the state's male residents, compared to a national average of 58.9 deaths per 100,000. Kentucky's Appalachian counties averaged 84.2 deaths per 100,000 males, while the rest of the state averaged 64.4.

John and his younger brother went through basic training together, and in 1968, the war's bloodiest year, they shipped out for a tour on a gunnery crew. They survived combat together, were exposed to Agent Orange together, and, as John said, "saw a lot of bad stuff together." He did not elaborate.

John married soon after returning home and worked a string of odd jobs in construction, truck driving, and "whatever I could do" to earn a living. He finally settled in as an electrician at a local printing company, retiring after a quarter-century there. Now, he was a nicely prosperous good ol' boy who played a lot of golf and lived alone with his dog. He had been married and divorced six times.

"I just can't get along with people," he told me later. "I came back from Vietnam pretty messed up, but I didn't know it then. I had post-traumatic stress disorder. It took a while to figure out; I just kept bottling it up. You think about it all the time. You can't trust anybody. You want to be alone. My family, even my brothers and sisters, we don't get along. I still feel like I'm in the army. I'm supposed to be out. It's not as bad as it used to be, but I still have dreams sometimes."

A white city utility truck pulled up, and John waved at the chunky young man in a fluorescent orange vest who had climbed out, pulled a gas-powered line trimmer from the truck bed, and started cutting tall grass and brush near a culvert across the road. Within a few minutes he returned to the truck and drove west. I would follow that route shortly.

John has taken his sister's word that Daniel Boone was their great-great-great-grand-something. She looked it up on the family tree, John said, but he did not have many details. He and his sister didn't much talk about it. In fact, they don't talk much at all. What *is* certain is that John's famous possible ancestor passed close to where his house now stood.

Daniel Boone was born in 1734, the middle of eleven children born to Squire and Sarah Boone. Squire, a weaver, had emigrated with his family from Devonshire, England, settling in eastern Pennsylvania in 1717 with a growing and prosperous colony of the Society of Friends— Quakers—from England and Wales, including his future wife, Sarah Morgan.

The tales surrounding Daniel's childhood and early adulthood mix verifiable facts, half-truths, and outright exaggerations, but they all point in the same direction: Daniel was a singular boy whose deep love and knowledge of the outdoors became evident early, whose prowess in hunting and tracking even by age fifteen was unparalleled, and whose curiosity and mischievousness were well recognized. When he was about fourteen years old, for example, he wandered off to hunt in the Pennsylvania hills, as he often did, but instead of coming home at dusk as usual, he did not return that night, or even the next day. Frantic, his parents gathered neighbors for a search party, which found him at last, almost at the end of the second day. The boy was calmly sitting in the woods nine miles from home, tending a fire on which he was cooking meat from a bear he killed. (At least one early biographer compared this story with the one in Luke's Gospel about young Jesus in the temple, who had gone missing on his own noble errand.)

The Boones uprooted from Pennsylvania and moved to the Yadkin River Valley in the hills of North Carolina in approximately 1750, when Daniel was almost sixteen. While the catalyst for their move isn't certain, Squire and his family departed soon after a falling-out with the Friends community over the marriage of two of their children to "worldly" mates—that is, not Quakers. Squire and Sarah had both publicly confessed and apologized when their daughter married in 1742— already pregnant, it turned out—but circumstances or attitudes changed over the next five years so that when their son Israel married outside the Society, Squire did not apologize and was eventually cast out. (Sarah did confess, however, and continued taking her children to monthly meetings.) His father's refusal to submit to the community's pressure and his tendency to go his own way apparently made a strong impression on Daniel. By all accounts, Daniel grew to be a sociable, humorous, and family-minded man, but one who ultimately found more pleasure on his own in the woods.

Boone got his first taste of combat in 1755, as a teamster for General Braddock's campaign to take Fort Pitt during the French–Indian War. That debacle, one of the worst defeats the British army ever endured, made a mark on the young Boone. Although he was often assumed to be one of the fiercest Indian fighters on the frontier, he claimed to have killed only three people in his life, all in self-defense.

In 1756, Boone married a neighbor, Rebecca Bryan. James, the first of their ten children, was born within a year. Boone was already a successful professional long hunter—so called because of the backcountry expeditions that could last weeks, months, and occasionally years. Between his own journeys and the tales he heard from other travelers, the wilderness of "Kentucke" and its forests and rivers and big game captured his imagination, and he began edging westward. By 1760 he had explored the

Holston River area, now the northeastern corner of Tennessee where John and I stood talking. Daniel moved his family to the region by 1772. He tried to lead a group of forty or so settlers into the wilderness in the autumn of 1773 but was turned back when a band of Shawnees, Cherokees, and Delawares ambushed a resupply party and killed five of its eight members, including Boone's son James. Even so, when Richard Henderson hired him to assist his newly formed Transylvania Land Company, Boone saw the opportunity to head for his promised land. That prospect, of course, is what led him to blaze a route into the wilderness in 1775—a venture that, among more notable things, brought me to John Wayne Boone's front yard two hundred thirty-eight years later.

Another city truck parked across the road, and a woman, also in a florescent vest, climbed out. John waved at her. They were friends, and John wanted to talk. He and I exchanged goodbyes and phone numbers.

I caught up with the trimming guy in the orange vest just before the intersection with the road to Kingsport. His name was Dale, and he had been working for the city for only three weeks. He liked his new job, except for the snakes. "I've just seen a lot of black snakes, but you never know how they're breeding these days," he said, and then added ominously, "Watch where you step."

The area around Carroll Creek Road and Kingsport Highway is a busy retailing intersection in the Boone's Creek area, which was named for Daniel, of course. He not only passed through; he also "cilled a bar" at the creek in 1760, according to an old carving on a tree that once stood about a mile from the historical marker posted in front of Curvacious Consignment (catering to women sizes 12 and up). The archeological jury is still out as to whether that was really Boone's carving or the work of an imposter, and with the tree long gone we may never know.

The road north is straight, a rarity in this area. The only curves are vertical, as the line of asphalt follows rolling hills gradually rising into the distance. Boone's Creek itself at this point is a nondescript narrow stream with steep banks overgrown with brambles and bushes, spanned by a plain concrete bridge. Heavy road construction dominated the next five miles, the latest phase of a multiyear project to widen the road from two to four lanes. The work required excavations, often ten to twelve feet below the road surface, where the recent rains had turned the dirt and clay into a burnt-orange sludge. Jersey barriers, orange-and-white barrels, and constant traffic made walking slow, sometimes slick, and occasionally treacherous. What at first looked like a roll of tawny carpet lying atop a five-foot-tall pile of debris turned out to be a deer carcass, with four reddish-brown stumps sticking up from the top, its legs either chewed off by other animals or torn off by machinery. I added the deer to my tally of roadkill spotted during the past twenty-six hours: three possums (two of them split open, as if prepped for biology lab), a dog, and an unidentifiable mammal about the size of a raccoon.

I had not even left the city limits when I almost became roadkill myself. On short stretches of road, usually at bridges spanning the numerous creeks and other low spots, the road crew had placed Jersey walls—those ubiquitous three-foot-tall concrete barriers—on the painted line edging the road, usually on the side where I walked to face oncoming traffic. At one of those bridges, I started walking as fast as I could when traffic was clear, but I had gone about ten yards when a semitruck suddenly appeared ahead, barreling up a hill that had hidden it from sight. If I stayed where I was, the semi would crush me. I checked behind me: a white cargo van was coming from the opposite direction. Directly across the two lanes, a permanent guardrail hugged the opposite edge of the road. I glanced over the Jersey wall, but jumping it would mean a fifteen-foot fall with a forty-two-pound pack onto sharp rocks. With no room to stand or maneuver, I turned around and scampered toward the end of the barrier. The semitruck was coming fast. With a quick glance, I figured—hoped, prayed—that I could make it across the road where the guardrail on the other side flared back enough to offer a space to stand. I dashed across the road, my metallic trek pole tips clacking on the asphalt, my backpack heaving with each step. I started counting as soon as I reached safety (*one-thousand-one, one-thousand-two, one-thousand . . .*). The semi and cargo van whisked past me before I got to three.

"Idiot!" I shouted at myself. I stayed on that side of the road until I passed the bridge and the barriers and then crossed to face traffic as usual. For the first time, I seriously considered that there was an actual risk of getting killed on this trip. Lesson learned.

A half-mile or so later, the excavation dropped eight to twelve feet immediately next to the guardrail, down to mud and shelves of shale punctuated by random patches of grass. I climbed to the outside of the guardrail and clung to it, inching along until the ground beneath my feet narrowed into a small cliff and then crumbled completely, forcing me to jump down into the mud. Using my trek poles for balance, I picked my way over orange mire, hopscotching onto small islands of gravel, shale, or grass when I could. The whole section was maybe fifty yards long, but it felt longer. Daniel Boone faced more dangerous and tougher obstacles than I could imagine, but I couldn't help wondering what he would have made of this construction zone.

It is impossible to know what route he took from Sycamore Shoals to "the Long Island of the Holston," the initial rendezvous point for his crew, but he likely followed the Watauga River northwest to where it flowed into the Holston River, before tracing the Holston to Fort Patrick Henry and Long Island. Present-day roads roughly parallel the rivers, but the point of confluence of the Watauga and Holston rivers doesn't look anything like it did in Boone's time. There, on the northern edge of Johnson City, the TVA dam system created Boone Lake, a wide spot in the river where boats and jet skis zip around, overlooked by waterfront mansions that cling to the steep, heavily wooded banks.

I felt mildly elated when, after almost four hours of walking, I passed an "End Construction" sign and came to a wide intersection with a gas station and convenience store. In the men's room, I ran my fingers over my head and saw on them a few drops of blood and the partial remains of a tick. I searched for the bug's head with my fingers and pulled, hoping I didn't leave anything behind.

The road beyond narrowed to two lanes. I came upon the shell of a retired, gray gas station where three men sat, one on a folding chair and the other two on a tattered, overstuffed sofa. Looking for an excuse to stop, I asked if this was a machine shop. "No," one of them answered. "It's a loaf shop." Laughter all around.

One of them—a thin, bespectacled man with neatly parted salt-and-pepper hair—wore a gray Boy Scout jamboree T-shirt tucked into his blue jeans. Another was a huge man in jeans and a plain T-shirt that somehow hung loosely on him. Their companion, in bib overalls, had a long, unkempt beard and held a cigarette daintily between his fingers. When I told them where I was headed, they started discussing directions to Warriors' Path State Park, which they claimed was just about five miles up the road. *Turn at Colonial Heights Road. That's at the Zoomerz gas station, not far past the . . . and then you'll see . . . if you pass this place you've gone too far . . .* and so on. They seemed to think I couldn't read road signs. One of them asked if I was hiking the Appalachian Trail, which was nowhere close—a fact that either they didn't know or, more likely, thought I didn't.

The day and the road felt long and tedious after that. By the time I reached the Interstate 81 overpass, perhaps five miles later, a blister had formed on the second toe of my right foot. I sat on the concrete embankment under the interstate and pulled out my canteen and a small plastic bag packed with bandages and moleskin. When I took off my shoes and socks, the fresh air that brushed my feet felt almost erotically good. Just then a Kingsport police car pulled onto the shoulder. A thin, blondheaded police officer stepped out, chewing gum or tobacco. His nametag identified him as B. Conkin.

"Howdy," said Officer Conkin. "I bet you're coming from Trail Days," referring to the recent celebration of the Appalachian Trail in Damascus, Virginia. This was a better guess than the Appalachian Trail.

I told him where I was going, adding that I just wanted to make it to the state park tonight.

"You're not far; just a couple more miles," he said. "Could I see some ID, please? You're not doing anything wrong. Just standard procedure." *Standard procedure*, I assumed, *to make sure a vagrant wasn't setting up under the interstate for the night.*

He called in my driver's license, and we chatted while waiting for the response. He obligingly agreed to search the back of my neck for signs of ticks, finding nothing but a spot of blood. He had heard of Daniel Boone, of course, but to my surprise he also was, like several people I met, passingly familiar with the history of the Wilderness Road. Three minutes later he had the information he needed. He wished me luck and drove off. Just beyond the interstate, the road builds up to a four-lane suburban retail stretch of strip malls, banks, restaurants, and gas stations. Rush hour was approaching, and so were chimneys of ominous cumulus clouds. I found the Zoomerz station, crossed the highway, and entered the sudden quiet of a side street lined with ranch-style and split-level houses and a few churches. These gradually gave way to open ground as the houses spread out along a valley. The road then made two sharp turns as it entered a bank of small hills and crossed train tracks, and Warriors' Path State Park lay before me.

The campground was almost empty—it was the middle of the week, after all—and the young woman at the registration booth said she was giving me one of the best sites in the park. If so, then that raised questions about the others: My site sat on a shelf of land six feet above the road, accessible by climbing up tree roots and strategically placed stones. There was plenty of space to pitch a tent, but none of it very good. The ground was almost bare on one half of the campsite, and half-buried rocks and roots poked through the grass on the other. Given the choice between smooth, bare ground and grassy, knotty ground, I went for the smooth. My tent was a lightweight model called the "Double Rainbow" that featured a greenish-gray fabric oval dome body, a bright yellow spine (the sleeve for the supporting tension rod), and winglike flaps that opened to let breezes flow through. It resembled a very big bug or a very small space capsule, depending on how a person looked at such things.

Big raindrops started pelting the ground almost as soon as I finished setting up, and I dove inside, leaving my shoes underneath the small vestibule formed by the pegged tent flaps. Inside, I organized my gear: *Put the stuff bags here. Unpack the sleeping bag.* The rain hit harder. *Stove, fuel canisters, and water bottles outside, underneath the flap.* The rain slowed for a few staccato beats and then fell harder than before. *Inflate the air mattress.* A few dribbles of water followed a tent seam and ran beneath the silicon fabric floor, no doubt forming a puddle underneath my tent. The rain eased after about twenty minutes, and I looked out to find the soil around my tent had turned into black goop. My shoes sat like miniature tankers in a dark sea. I moved them to the single, tiny tuft of grass under the vestibule.

I climbed out and headed to the bathhouse across the road for a shower, skidding down the rooty–stony steps on the way. I returned to camp and fired up my stove, a compact marvel of engineering with the evocative name of Whisperlite and the spidery profile of the Apollo lunar-landing vehicles. The water in my tiny saucepan was boiling furiously within three minutes and, per instructions, I tipped it into a pouch of freeze-dried beef stew, stirred it with a long spoon, and let it simmer. Just as I poured the water, the rain started pouring, too. I shut off the stove, grabbed the pouch and my canteen, slid more than stepped down from my camp to the road, and sprinted for the picnic shelter, which was connected to the bathhouse.

Three teenage boys sat under the shelter playing a board game while an older couple waited out the storm at another table. We exchanged hellos when I took a neighboring table and opened my pouched meal, but I did not feel sociable. I ate silently, chasing the thick, salty stew with drinks from my canteen as rain ricocheted off mud and concrete. I did not feel triumphant or adventurous. After muck, trucks, and ticks, I felt tired, frustrated, and grumpy. *Could I devise an honorable excuse to call it quits?* Maybe my hip would get so bad that I couldn't go on. *Should I pray for that?* Maybe I could bribe those boys to steal my gear while I slept.

As the rain eased, I dashed back to my site, cleaned and stowed my cooking gear, made another trip to the bathhouse, ran back to the tent, and waited to feel miserable. But a few minutes after zipping myself into my bright green sleeping bag, with hot food settling in my stomach, the rain easing, and daylight fading, I felt a surge of something like encouragement. My mind cleared enough to write in my notebook, to think about what to do in the morning, and to discard the idea of quitting. Soon after sundown, I turned off my tiny reading lamp and cozied up in the sleeping bag, telling myself it wasn't so bad after all.

I slept fitfully, wakened at least once by the scritching of some animal exploring the edge of the tent. *A raccoon maybe?* Later, a flash of lightning and the following thunder hit so close that, for a second, I felt pinned like a mounted insect. It seemed like I had just dozed off again when birds suddenly started quarreling, a wan light filtered through the greenish tent, and a diesel engine roared by on the road below. Day three.

3

TO THE BLOCKHOUSE

All conservation of wildness is self-defeating, for to cherish
we must see and fondle, and when enough have seen and
fondled, there is no wilderness left to cherish.

—ALDO LEOPOLD

C rawling out of my tent, I noted three facts: the weather was cool and breezy for mid-May, my right knee dully ached, and I felt like I hadn't eaten in a week. I set up my stove and boiled water for instant oatmeal and coffee and finished with peanut butter on a thin bagel—a combination that became my regular breakfast. I strung a thin nylon rope between two trees to hang up my clammy shirt and pants, sleeping bag, small camp towel, and tent to dry.

I had packed three changes of clothes, planning to rotate between a garish yellow short-sleeve T-shirt and a white, long-sleeve T-shirt, and between an old pair of green hiking shorts and a new pair of beige cargo pants with legs that could zip off to make shorts. I reserved a blue button-down short-sleeve shirt and khaki nylon pants for times when I needed to be presentable and relatively stink free. But after two sunburned arms and a couple of ticks on my second day, for the rest of the trip I hiked in the long-sleeve shirt and beige pants, topped with a wide-brim hat that almost matched the pants. So, without meaning to, I walked mostly in a slightly grimy white-to-beige palette, a low-grade homage to Gandalf, the white wizard in the Lord of the Rings.

A two-mile road brought me out of the campground and farther north on Fort Patrick Henry Highway, the same retail-friendly boulevard I'd followed into Kingsport the day before. I had planned to take the road downtown but was turned back in a quarter-mile by the convergence of a short, shoulderless bridge on a blind curve with traffic whipping past at what seemed like forty miles per hour. I instead followed More-land Drive, a broad four-lane arc around Kingsport. The road seemed custom-built to attract office buildings and heavy traffic, but much of it was almost deserted, lined by sparse trees and open fields. This five-mile stretch of road turned out to be so boring that I found myself taking inventory of roadside trash. In one short section, I saw one Starbucks cup, one Chick-Fil-A wrapper, four Mountain Dew cans, seven crushed cigarette packs, two dozen or so gum wrappers, a tire-balancing weight, and an infinity of cigarette butts. The roadkill tally increased, too: a cardinal, a cat and, ten yards past a flattened dog collar, the bone and fur remains of a dog.

If I wanted to meet people, I needed to stay on narrower roads. Wide highways, even busy ones, were paradoxically isolating, with people zip-ping past, cocooned in their cars.

By noon, my brain was gnawing on a different problem: pain. Sharp, electrical burns had begun to sporadically ignite in my right thigh, espe-cially on downward slopes, making me think of cattle prods and enhanced interrogation techniques. I stopped, took off my pack, and leaned against a guardrail to rest. After about ten minutes, the pain eased enough that I could start walking again.

Moreland brought me to Long Island on the Holston, a four-mile-long paramecium-shaped island tucked between two bends in the Holston River that had served as a meeting place for Cherokees and whites in the eighteenth century. Here, Boone rendezvoused with some of his trail-blazing crew before setting off for John Anderson's blockhouse, some twelve miles away. There they met the rest of their party and started their work. Today, however, they would have had to contend with East-man Chemical Company.

Long Island itself, with a snatch of physical and psychological distance from the town of Kingsport, had developed into a distinct and somewhat shady community of small farms, churches, roughnecks, and moonshin-ers by the start of the twentieth century. Then George Eastman, the in-ventor of the Kodak camera, came to Appalachia. After coping with sup-ply shortages during World War I, he wanted an independent source of raw materials for his photographic chemicals, particularly methanol and acetone, and Kingsport offered easy access to the water, wood, minerals, and railroad system required to manufacture and transport them. So, he launched the Tennessee Eastman Company here in 1920. The company struggled for a decade before expanding rapidly in the years leading up to World War II, its progress spurred by more efficient technology, a growing hunger for synthetics, and, in the 1940s, the needs of war. The company helped build weapons during World War II, including a plant near Oak Ridge that worked on the atomic bomb. It later produced more mundane materials such as polyester for clothing and furniture. Spun off from Kodak in the mid-1980s, Eastman Chemical Company still employs more than 13,000 people worldwide, more than half of whom are based at the Kingsport headquarters. Not surprisingly, Eastman defines the economy of Kingsport (2013 estimated population: 52,892) and much of the "Tri-Cities" of Johnson City, Kingsport, and Bristol.

The Eastman facility almost covers Long Island, although "facility" barely does justice to the techno-maze of silvery skeletal vent pipes, discharge stacks, four-story-tall spherical storage tanks, roads, railroad tracks, and other links in a chemical production chain that brings in more than nine billion dollars annually. Blocks of laboratory buildings and brick-faced office buildings stand at the perimeter of this industrial rabbit warren, like clean-shaven assistants in a rock star's entourage. While the main plant covers nearly eight hundred sixty acres, the entire site includes about four thousand acres and almost six hundred buildings.

Locals joke about the smells that often hang in the Kingsport air—sometimes sweetly metallic, at other times pungent and sour—but I did not smell chemicals as I descended to the western edge of the Eastman compound. And to my surprise, small fish were swimming in a drainage stream alongside the road. Crossing a short bridge over a slender creek placed me firmly on Long Island. Then, sure enough, twenty-five yards later, a sweet chemical odor slapped my nose.

Eastman enjoys a reputation as a good corporate citizen, winning several awards for sustainability and environmental responsibility. (The company consistently appeared in *Newsweek*'s "Green Rankings," which named it the fourth "greenest" materials company in 2012.) It has underwritten a series of environmental studies of the Holston River conducted by Drexel University's Academy of Natural Sciences over the past forty-five years. The last major study, in 2010, concluded that there were "continued improvements in the ecological condition at most of the zones throughout the study area," compared to earlier surveys. However, the company was fined by the state for various violations between 2009 and

2013, including releasing volatile organic compounds into the air. The fines totaled $340,000 over the four years—less than 0.0001 percent of its revenues. No one's perfect.

Soon the road was flanked by twelve-foot-tall chain-link fences topped with barbed wire, demarcating sections of land given over to various company functions. Trucks and railroad cars waited in perfectly spaced columns, followed by wooden-sided buildings the size of mobile homes that lined a central road like military barracks. Clusters of storage tanks and discharge stacks followed, connected by pipes wrapped in weblike scaffolding.

But there were also reminders of the island's preindustrial past—or perhaps signs of ongoing passive resistance. Long Island Evangelical Methodist Church, a small, white frame church building with a new, bright-green metal roof, stood about a hundred yards from scaffolded tanks and discharge stacks. *Who worshipped there now?* The only remnants of a neighborhood seemed to be some moldering shacks, abandoned except for a few big barking dogs. A dilapidated country store next door was for sale. The strange chemistry between old and new Long Island was even more visible a half-mile away, where three Canada geese stood in the middle of the road, keeping a Ford pickup truck at bay until a semitruck slowly approached and sent them skyward. They flew over the silver superstructures of Eastman before wheeling back over my head and buzzing a small white farmhouse standing on a lone acre of grass—a defiant patch of green bordered on three sides by tall chain-link fences that enclosed parked semitrailers. I wanted to meet whomever lived in this holdout farm, but no one answered the door.

The road ended at Wilcox Drive, a busy thoroughfare that connects Interstate 26 to downtown Kingsport. I turned toward town and stopped at a series of historical markers that I had never noticed while driving. One stated that the Avery Treaty between Indians and white settlers was signed here on July 20, 1777, adding with rare candor that it was the settlers who violated the treaty.

A second marker erected near the bridge over the Holston River described the flotilla of flat boats launched from the spot on December 22, 1779, led by John Donelson and wrecked barely a mile away. Donelson's flotilla resumed the following February and arrived two months later at what would become Nashville. In the bottomland below the bridge, presumably near the place where Donelson put in, stood four white globes—storage tanks—each four or five stories tall.

By now, the cloudless day had grown warm and humid, and I had grown hot and hungry. I made my way past the Eastman headquarters, a sprawling three-story brick-and-glass office building that would fit well in suburban Atlanta. Then came a section of down-at-the-heel houses, shuttered stores, and abandoned warehouses. I approached the modest skyline and wide streets of downtown Kingsport, where a civic renaissance has been attempted in the past decade. Old storefronts now housed boutiques and bistros. Large planters dotted the sidewalks. I was looking for an early dinner, but businesses were already closing, counterintuitively, in advance of a concert scheduled outside the refurbished train station that night, the Friday before Memorial Day.

The JanMar Diner was open, however. I parked my pack at one of the black metal bistro tables on the sidewalk and stepped inside for the air conditioning. The long counter was orange. The tabletops were orange. Three of the walls were cream-and-orange. Only the fourth wall of exposed brick and the black-and-white checkerboard floor offered any variation.

I ordered the biggest pulled-pork barbecue sandwich on the menu. As I waited, two elderly women, both dressed smartly in black and white, made their way to the exit. While her companion held open the door, the older woman—maybe in her eighties—abruptly stopped. Framed in the doorway, she pointed at the planter standing just outside the door.

"This plant needs watering," she nearly shouted to the man behind the counter. She sounded like Jessica Tandy in *Driving Miss Daisy*. "It's as dry as a chip."

"It just got planted today," the man answered, defensive. A pause hung in the air, and the other customers grew quiet.

"It's as dry as a *chip*," the woman repeated, annoyed. Another pause. Then the tall, muscular waitress who had been pouring water at another table stepped up as the peacemaker.

"I'll water it tonight," she said cheerfully. The older woman gave a single, sharp nod and left. As the door closed, the waitress said to no one in particular, "It'll make her happy."

By then it was clear that I would not make it to the blockhouse site that day, as I had hoped. The walk into Kingsport had taken longer than expected, thanks in part to that shooting pain in my hip. Unbidden, a worry crept in: *I might need to quit.* Shoving it aside, I focused intently on my sandwich and decided I was in no mood to search for a camping spot. There was a Super 8 motel somewhere in the vicinity. After three wrong turns and forty-five minutes of searching, I found it.

The lobby was open but empty, which was both surprising and disturbing on the Friday afternoon of a holiday weekend. Five minutes and no one, and then ten. A few cars dotted the parking lot. After twenty minutes, I started scanning a tourist map in the lobby for another motel, when in walked the twenty-something clerk. With a friendly voice and without apology, she booked me into an upstairs room in the back of the building, equidistant between the stairwells. As best I could tell, it was the farthest possible room from the lobby of an almost empty motel. For $67 I had a bed, hot and cold running water, a coffee carafe with a missing lid, a broken radio, a cracked toilet seat, a TV with a missing remote (which the clerk replaced), and a rattling heater–air conditioner with a broken thermostat, where I hung my socks and underwear after rinsing them in the bathtub. Even so, I slept soundly.

The temperature dropped into the thirties overnight, and the morning was cool and clear. I followed Bloomingdale Pike northeast, past shopping centers, apartment buildings, and houses. A few miles out, at the crest of a hill in Bloomingdale, I came to Karen's Kloset, a one-story house that served as a secondhand shop. On the porch a bulky, bald white man in bib overalls and oversized glasses sat talking to a young black man in jeans and a button-down shirt. The view from the porch featured a loose scattering of mobile homes across the road. I asked how far it was to Wadlow Gap Road. "Ten steps," the big man deadpanned. Pause. "But really big steps." When he stopped chuckling at his own joke, we introduced ourselves.

Michael Dugger, in his late sixties, owned the shop and preached on the side. I asked about the area. "This is the worst place for drugs in the Tri-Cities," he said. "That's what the police tell me." He asked if I was carrying a gun and shook his head in dismay, or disbelief, when I told him no. Then he and his friend left to run an errand.

By then a plump young woman with friendly eyes had emerged from the store. This was Michael's daughter, Jennifer, and a moment later she was surrounded by a quartet of kids: her ten-year-old red-haired daughter, Katelyn; cousins Halley and Troy, eight and nine; and Troy's friend, Bradley. The two boys eagerly showed me around the shop, which was better organized and cleaner than its ramshackle exterior suggested. Jennifer explained that the shop was named after Michael's second wife, Karen, who "is about half his age"—that is to say, about her own age. I asked how they got along. She raised one eyebrow. "It's complicated," she said. They had been friends and roommates in Johnson City before Karen and Michael moved in together, eventually married, and then brought the whole family to Kingsport to be closer to Karen's folks. The tightness around Jennifer's mouth suggested that she was not happy about the arrangement. I asked where Michael did his preaching. "All over," Jennifer said. That was that.

Wadlow Gap Road was more than ten steps but less than a mile past Karen's Kloset. Less than a mile beyond that was Lucy Road, which cut north through a quiet neighborhood of single-wide and double-wide trailers, old farmhouses, and sporadic groupings of 1960s-era brick houses. The road felt lonesome. Almost every lot on Lucy Road displayed a "No Trespassing" or "Private Property" sign, and several featured the familiar blue hexagons of ADT Security Systems. Late on a sunny Saturday morning, few people were outside.

The road eventually crossed into Virginia and ended at Carter's Valley Road, which runs parallel to the ridge of Clinch Mountain. A quarter-mile into Virginia, the road turned entirely rural, with trees and brush hugging the sides. A tilting barn high on a knob looked fragile enough to be brought down by one good kick from the chestnut horse standing in its shade. A creek flowing alongside the road would have made this spot an image of mountain paradise were it not for the two full sets of tires strewn in the streambed and the mud-smeared plastic bags and empty Mountain Dew cans tangled in the roadside weeds.

Prompted by the rugged landscape—or perhaps by the trash that rendered it imperfect—I felt more peaceful than I had the first few days. After checking into the motel the previous night, I felt sullen and idiotic. I had camped only one night, and that had been difficult. I had talked to only a few people. My hip was worrying me, and resorting to a motel only reinforced my sense of weakness. But lying in the dark, praying more intensely than usual as I waited for sleep, I was reminded that this was the life I had chosen for the next several weeks. I would do better,

I concluded, if I stopped thinking of home as a house behind me and instead thought of home as what I carried with me.

Recalibrating home seemed to help my spirits. My feet felt good, and the dull ache in my right knee and the hot bolts firing down my right leg were less severe and frequent than yesterday. By the time I emerged from a stand of trees into an open valley, I had made some kind of mental shift. I even broke into a *Fiddler on the Roof* tune: "*L'chaim!* . . . To life!" I felt like the setup for a joke: *A half-Jewish guy from New York walks through Appalachia singing Broadway show tunes.* . . . That seemed weird even to me.

Approaching Carter Valley Road, however, I still felt twinges of guilt for breaking my "rules" for the trip, even though I had never actually spelled them out. The time had come to make them more definite, so I composed a draft in my head as I walked.

Rule no. 1: I will walk the historic routes as best as they can be determined. That is, avoid the modern bypasses or shortcuts when practically possible.

Rule no. 2: Even more importantly, I will *walk* and not ride. I may ride around, as with Sarah on the first day, but only if I restart from where I left off. No skipping.

Rule no. 3: I will carry my belongings.

Rule no. 4: I will put people before places. That is, I will aim to pay more attention to people and their lives than to locations, architecture, and landscapes. Ideally, places and people will blend—it's difficult to understand one without the other, after all. But if forced to choose, people take precedence.

Rule no. 5: I will not trespass.

Rule no. 6: I will try not to be stupid. I'm up for the unknown, the adventure, the unexpected, and even the prospect of chaos. I will not, however, knowingly gamble with permanent injury or death. The trip will involve a certain amount of discomfort and risk, but I won't wade recklessly into blind thickets or get into any more right-of-way arguments with trucks.

Rule no. 7: I will keep my head up, literally and figuratively. I tend to watch the road directly in front of me and sometimes even watch my own feet. I also tend to get distracted by memory (the past) and by speculation (the future). Instead, I will pay attention to the present moment, to the scenes and experiences as they come.

Carter's Valley Road is an unremarkable two-lane blacktop, with two exceptions. First is the beauty of the route, which runs between soaring green ridges that seem to safeguard scattered houses, fields, barns, cows, and perhaps an old way of life. Second, more than two centuries ago, this road linked the Great Wagon Road, which originated in Pennsylvania, with the last station before the "wilderness" began, namely a blockhouse built by Captain John Anderson of the Virginia colonial militia.

Anderson arrived from central Virginia in the migration that was inching southwest toward the Carolinas and present-day southwest Virginia, where settlers found cheap, fertile land. Most of them took the Great Wagon Road out of Philadelphia, turning south at Fort Pitt—now Pittsburgh—to follow a path through the Shenandoah Valley that was first trampled down by buffalo herds en route to salt licks. The animals, in turn, were followed by Native Americans, who were followed by European migrants. This pattern repeated over and over, and thus it is no exaggeration to say that many present-day American roads, including numerous federal highways and interstates—such as Interstate 81 and US Highway 11 in Virginia—were originally laid out by herds of buffalo and elk. Small stations and forts grew into settlements and towns that dotted the route at strategic points, often hugging the rivers that flowed out of the mountains and merged into the great rivers of the region— the Shenandoah, the New, the Clinch, and the Holston.

Anderson settled a little farther west than most people at the time, about thirty miles north and west of the white settlements around the Watauga and Nolichucky rivers. When he finished building his blockhouse in late 1774 or early 1775, it was literally the last outpost of white man's civilization, on the edge of the so-called wilderness, approximately a day's journey from Wolf Hill (present-day Abingdon, Virginia), where the Great Wagon Road ended.

A typical blockhouse, such as Anderson's, showed a certain practical genius. The structure resembled a simple log building, but the modifications made it harder for attackers—read: Indians—to force open. The timbers were cut square instead of rounded, for instance, so that the joints fit tightly and did not require much chinking, which would have been easily shot out during a raid. Chimneys were typically built inside the wall, so that attackers could not pry out the stones as they might with the more common exterior chimneys. The windows were narrow, often only slits, to offer maximum protection from bullets and arrows.

The most distinctive feature of a blockhouse was that the second story overhung the first story by about two feet on all sides. Slots that could be locked shut were cut into the second-story floor overhang, allowing defenders to shoot down onto anyone attacking the base. Builders often incorporated blockhouses in the stockade walls of frontier forts, sometimes building a blockhouse on each corner of a fort. Many blockhouses, such as John Anderson's, stood on their own.

Anderson's structure is long gone. Its place is marked by a stone monument, four feet tall, three feet across, and almost a century old. A tarnished bronze plaque bolted to the front reads:

The Blockhouse.

The starting point of the road through the wilderness to Kentucky, and the station where travelers used to wait until parties collected large enough to defend themselves against Indians on the journey.

Built about 1777 by Captain John Anderson, who died here in 1817, it stood until burned in 1876.

Surveying the valley from the site, it is easy to see why Anderson chose this location: A gentle slope provides a clear view up and down the valley, at least a half-mile in either direction. Potential enemies would find it hard to sneak up on the place.

The blockhouse did not remain the last outpost of white settlement for long. Lured by tales of rich land teeming with game (*true*) that was virtually free for the taking (*mostly not true*), Anglo-American settlers looked farther west, to Kentucky. That journey, however, was complicated by several factors. First, while virtually no Native American settlements existed in Kentucky, the Shawnee, Iroquois, and Cherokee nations hunted there, usually shared it, and sometimes battled over it. Second, in the aftermath of the Seven Years' War, the Indian nations and the British government had forged a treaty in 1763 that barred white colonists from settling in lands west of the Allegheny Mountains. That arrangement, for obvious reasons, suited the Native Americans and, for somewhat less obvious reasons, also suited the British government, which had its own designs on the territory and did not want freelance encroachments. Finally, there were questions over who had legitimate claim on the land.

Virginia, North Carolina, the Cherokee, the Shawnee, and the British Crown all asserted interests.

Even so, a few adventurous, perhaps reckless, white settlers breached the 1763 "Proclamation Line" to plant small communities, such as the Watauga settlements, Martin's Station in southwest Virginia, and, deep in Kentucky's interior, a small fort led by James Harrod. But Richard Henderson's audacious purchase in 1775 topped them all. By the time Virginia's colonial governor nullified the sale, new Kentucky settlements were already springing up, and the American Revolution had begun. The Transylvania Land Company lasted only until the end of 1775, when the embryonic American Congress voided its charter. But that was long enough to give pioneers a foothold, and the purchase stands as the largest private real estate deal in American history.

Henderson hired Daniel Boone both for the long hunter's reputation of being able to work with Indians and for his uniquely fine knowledge of Kentucky. As he departed from Sycamore Shoals in early March 1775, Boone put out the word, and a few days later he and a crew of almost three dozen people gathered at Anderson's blockhouse to start the work. The expedition included his newly married fourteen-year-old daughter, Susannah, and a slave woman to keep camp and cook.

Boone's party did not create an entirely new route. Instead, they followed a narrow Indian path through nearby Moccasin Gap, a natural gateway in Clinch Mountain, clearing underbrush, hacking down trees, slightly widening the route and blazing it as they went. So, their three-week expedition was not a major road-building project; that would come later. For now, the job was simply to find the best way into the Kentucky interior and make it recognizable and passable to people and pack animals. The road was still rough and treacherous. "Boone's Trace" was little more than a well-marked walking trail, but it was a start. Another twenty-one years would elapse before the road would be widened and improved enough to accommodate wagons north of the Cumberland Gap—long after American independence and soon after Kentucky statehood. Boone, however, would have no part in that later project.

Even so, the route, quickly nicknamed "the Wilderness Road," became the favored route to the lands beyond the mountains, despite its hardships and risks. Some settlers dared a shorter but more dangerous course by boat down the Ohio River from Fort Pitt to the Falls of the

Ohio, but Shawnee and Iroquois defenders quickly realized that settlers on boats made easy targets. It would be years before the river passage became safe enough for regular travel.

Thus, in the thirty years after Boone cut his trace, more than a quarter-million men, women, and children—an average of ten thousand people per year—took to the Wilderness Road, creating the first massive westward migration into the heart of North America and setting the stage for the push to the Pacific in the following century.

Thousands of travelers would have stopped near Anderson's blockhouse. This was the frontier equivalent of a base camp, a launching pad for people who were waiting for members of their party to arrive or for the weather to clear or for enough travelers to gather so as to provide safety in numbers against Indian attacks. In another era Anderson might have erected a sign that read "Last gas before the wilderness. Next rest area: 300 miles."

The place is a cow pasture now, fenced with barbed wire. I arrived at noon. No one else was around. After three days of walking, I stood on the Wilderness Road, or what remained of it. Standing where I had the previous November, a few days after Melissa died, I raised my canteen to toast her with a drink of water.

4

KICKED IN THE HEAD

*Being in so alien an environment is the first step towards living
more slowly . . . an equivalent of living in the wilderness.*

—PICO IYER

The gravelly bends of Smith Hollow Road follow a creek twisting
past thick woods and smatterings of houses for a mile, ending at
the gated entrance of the Wilderness Road Shooting and Conservation Club. There, a three-foot-wide wooden footbridge is suspended
above the north fork of the Holston River. A sign warns: "Notice: Bridge
use restricted. Pedestrians only. Limited to 3 pedestrians. Do not run.
Do not cause bridge to sway."

The bridge started to sway as soon as I stepped on it. I glanced down
at the river, running fast about fifteen feet beneath me. Milk-chocolate-
brown with mud after recent rains, the river was about a hundred yards
wide at this point. Indiana Jones scenes looped through my head as
I gingerly crossed the span: *My foot will crash through a slat! A steel
cable will suddenly break, sending my pack and me plummeting into
the muddy water, and they'll fish out my body a hundred miles away in
Knoxville!* The bridge steadied in the middle, and I relaxed, but it began
swaying again during the final third. With my first step on terra firma,
I felt triumphant. By the third step, I just felt silly.

Looking back at the south bank of the river, I saw a sheer, brambly
cliff, a reminder that rivers were severe and constant hazards in the pioneer days. "[F]or nearly its whole length the Wilderness Road followed
the streams," wrote historian William Allen Pusey. "And when it left
the water-courses and took to the mountains, it went up the mountains
and down them along streams that made the grades easier. The traveler
over the road, therefore, had constantly to meet the obstacles offered by

A footbridge over the North Fork of the Holston River

streams, boggy lands, drift wood and fallen timber." He noted that the Wilderness Road crossed five rivers "of considerable size" and "between these it crossed creeks innumerable," with the greater ones fordable only when the water wasn't high. "They were troublesome at their best," he wrote. "In times of high water, they made impassable obstacles."

A river like this—a mere stream compared to the Ohio or the Mississippi—could stop a caravan for days while travelers searched for a ford or built makeshift rafts to ferry people and their belongings. Even then a single misstep, a spooked horse, or a moment's inattention could send all of a family's possessions—or a family—to oblivion. Pioneers commonly made the journey in winter so they would be settled in time for spring planting, but the weather made the trip especially treacherous and brutal. In 1781, for example, a group of more than five hundred settlers from Virginia encountered the rain-swollen Clinch and Powell rivers, forcing them at each crossing to unload their packhorses and ferry people on rafts. By the time they slogged through the knee-deep mud on the trail and in December reached the Cumberland River in Kentucky, the water was "full of floating ice," according to Kincaid. "There was no time for delay. The women and children rode across on the horses and the men and boys waded waist-deep in the icy waters. Once across they pushed on ahead, their wet clothes freezing stiff in the bitter wind."

I do not take the presence of a footbridge for granted.

The gravel road on the north side of the Holston—level, attractive, and lonely—traces the river's S-bend generally westward, just wide enough for two cars to pass. It is lined by sycamore, birch, oak, and occasional pines, with honeysuckle cascading down the bank to the river's edge. Houses and barns are scattered among the river, the road, and the surrounding foothills. Down at the river, at least a dozen dead trees, uprooted from the bank upstream by rains or TVA water management, were stacked up on a sandbar.

The road turned me back to Wadlow Gap Road, the busy thoroughfare I had crossed earlier, but I was farther north now. The noise and vibration of heavy traffic were jarring after several hours of relative isolation. At one bend in the road, a collection of old log cabins was scattered around a field behind a split-rail fence. I was greeted by Ryan McCarty, a barrel-chested man in his mid-twenties, sporting thick dark hair, aviator sunglasses, and a goatee. Ryan assured me that he was a local boy, even though his accent didn't seem to indicate that.

"I get that a lot," he said. "I was born in Wise County, grew up in Lee County, and we moved to Scott County when I was twelve. I can turn on the accent, believe me. But I can turn it off, too. It's a gift."

His dad, Rex, had dreamed of creating a museum of old cabins, and for fifteen years had collected them from around Scott County. He had so far dismantled, hauled, and reassembled fifteen structures on this thirteen-acre field. Then the economy soured in 2008, and Rex realized no one wanted to spend money to look at old cabins. He changed direction and started refurbishing them as vacation rentals for people who might want to stay in an authentic old cabin while enjoying authentic modern amenities. A two-story cabin with a large arched central window stood at the far end of the property, a sample of things to come.

Ryan and his wife would not be around to see the first guests arrive. Instead they would be moving to China that summer to teach English with the Peace Corps. He asked where I would camp that night. I had considered Gate City, I said, only a few miles up the road, but had no definite plans. A moment before I could ask if I might pitch my tent here, he suggested I check for a room at a bakery in town. ("The owners are really nice, and they used to own a bed-and-breakfast.") Or maybe at one of the churches in town because it owned an open field next door to its building. ("I think it's the Methodists, but I'm not sure.")

A mile past the McCartys' cabin collection, the road met US Highways 58 and 23, an intersection familiar to me from dozens of previous drives. I knew that if I turned to the right—eastward—and walked about five miles, I would come to Hiltons, the home of the famous singing Carter Family: husband and wife A. P. and Sara, and Sara's cousin, Maybelle. Maybelle was the mother of three girls, including June Carter, a famous singer in her own right and Johnny Cash's second wife. The old Carter family home and general store had long ago been transformed into the Carter Family Fold, which hosts concerts every Saturday night with old-time, country, and bluegrass music, a place where people get up and dance in front of the stage in their clogging shoes. Johnny Cash played his final show here in July 2003, two months after June died and two months before he joined her in the sweet by-and-by.

I turned west, however. A Food City supermarket overlooks the intersection with US Highway 23, and I decided to pick up a snack. An elderly couple pushing a full cart to their car stared as I passed them in the parking lot, my metal-tipped trek poles clacking on the asphalt. Inside, after stowing my gear near the store office, I walked the aisles in search of beef jerky, chocolate milk, and fresh fruit. Only when a woman almost crashed her cart into a Doritos display to let me pass did I think what a sight I offered: short hair ironed to my head by sweat, a few days' growth of grizzled stubble, a sagging shirt clinging with sweat, grimy cargo pants tucked into socks. I could only imagine the smell. All this felt normal to me after just three days, but looking at it from the other side, I might have given me a wide berth, too.

Back on the road, I crossed the highway's four lanes and walked through Moccasin Gap, a natural cut in Clinch Mountain that has been used for centuries by big animals, Native Americans, white settlers, and now the Virginia Department of Transportation. The narrow shoulder, with a sweeping curve in the road just beyond the gap, created the feel of a bottleneck, and I pressed close to the guardrail as semitrucks and SUVs rumbled past.

Turning off the highway, I headed to the center of Gate City. The road gradually ascended past a looming concrete retaining wall on which the local high school squatted like a massive two-tier cake. A couple of historical markers stood in front of the Pizza Hut. One described Blackmore's Fort, which had stood about ten miles to the northeast, "on the Clinch River near the mouth of Stony Creek." The defensive outpost was named for John Blackmore, who had bought the land in 1773. A group of pioneers led by Daniel Boone stayed there during an early attempt to move to Kentucky that same year. The following year, Boone was put in command during Dunmore's War, a yearlong escalation of native-versus-settler hostilities. The marker noted with admirable understatement that during Dunmore's War and the American Revolution, "periodic conflicts between Native Americans and settlers occurred there, in part because of increased settlement." Dunmore's War ended in late 1774, only a few months before Henderson hired Boone to cut the Wilderness Road.

According to the next marker, the town claimed at least three names in the course of seventy years: "The original name of Winfield, for General Winfield Scott, was changed to Estillville for Judge Benjamin Estill. In 1886, the name was changed to Gate City because of its situation in Moccasin Gap, through which the old Wilderness Road to the West passed. It was incorporated, 1892."

The reference to Winfield Scott confused me because I'd always connected him with the Civil War: the old, bloated, inept commander of the US Army who was pushed out of office in favor of General George McClellan. But I later learned that, as a younger man, Scott had gained a reputation during the War of 1812 as a bold and brilliant tactician. He emerged as a bona fide national hero during the Mexican-American War of the 1840s, popular enough to be the Whig Party's presidential candidate in 1852, but ultimately losing to Franklin Pierce. By the time he retired from military service in 1861, he had served as commanding general of the US Army for twenty years, longer than anyone in American history. At the outbreak of the Civil War, he offered the command of the federal army to a fellow Virginian named Robert E. Lee, whom he called "the finest soldier I ever knew." Lee, of course, turned him down and returned to Virginia to command the Confederate Army. Scott remained loyal to the Union. Small wonder, then, that a local lawyer named Benjamin Estill was smitten by Scott. Estill, whose lone surviving image shows a thin man sporting thick white hair and a slightly bemused expression, went on to serve as a one-term congressman—elected almost unanimously—and as a circuit court judge before dying at the ripe age of seventy-three.

Jackson Street, Gate City's main drag, is sprinkled with a few boutiques and restaurants, including the family bakery Ryan McCarty had mentioned. It was closed. The Scott County Courthouse resembles a colonial-style church building with a clock tower rather than a steeple. Side streets branch from Jackson and climb steeply toward the hills. The streets are laid out on a grid, but from a distance the houses and churches buildings somehow look as scattered as thrown dice.

Three monuments stand in front of the courthouse: a bronze statue of a World War II infantryman, a DAR plaque honoring Daniel Boone's travels, and most prominently, a monument dedicated to the Confederate soldiers of Scott County, which urged onlookers to "Let not ignorance of fact or time overshadow their acts of patriotism, bravery, and courage for Virginia and the Confederacy." It was also inscribed with the Confederacy's motto: *Deo Vindice.* . . . "God is our vindicator." The Sons of Confederate Veterans erected the monument on October 16, 1988—by coincidence, surely, the 134th anniversary of Abraham Lincoln's speech in which he first called slavery "immoral" and also the 129th anniversary of John Brown's raid on Harpers Ferry in present-day West Virginia. This all felt a little jarring. The mountainous parts of the South, with no large plantations and relatively few slaveowners, was not strongly Confederate. In fact, most northeastern Tennesseans opposed their state's secession in 1861, and their independent streak asserted itself as many of them fought for the Union. Only two miles from the state line, however, Gate City is decidedly a Virginia town.

A sign at the corner pointed to the United Methodist Church, a block away. Sure enough, just as Ryan McCarty remembered, next to the large brick colonial church building was a half-block green space enclosed within a three-foot-tall stone wall. A small brick house stood close to the north side of the church. Its front yard provided clues to who might live there: a Big Wheel, a modest jumble of a preschooler's toys, and a sign at the corner for "Gate City United Methodist Church, The Rev. Betzy Elifrits Warren, Pastor." Across the street, a brown tabby kitten mewed incessantly. Drawing a deep breath, I knocked on the door of the house. For the first time in my life, I was about to ask a complete stranger for a place to sleep. It felt like I was starting a career as a beggar.

A thirty-something woman with soft eyes, dark blonde hair, a Duke University T-shirt, and a slightly disconcerted expression answered the door, opening it shoulder wide: This was the Rev. Betzy Elifrits Warren. I introduced and explained myself as quickly as I could, including the part about wondering if I might camp. She hesitated, obviously reluctant as she glanced past my shoulder. (*Is he alone?* she must have wondered.) She surprised me by saying yes. She sounded like she was from the Midwest. I thanked her repeatedly and sincerely.

As I set up my tent, a lean, fidgety man with a shaggy beard and a ball cap approached, accompanied by a blonde, heavy-set woman wearing owlish glasses. They stood on the sidewalk by the church wall and asked where I was hiking. The man had long dreamed of hiking the Appalachian Trail, he told me. "I like to walk. I walk everywhere."

Wes and Tammy Dingus lived just two blocks from the church, but they never had liked "the city." (The two square miles of Gate City housed just over two thousand souls in the last census.) Wes was thirty-three; Tammy's age was not mentioned, but she looked older. They had been together thirteen years. Her family was from Gate City; Wes moved here from near Fort Blackmore so they could be together. Most of her family was gone now, except for a niece, but I had the impression Wes and Tammy were stuck here for financial reasons, living on his monthly disability payments of $750. His disability was one of the dominoes of life that fell after he was kicked in the head by a horse when he was seventeen. That blow kept him out of his final year of high school and left him stricken with occasional seizures. That condition disqualified him from a driving license, which in turn limited his job prospects to places where he could walk, and jobs were scarce in Gate City.

Wes told me his story matter-of-factly, with no self-pity, but his face brightened and his voice picked up steam when he started talking about the countryside. He grew up on a family farm, reared with six siblings by a father who believed a nineteenth-century rural upbringing was best.

"It was just his way," Wes said. "We'd make apple cider vinegar and give it to the horses, because when they sweat the flies leave them alone. I learned how to make a bow from a willow tree. We made everything." When the family's mule died, Wes and one of his brothers had to pull the plow. He benefited from a grandmother who was full-blooded Cherokee—the Turtle clan, he added—who took him to the woods to teach him about native plants and their nutritional, practical, and

Tammy and Wes Dingus

medicinal uses. ("You'd be amazed how much water you can drink when you cut open a wild grapevine. It's like drinking from a faucet!") Wes told me his Cherokee name, which sounded like "Keehawday" and means "man from the field," he said. He was the proud possessor of a redtail hawk feather, which he said was allowed only because of his Cherokee heritage. "There's a $10,000 fine for having one of those, unless you're Cherokee," he explained. He still roamed the hills, looking for raw materials to carve into walking sticks or jewelry, and sometimes just to get out of the city.

As Wes talked, I found myself entranced by his easygoing, natural profundity. "I love to watch a mourning dove take flight," he said at one point, "and the way that iridescent neckband just glows." Later, when another man walked by and briefly joined our conversation, the talk turned to religion. Wes complained that many local people thought all snakes were bad and should be killed, citing the Bible to justify it. "They use that verse about 'crushing the serpent's head,'" he concluded, "but that's a metaphor. God talks in metaphors!"

Wes told me that he liked to read but found it difficult because of the damage from that horse's kick. When I asked him to write their address in my notebook, he did so slowly in block letters, asking Tammy to help him spell the name of their street. Later he brought me a few samples of his craftsmanship: a walking stick he had carved from one piece of wood to look like a chain with distinct links, and a few pieces of jewelry he had made, including a cedar-and-wax pendant hung on a leather strip.

"Do you ever sell your work?" I asked.

"No," he said. "My heart's too big. I just want to give it away. That's what makes me feel good."

I swallowed an urge to suggest that he could not afford the luxury of such generosity. After he explained the finer points of locating good branches to make walking sticks and recognizing the difference between a tooth and a tusk—tusks are hollow, he said, handing me a couple wild boar's tusks he'd found—I asked if he ever considered offering classes at a local high school or community college. I imagined him leading field trips for teenagers or groups of senior citizens who would lap up his folk knowledge.

"Nah, I don't think they'd have anyone like me," he replied, and I realized he was probably right. Tammy—who was feigning annoyance at the mewing kitten that had followed us down the street—said they did "nothing" most days, other than check on her niece, visit friends, and take care of their dog, cat, and a fish that "had babies today."

Wes handed me the cedar-and-wax pendant, insisting that I keep it as a good-luck token for my trip, and invited me to visit whenever I passed through. "We live just up around the corner," he added, "so come on up there tonight if you need anything." We said goodbye, and as they walked away, with Tammy cradling the kitten, it occurred to me that a person with his background and skills would have been highly valued, back in the century that his dad had prepared him for. Now there didn't seem to be a place for him.

Wes and Tammy often came to mind long after I left Gate City. I liked their openness, generosity, and easygoing way, but their story nagged me. He was bright and inquisitive, the possessor (as best I could tell) of a trove of Cherokee knowledge, a man who readily summoned words like "iridescent" and "metaphor" and noticed how hatchlings would imprint on him. I wondered how their lives would be different were it not for that literal kick in the head. The accident had crippled his ability to read and write and to get around, which left him without a place in our economy. They get out and walk and he makes things with his hands, but the sum of their days seemingly does not add up to much. The thought of Wes and Tammy watching their lives drain away, day by day, unsettled me. *There could be so much more!* But almost as soon as that thought crossed my mind, I recognized my prejudices, shaped by assumptions of what fills a life. I was comforted only slightly by knowing that mine was a common instinct. Even so, meeting Tammy and Wes reminded me that it does not take much to alter the trajectory of a life. A horse's hoof. An icy riverbank. A renegade gene.

It was almost half past five, and I suddenly felt hungry but unwilling to cook. I had noticed a small Mexican restaurant on Jackson Street, but I needed to wash. Even I could smell my stench. With the church locked, I sheepishly walked back to the parsonage and knocked.

When I explained my predicament to the pastor, she offered me the use of their guest bathroom. She led the way, poking her head into the kitchen as we went to check on her towheaded nineteen-month-old son, Benjamin. Then we stood talking for about twenty minutes, me in the small, tiled bathroom and she in the hall.

After almost two years in Gate City, Betzy was down to her last three Sundays because she had accepted an appointment to a church in a town seventy miles to the east. They would be no closer to her husband's job as a music teacher in Pound, Virginia, but his commute wasn't the main reason for the move.

Betzy grew up in Missouri intending to teach high school English, but she began a lengthy career change soon after starting graduate school at the University of Tennessee.

"I was still in my first semester when I realized I didn't know why I was doing it," she said. She had been drawn to religion courses during her undergraduate years at Simpson College in Iowa, and her professors there had encouraged her to go into pastoral work, but it "took a few extra years to click." After finishing her master's degree in English and working a couple of years with an inner-city mission in Knoxville, she entered the master of divinity program at Duke University.

She was the first female pastor in the Gate City congregation's century-long history, and I wondered if she had felt discrimination. A little, she admitted—such as when some members were baffled that she would willingly participate in trustees' meetings. (A male pastor typically would have been expected to attend.) She wasn't surprised when a few nonmembers phoned to speak with the pastor, only to stumble over themselves when they discovered that the pastor was a "she."

More to the point, Betzy felt frustrated with some of what she had experienced at this church, which, like many big churches in many small towns, had seen more prosperous days. Congregations in such situations might expect more from a young pastor than could be accomplished with the resources at hand. She was concerned how churches could lose connection with the communities around them and fail to minister to young people and families as the congregation aged.

"It can be difficult for church members to see why people outside their doors aren't showing up," she said. "People have other things to do, and of course mainline churches in general are declining."

The church in Gate City is not alone. Religion is changing everywhere in the United States, even in the traditional Bible Belt, even in Appalachia. Regular church attendance is not greater than in other regions of the country, as would be expected, and often is less. Small country churches still exist, strung through the hollows almost by the mile—Baptists of various stripes (Southern, Freewill, Missionary, Primitive, Independent), Pentecostals, Methodists, Churches of Christ—but many struggle as improved roads make larger towns and their larger churches more accessible to the declining numbers of people living in the country. As rural communities shrink and become more connected to the world, their religious makeup changes, too. For example, what began as a gathering for Muslim students at East Tennessee State University in Johnson City more than thirty years ago has matured into a thriving Muslim community with more than three hundred families who opened the city's first purpose-built mosque in 2007.

As our conversation wound down, Betzy looked a little rueful, but I couldn't tell whether it was because we were carrying on a conversation on the threshold of her bathroom or because she thought she had said too much about the church. She excused herself to corral Benjamin for dinner.

I wanted to linger in the shower's warm massage but moved quickly. I hadn't yet washed away the feeling of being a beggar and an intruder. On the way out, I thanked her and said I planned to be in church the next morning. She said she was working on the sermon.

"How's that going?" I asked.

"Trinity Sunday is always difficult," she said with a sly smile. "You always risk committing heresy."

- - - - - - - - - - - - - -

Sunday dawned with a gray sky and gentle spitting rain. I fixed my usual breakfast, using the church's stone wall as an impromptu table for my oatmeal, coffee, and bagel. Just as I finished eating, a red pickup truck stopped in front of the church. The man who climbed out and entered the church did not notice me. I grabbed my clothes and ditty bag and trotted to the front door: locked. Just as I reached a side door, the man opened it from inside, and we both froze a second, startled. We introduced ourselves—he was Josh—and after I told him about the pastor's permission, I asked if I could use a restroom. He hesitated for two beats, then said cheerfully, "Sure, follow me." He led me through a maze of white walls decked out with framed photographs and notice boards, through a large hall with an industrial-grade kitchen, and into a small lobby with modern restrooms. I quickly combed my hair, brushed my teeth, washed my face, and changed clothes. I wiped down the sink with paper towels to make sure parishioners would not criticize Josh for a messy restroom or, for that matter, criticize Betzy for allowing a camper at all.

Betzy and Benjamin were in their front yard when I left the building, and I went over to say good morning. I asked if she was prepared to commit heresy. "Not if I can help it," she replied with a big grin.

I worried about leaving valuables in the tent while I went to church but decided to start trusting people—they had been trusting me—and so I packed what I could, grabbed a notebook, walked into the church, and sat near the back of the sanctuary while the choir warmed up. Before I was settled, four members introduced themselves and welcomed me. The interior was as traditionally Protestant as the exterior: plain white walls under a high ceiling, with painted faux stained-glass windows. The pews were white with oak-colored trim, upholstered in burgundy that matched the carpet down the aisles. The stained-glass cross over the square-framed chancel was flanked by resurrection-themed banners, all below a halo of indirect fluorescent lighting that ringed the ceiling. The room could easily accommodate four hundred people, but a wooden board hanging on the front wall indicated that last week's attendance was just over one hundred. Family Night attracted thirty-five people, and a faithful remnant of eight came on Wednesday night.

The choir—seven women, three men—was conducted from a parlor grand at the side of the platform by a man in a charcoal-gray suit, glasses, and a graying ponytail that fell to the middle of his back. They sang an old hymn, "For the Beauty of the Earth," with a bit of swing. The director looked loose, like a jazz musician. The robed choir looked stiff, a squad of soldiers not quite at ease.

With about fifteen minutes until the service began, I explored the building. A wall in the hallway behind the sanctuary featured a photo gallery of the church's thirty-one pastors, dating back to 1900. Six of them held doctoral degrees, impressive for a town the size of Gate City. Counting the slightest hint of a grin, the first pastor who smiled for his portrait was Dr. Sydney O. Frye, who served from 1937 to 1940. Betzy beamed broadly above the nameplate that already listed her tenure: 2011–2013. Back at the front entrance, I signed the thin guest book lying on the tall stand. The book's first entry was dated June 11, 1988. The most recent entry until today was July 27, 2012—ten months earlier. The scrawled handwriting made me think of my third-grade self who occasionally wrote in our church's guest book for fun, and I wondered if bored church kids made the last few entries.

As the service started, a stout woman stood at the pulpit to read the announcements printed in the morning program, adding a few remarks as she went. She also announced that Janice and Stan were celebrating birthdays, and someone in a pew spontaneously started up the birthday song, separately for each of them. After almost fifteen minutes, Betzy stood up in her white clerical robe to report that the congregation "helped save eighty-six lives" with the $864 it contributed to the denomination's "Imagine No Malaria" campaign.

A five-piece combo—drums, bass, twelve-string guitar, rhythm guitar, with the pony-tailed jazzman at an electronic keyboard—accompanied the hundred-strong congregation, whose singing was barely audible. Jazzman played "America the Beautiful" on the piano while the offering plates were passed. For a moment, I thought he would segue into a minor key, but that tonal trail turned out to be a dead end. (Was I really expecting an ironic musical question mark on Memorial Day weekend?) Betzy indeed preached about the Christian mystery of the Trinity, a message she delivered with humor and a hearty challenge to live—like Father, Son, and the Holy Spirit—in harmonious community, and she did it all without a whiff of heresy.

Many of the worshippers put their pastor's advice to practice as soon as the service ended, lingering inside and out, catching up on the week's news, and sharing new jokes. Back in my tent to change clothes and pack, I caught passing snatches of conversation about cattle, about how nicely the sky had cleared, about someone's cancer diagnosis. As I rolled my tent, several people stopped to chat and invited me to return. A few minutes later I started walking—not quite wanting to leave Gate City yet, but not having a good reason to stay.

5

DOWN AND OUT IN SCOTT COUNTY

*What is straight? A line can be straight, or a street, but the
human heart, oh, no, it's curved like a road through mountains.*

—TENNESSEE WILLIAMS

After leaving Gate City, Jackson Street becomes the two-lane Daniel Boone Road, which runs surprisingly straight and level for almost eight miles. It follows a valley due west, flanked by Clinch Mountain to the south and Moccasin Ridge to the north, until it joins the four-lane US Highway 23, just past a little gap where Troublesome Creek pours into the Clinch River. This ribbon of asphalt had been designated as US Highway 23 until the big highway was built in the 1960s. Now it's a peaceful byway with scattered farms and churches and a diner with a reputation for excellent milkshakes. A railroad track runs parallel to the road, fifty to a hundred yards from the shoulder, just visible beyond the trees and fields and occasional homes. On the front steps of one small fading gray house, a tanned, bony man with gray hair and mustache sat smoking a cigarette. I asked if I could stop and take a breather.

"Sure. Take your pack off and come sit up here if you want," he said, waving me over. His name was David and he lived, coincidentally, in the town where the Reverend Betzy and her family were soon moving. He owned a landscaping business there, but his sister and "her old man" lived here. David had come to mow, a favor he did for his sister every few weeks, gesturing toward a white pickup truck parked on the gravel shoulder, a bright orange riding mower and two gas-powered trimmers loaded in the back.

Stealing a glance inside at the small front room, I saw a dull brown overstuffed recliner, a sofa, and various small tables cluttered with beer and soda cans, ashtrays, and an opened bag of chips. David and I had talked a few minutes when his sister, Kathy, emerged, sat on the chair on the porch behind us, and bummed a cigarette from her brother. She was only a few pounds heavier than gaunt, and her face did not seem wrinkled so much as grooved like an eroded hillside. Her deep tan made her short, blonde-gray hair look especially pale.

Soon, Kathy's "old man" lumbered onto the porch. Gary was big, his round face framed by a black mullet and a ragged goatee flecked with white, which highlighted wide-set, bright blue eyes. He wore flip-flops and shorts but no shirt, exposing a taut, globe-shaped belly parted by a pinkish butterfly-shaped keloid scar the size of a dinner plate. Kathy joined David and me on the top step, and Gary sat in the chair behind us. David told him who I was and what I was doing. Gary did not seem impressed.

"Headed to Kentucky, huh?" he said. "Those people in Kentucky, they're crazy." We all laughed.

"There are some crazy people in Tennessee," I said.

"Yup," Gary answered. "And I'm crazy too."

He wasn't kidding, he added quickly. "I've been in the nuthouse a lot of times. I've tried to kill myself three or four times. I tried to gut myself once," he said, pointing to the scar on his stomach.

"I've cut myself," he added, extending his arms. He had checked into the "nuthouse," a mental health hospital in Johnson City, only a few months earlier. "I think of it as a vacation now."

Gary, who was 51, unrolled his life story as readily as a rug salesman displays his wares. The son of an Irishman and a woman who was three-quarters Cherokee, Gary had married and divorced three times, the first time when he was seventeen. "That didn't last long, just six months," he told me. His second marriage lasted eighteen years and produced a son. He and his wife were regular churchgoers, and he sang in a gospel group.

"Then I find out my wife was screwing the preacher, and that really messed me up," he said. He was ready to kill the preacher, with the man literally in his gun sights. "I thought I felt someone tap me on the shoulder and say, 'Don't do that. It's not worth it.' But when I turned around, there was no one. I figure it must have been the good Lord."

After his third divorce—he didn't say much about that marriage—he lived with another woman four years and had a child with her, but then broke up when he realized "she was nothing but a druggie." He and Kathy had been together four years, mostly on but occasionally off, and he accepted the blame for their temporary splits. He knew he made her life hard. On the other hand, he continued, she suffers from depression and when she doesn't take her drugs, "she can be a witch, and I'll tell her. She knows it."

By then, Kathy and her brother were unloading the riding mower from the truck and stowing the weed trimmers in a shed so David wouldn't need to haul them back and forth. I couldn't tell if they were listening to Gary's monologue. Surely, they had heard it all before. He moved on to describe his cocktail of prescription drugs, including Ambien.

"I'm supposed to just take that at night, but sometimes I get bored and take one or two during the day and go lie down," he explained. His bed was in the living room. Gary told me he paid $250 a month from his disability payments for "this shitty little nothing house with blacktop in front and trains in my ass, with diesel and coal dust all the time." Not to mention the black mold.

"Life has just happened to me," he summed up. I asked if things were getting any better.

Yes, he said, but he sighed deeply and repeated that he'd been in "the nuthouse" a few months ago. He had the sound of a man who was trying to convince himself more than anyone else that things were looking up.

David and Kathy returned to the porch steps with me, and we chatted about things I don't recall—maybe the weather, maybe what to expect on the road ahead. After a few minutes I hoisted my pack, and we said our goodbyes. Gary told me about a good camping spot about five miles away, where Copper Creek flows into the Clinch River. I could even swim down there, he said—about a half-mile off the main highway, underneath a long, tall railroad trestle bridge.

"But just watch out for snakes and bears," he casually added. "Yeah, the snakes are really bad this year."

For a few miles the road was level and mostly treeless, but at one cluster of trees a maroon minivan slowed down and then stopped beside me.

"What are you into?" the driver asked, leaning out the window. Forty-ish, he could have stepped out of a Kohl's clothing ad. As I answered he reached down beside him. "I saw you walking and thought you might like one of these," he said, extending a vanilla soft-serve ice cream cone that looked huge and delicious. "I was going to get one for my wife and me anyway. My name's Kevin Barnett, and I'm at the little brick church up here," pointing in the direction I was walking. I thanked him and watched him drive away, mildly stunned by this impromptu gift. I took off my pack, propped it up with my trek poles, and leaned against it like a beach chair to eat ice cream in the shade.

Roughly at its halfway point, the road passes through the small, un-incorporated community of Daniel Boone, the only place along the Wilderness Road named for the man. Neighboring churches—the white-sided Church of God and the brick-faced Missionary Baptist Church, Kevin Barnett's, perhaps—seemed to define the community. Across the road was a side street named Mingo Private Drive. Was it named for the actual Native American tribe, or was it an ironic nod to the televised Daniel Boone's fictitious Indian sidekick in the 1960s? *So much was wrong in that series, starting with Boone's coonskin cap.*

A long CSX train rumbled east, all but a couple of its sixty-plus cars piled high with coal and half of them decorated with simple graffiti: *Billy* ♥ *Chris.* A cartoon face peered out near the bottom of one of the train cars. In a few minutes, the train would pass behind Gary's small, moldy house—another train in his ass.

In its last mile or so, the road starts to undulate and to feel pinched between hills as it gradually ascends to the gap where Moccasin Ridge abruptly butts up against Clinch Mountain. The open, flat landscape that had defined most of the miles since Gate City now gave way to out-croppings of rocky cliffs and tall trees. Thirty feet down to my left was Troublesome Creek, named for the problems it gave the first settlers. Beyond the creek and up a steep bank was the railroad track. Roads followed the rivers, and railroads followed the roads. Eerie green kudzu vines were taking over the trees between road and river. One tall, dead remnant of a tree looked like a giant, shiny, elongated insect with mul-tiple green arms, the weird offspring of Godzilla and a praying mantis. In a few weeks those kudzu leaves would grow to the size of a hippo's footprint—something the pioneers never saw because the vine was in-troduced into America a century after they walked through.

Just before three o'clock, I paused where Daniel Boone Road ends at the newer, wider, faster version of US Highway 23. Studying a map while munching trail mix, I estimated Natural Tunnel State Park to be another two hours away, prompting an internal debate over whether I should try to find Gary's camping spot at the Clinch River or just head for the park. I was still weighing the options as I resumed walking along the wide but uneven shoulder. The rush of vehicles felt jarringly fast and relentless after hours of relative quiet, and I was so focused on it that I almost stepped on the first snake of my trip: a four-foot-long black snake on the shoulder of the road, split open almost its entire length. Tiny shards of tissue were dried like jerky, and the ribs were folded down, almost flat, like rows of white upholstery needles.

I came upon a live animal a few minutes later: a young whitetail deer grazing near the concrete pier of a railroad bridge, standing only a few feet from the shoulder of the highway as cars, motorcycles, and semitrucks rumbled past. I was still about fifteen yards away when the deer suddenly lifted its head, spotted me, and broke for the wooded hill behind it. *How strange,* I thought. *Or how revealing.* The animal had grown comfortable with the roar of engines and the buzz of tires but was frightened by the peculiar sight and muted sound of a single walker.

In another hour I reached the broad, barren concrete bridge over the Clinch River and a decision point about where to spend the night. I chose to skip Gary's camping spot, reasoning that reaching the state park tonight would allow me to rest the entire next day. Besides, after adding a few extra miles, who knows what I might find at the creek? This all sounded rational. In reality, the prospect of snakes and bears had unnerved me, and as I crossed the bridge I scolded myself for being afraid. *I should turn back and camp down there,* I told myself. But a moment later I still managed to hedge: *I'll be more adventurous after the state park. I'll have other chances for a wilder night than the one I'd chosen today.*

But the true reason continued to needle me: *Watch out for snakes and bears.*

At this point, US Highway 23 is a broad curve of four-lane, almost-interstate-grade divided highway, with a wide shoulder meeting a sheer rock face rising almost a hundred feet. Vertical grooves score the rock like pinstripes, spaced two feet apart, evidence of the drills and dynamite that split these hills in the 1960s to create the thoroughfare. Before that time US Highway 23, like most federal highways in Appalachia, was predominantly a two-lane road that twisted around mountains rather than blasting through them, winding through towns and past houses, churches, and farms. In the first half of the twentieth century, these federal highways were valued for two main benefits: They were paved, and they linked places directly. A driver could get on US Highway 23 in Sault Ste. Marie, Michigan, and follow the road almost 1,300 miles to Jacksonville, Florida, passing through towns like Big Stone Gap, Virginia; Johnson City, Tennessee; and Asheville, North Carolina. Even though many roads were nothing more than narrow threads of blacktop, the federal network accommodated the great outmigration after World War II, when thousands of families headed north to find work. "It was not uncommon on Friday nights in the 1950s to find the highways flowing south from Akron, Dayton, Cincinnati, Detroit, and Chicago filled with Appalachian migrants heading to West Virginia, Kentucky, and Tennessee," wrote historian Ronald E. Eller. "Migrants quipped that the only things taught in mountain schools after World War II were the three Rs—reading, writing, and Route 23, or whatever the local highway to the North was."

This particular section of US Highway 23 in extreme southwest Virginia bears a few different signposted nicknames. It's The Crooked Road, Virginia's designated music heritage route because so many country and bluegrass artists were born and reared within shouting distance of the highway. It's also the Coal Heritage Highway, for obvious reasons. Those labels are mere memorials now, hearkening to a day when the early version of the route passed literally within feet of those musicians' front doors or through coal camps. The new highways, by contrast, remade the road system into a kind of little-brother image of the burgeoning interstates. These still offer the benefits of speed, efficiency, and occasional magnificent mountain views—in a word, progress. Charming, however, they are not.

Walking the steeply cambered shoulder, I picked my way past boulders, litter, and scattered tufts of weeds. With each step I grew more convinced that I had made a sound decision about not stopping. The sooner I could get past this tedium of rock and road, the better. I let my mind wander to the first explorers, long hunters, and pioneers. What did they think about as they traveled? With sweat pouring, feet aching, and hip burning, I couldn't imagine them spending much time contemplating the meaning of life or the historical impact of their journey. They would have focused on the plain, blunt work of survival, their thoughts dominated by the physicality of travel. Philosophical musing was a luxury reserved for the day they stopped moving, if they ever did.

It was well past five o'clock when I exited the highway onto the two-lane Natural Tunnel Parkway and came to the Redstone Drive-In, a white building outlined, predictably, in red. Telling myself that I had earned a cheeseburger and maybe even a milkshake, I dropped my gear at the door and walked in. The decor was 1950s retro: black-and-white checkerboard tile floor, a half-dozen chrome-trimmed booths and tables with fire-engine-red padding, Betty Boop signs, and a jukebox that looked vintage but played MP3s instead of 45s. The place was about half-full, and I could feel eyes following me to the counter. Between delivering food to other customers and flirting with a brawny guy at the register, the high-school girl working the counter took some minutes to get to me. While I waited I leafed through a leftover copy of that day's Kingsport *Times-News*, a reminder that after five days of walking, I hadn't even left my own neighborhood. I was still in the Tri-Cities! I left the Redstone about forty-five minutes later, after a cheeseburger, onion rings, four glasses of water, and a bout of diarrhea, which I got out of my system with several trips to the men's room, fortunately located in a separate building on the far side of the gravel parking lot.

Natural Tunnel State Park is named for a limestone oddity created by a million years of percolating water that produced a passage spacious enough to accommodate a railroad track, currently two hundred feet wide and eighty feet high in places but still growing. William Jennings Bryan—lawyer, Woodrow Wilson's secretary of state, and three-time presidential candidate—called it the "Eighth Wonder of the World," a piece of trivia that made me wonder what John Scopes' old Presbyterian prosecutor believed about its age.

Less than a half-mile from the park entrance, a young man wearing a fluorescent orange trucker's cap, aviator sunglasses, and a spotless white polo shirt sidled up and started walking with me. Within two minutes I knew that J. E., age twenty-two, lived with his parents—or maybe not, as he contradicted himself a few minutes later—and dreamed of becoming a park ranger.

"I used to volunteer here all the time," he told me in a march-tempo voice that had an odd, flattened quality. "I know all the trails. I know just about everyone who works here."

They knew him, too. He apparently was a local fixture. The rangers treated him kindly but addressed him with a hint of condescending politeness, like they might talk to a very bright first grader. A local woman later told me that "J. E. has issues."

Whatever his issues, he made good on his boast about knowing the trails. The ranger at the entrance directed me to the campground store where I would check in, tracing a route along the park's main road on a map. Once outside, however, J. E. offered to lead me a different way, guaranteed to be shorter. I decided to trust him and we started ascending. I was stiff and winded after the day's long walk and still feeling the Redstone's onion rings. We seemed to climb a long time, passing people coming down. J. E. talked the whole way as I followed close behind with growing doubts about whether the route was shorter than the ranger's.

"Are you sure we're on the right path?" I asked.

"It sure is," he answered just as the trail reached a hairpin turn at the top of a cliff, offering a dramatic view of green ridges fanning toward the south like ocean waves and a chasm, almost straight down, where I could just make out the entrance to the famed tunnel. J. E. informed me that this fenced overlook was Lover's Leap, where, legend has it, a Cherokee girl and a Shawnee boy, forbidden to marry, jumped to their deaths as a hunting party closed in. When I compared the story to Romeo and Juliet, J. E. tilted his head quizzically and said, "Uh huh." The Shakespearean reference was lost on him.

Less than five minutes farther up the trail, we arrived at the camp store just as J. E. had promised. A woman ranger sat behind the counter inside the faux log cabin. "Oh, hi, J. E.," she said cheerfully. I got the last available site, located just over a small hill. J. E. led the way.

"Do you want any help setting up?" he asked. I could tell he was eager, but I told him that I'd be okay, thinking he might attach himself to me for as long as I stayed. As we shook hands, he said he would come by the next day to make sure I was doing all right, but I never saw him again.

My site was grassy and flat and, unlike the one at Warriors' Path, free of rocks and trash. Motor homes, pop-up campers, and the vehicles that towed them occupied the surrounding sites. My tent, plopped in the middle of the site, looked lonely and tiny by comparison. I was still setting up when a tanned man wearing a T-shirt, jeans, and the ubiquitous trucker's cap over his short white hair and matching mustache approached from an adjoining site dominated by a large camper, a few other adults, and a couple of kids tossing a ball. He and I shook hands.

"Where are you headed?" asked Robert Bledsoe, which sounded to me like "Bled-saw."

The usual words popped out almost automatically: *Wilderness Road... Daniel Boone ... writing a book.*

"Do you have a family?" he asked, maybe to determine what I was—adventurer, loner, shirker. I told him about my two grown daughters and braced for the next question. "Are you married?"

I was, I said, but my wife died six months ago. He looked stricken. "I'm so sorry," he said simply and honestly.

We chatted a few more minutes, trading small details about each other's lives. The Bledsoes lived less than ten miles away, on the other side of Duffield, and were camping here until Tuesday, an annual Memorial Day family tradition. When I mentioned that I needed to get cleaned up and eat, Robert invited me join them for dinner after my "share." *Share?* It took me a moment to silently translate: *Shower.*

A half-hour later, Robert introduced me to his clan as we gathered around a picnic table laden with plates of grilled chicken, steak, hot dogs, corn on the cob, potatoes mixed with onions and peppers, and rolls.

There was Patty, Robert's wife, a slim woman with shoulder-length chestnut hair, a quick, crooked smile, and wide-set almond eyes that were both friendly and sad. She told me to make myself at home and handed me a tall plastic cup of sweet iced tea. Robert explained that I was hiking to Kentucky. The second fact he told her was that I'd recently lost my wife.

Their forty-something daughter, Carrie Ann, and her husband, Jason Rhoton, had done most of the cooking. Both worked at Eastman. Carrie Ann told me proudly that Jason was one of only eleven specialty brick masons the company employed around the world. As we tucked into the feast, I noticed that each successive generation around the table was heftier: Robert had a paunch befitting a sixty-seven-year-old man but was not fat, and Patty was downright skinny. Their daughter and son-in-law were both larger, as were their children, fourteen-year-old Mily (pronounced "Millie," short for Emily), and eight-year-old Isaac. Mily played volleyball for her middle school. Isaac seemed magnetically attached to his handheld video game.

Our conversation casually ran toward plans for the next day, what was happening at work, how good the food was. (*Do you want some more?*

The Bledsoe family, including Patty (left front) and Robert (left rear)

Help yourself, there's plenty. They were not kidding. There was plenty, indeed.) After we finished eating—after the pie and the cake—Robert and I retreated to folding chairs while Jason, Carrie Ann, and Patty cleared the table. Isaac sat on the end of the picnic table bench with his video game.

"I used to do a lot of hiking," Robert said. "I've walked all over these woods, camping and hunting. I've thought about hiking the Appalachian Trail," he added wistfully, "but I don't know if I'll get the chance now."

"Sure, you could," I said. "You can take it in sections."

"I don't know. Maybe." He paused, signaling a change of topic. "Where are you going from here?"

"Over Powell Mountain, through Kane Gap."

The Wilderness Road didn't follow the route of the modern main road that climbs from Duffield along the mountain's south side. That new road offers a majestic view of the valley below, but it is busy and seems to head almost straight up for two solid miles or more. I did not know what the trail over Kane Gap was like, but I had been warned that it was rocky and full of snakes. Powell Mountain runs southwest to northeast some sixty miles from Tazewell, Tennessee, to Norton, Virginia. Just a few miles from its eastern end is a geological apostrophe where the ridge bends like a J to form a curving valley to the north and west of the mountain. The Wilderness Road traversed Kane Gap, a natural passage into the valley at the crook of the J's elbow.

For decades the present-day route was an old logging road that rose from Duffield, but now it is used mostly by maintenance crews to inspect water tanks planted on the side of the mountain. A trail to the gap peels off from the old road, leading to the valley on the other side. The federal government owns the land on the eastern side of the gap, part of the Jefferson National Forest. The land on the other side, inside the J, is privately owned.

"I used to go hunting up there all the time," Robert said. "You'll want to watch out for snakes." *Snakes again . . .*

At some point he asked if I was carrying a gun and shook his head in bafflement when I said no. He looked skeptical when I mentioned the Mace spray and Maasai club.

The evening had grown dark, and the day's long walk was settling into me when Robert's voice roused me.

"I need to head over to Stan's shop tomorrow to fix a mower." The image of a suburban-style riding mower popped into my head. "I don't know what you're doing, but you'd be welcome to come along, if-un you want." I said that would be fine. It took me a minute to recall that Stan was Patty's brother-in-law, one snowflake in the flurry of family facts that had whipped around during dinner.

The cleanup was soon finished, and the other adults joined Robert and me. We chatted until the subject of s'mores came up. Mily and Isaac had started a flame that burned anemically in the metal-ringed fire pit. Robert nonchalantly retrieved a quart-size container of charcoal lighter fluid from his camper, and, with Isaac and Mily eagerly looking on, squirted a stream into the pit. A six-foot tail of blue-tinged flame shot up, like an upside-down rocket. The wood caught fire, and in a few minutes, we were passing around marshmallows and chocolate bars. Robert good-naturedly razzed Isaac about charring his marshmallows. After a couple of s'mores, I sat contentedly with a full stomach, enfolded by the warm spring night and the banter around me. As I felt myself drifting off, I stood to say good night, but on a whim turned to Robert.

"Would you like to hike with me over Kane Gap on Wednesday?" I asked.

He flinched a little with surprise and then smiled.

"I'd just slow you down," he said.

I told him that I didn't think so, and I really didn't.

"Well, sure, I'd like that," he replied.

I would like that, too, I said, and so we agreed.

The Bledsoe clan was still talking and roasting marshmallows as I crawled into my tent, and their murmurs and occasional laughs soothed me toward sleep, as well as the thought of driving around the valley and walking over Kane Gap with someone who knew the territory. This night was as close to normal as I had known since leaving home, and I was grateful for it. And I was grateful for the Bledsoe family.

The next morning, Memorial Day, Robert invited me to join the family for breakfast: fried eggs, sausage, tomato slices, and homemade jam on toast. Mily and Carrie Ann were absent because they'd gone to school. Mily wouldn't mind, I was told, since this year's traditional camping trip bored her. (It apparently bored her brother, too. Later that day—a bright, breezy, and warm afternoon—Isaac hunkered in his parents' camper, watching a movie.)

Robert and I climbed into his red Jeep Cherokee around nine o'clock and headed toward Duffield by way of Natural Tunnel Parkway, the serpentine two-lane that formed part of US Highway 23 in the days before the four-lane was built. In less than ten minutes, we were through Duffield and bound for Pattonsville, a community of farms scattered in a valley defined by the tree-covered shoulders of Powell Mountain on one side and Clinch Mountain on the other. We pulled in at a two-story steel shed with large double doors opening to a central bay. An eight-foot-long pair of articulating saw-toothed blades, rigged behind a tractor, sat in front of the main door. "Of course," I mumbled to myself. *Suburban lawn tractor? Did I really think I'd see that, here?*

A short, balding man wearing a gray University of Virginia T-shirt and walking with a cane greeted us: "It's about time," he said. This was Stan, Patty's brother-in-law. He owned the shop and was by all accounts a mechanical genius. He was using a cane because his left knee had been replaced six weeks earlier. Mike, Robert's cousin, was inspecting

Mike, Stan, and Robert

the blade and stood up, wearing a trucker's cap, eyeglasses, and a yellow T-shirt under bib overalls.

Mike and Stan thought the blade needed a new bushing. As we bent over to inspect the machine, I noticed that the back of Robert's neck was the color of leather, but the skin behind his ears was pink. He and Mike did most of the work while Stan intently watched from a stool, leaning on his cane for support as he offered advice and occasionally retrieved a tool from the depths of his shop. Classic rock music blaring from a radio inside provided a soundtrack for the three men, each one sporting identical white brush mustaches, as they worked and swapped stories about bad mowing days and groused about how often mowers broke down, usually at the worst possible moment; how newer models of blades, like this one, required too many moving parts to be dependable; and how Triple 19 fertilizer was better than potash for hay, despite what the Virginia Tech extension office said. Mike and Robert were sweating hard and having trouble removing the old bushing when Stan suggested heating the area with an acetylene torch to expand the metal. That worked. Robert burnt his fingers as he tried to pluck the old piece with his bare fingers, which gave Mike a good excuse to joke about his cousin's hard head.

The whole job took about ninety minutes. When it was done, we stood around chatting, telling stories, and joking. I was not native to a world where men farmed and repaired tractors as a matter of course, but here I was surprisingly at ease. I had long felt inadequate around men who knew how to work with their heads and their hands, including my deceased father-in-law. I felt awed and even intimidated by their hands-on skills and what seemed an almost-supernatural ability to diagnose a mechanical problem or in a vacant space visualize a room they planned to build. I had attended a few shop classes through the years and learned to handle rudimentary jobs—how to do a brake job, how to lay tile—but more complex mechanical work or craftsmanship seemed beyond me, and all my slow, labored efforts were clumsy by comparison.

But that old insecurity was absent today. Maybe it was because I wasn't related to these men, but I hoped it was for no other reason than we were comfortable standing together in the intersection where they did their work and I did mine.

I mentioned being raised in New York and Tampa, and Mike asked if I thought people in southwest Virginia were different from people in New York. I started to say people in Virginia were more outgoing and friendly when he interrupted: "Yeah, people here will go out of their way to be friendly." I agreed and told him about the man who gave me an ice cream cone on Sunday. I started to say that while New Yorkers can be harder to get to know, they—*Another interruption.* "Yeah, they seemed rude." I was going to answer that yes, it can be that way, but once you get past that first shield . . . but the conversation had already moved on.

Mike left to mow—his seventeen-acre field would take about seven hours—and Robert and I climbed into the truck and drove five minutes to his house so he could feed his two horses and his dog, Lefty. Robert and Patty lived in a two-story house with brick face and pale-yellow siding, circa 1980, alongside the old stagecoach road that swept down from Powell Mountain. A garden half the size of a football field grew in front. Robert pointed out where an inn once stood. During Prohibition, Robert said with a little swagger in his voice, the stage stop had its own speakeasy, complete with a one-eyed tiger.

Bledsoe is a common name in the area, but unlike many local landowners, Robert and Patty did not inherit their eleven acres. They bought the property in the 1960s. They both grew up a few miles away, in the Red Hill area, on the Clinch side of the valley, where Robert took me next, to see the small white church where Patty attended and where her father used to preach. Robert didn't go to church much, he said, but he respected Patty's faith and loved her father. ("The best friend I ever had," he said of his father-in-law. "A fine, fine man.") The church stood on a knob overlooking a state department of transportation depot, which was built on the site of a house once owned by John McKinney, who was likely Daniel Boone's brother-in-law. (Details are sketchy and open to interpretation.) The house was famous for having collapsed into a sinkhole or maybe quicksand. (Again, details are sketchy.) Only a staircase was salvaged, which was then incorporated into the schoolhouse built on the site, which Robert had attended. That set of stairs eventually wound up in a barn a few miles away, near the north fork of the Clinch River. It was there that someone found a letter tucked under the stairs, apparently written by Boone himself, specifying the sale of sixteen hundred acres to pay off debts.

Robert casually narrated as we drove up and down the valley, through hills and past wide hayfields, several of which Robert had worked: "There was a house here, where we lived when I was a boy, but it burnt down. . . . This was where my dad leased land to farm. . . . A man used to live there who . . ." Finally, he turned down a long, narrow dirt lane bisecting two hayfields and stopped on the far edge, at the north fork of the Clinch River. Here was a wide, shallow, rocky stream where, locals say, Boone built a cabin on a sandbar. A few hundred yards away, on the edge of a hayfield, was the barn where, less than thirty years ago, they found Boone's letter. In a flash I realized that some people in this region remembered family members whose own memories reached back to ancestors from Boone's time. We are not so far removed from the frontier days.

It was midafternoon by the time we turned back toward the park, and I felt myself drowsily swaying as the truck bounced down the road. I asked Robert to drop me at the replica blockhouse so I could meet Joan Boyd Short, the president of the Daniel Boone Wilderness Trail Association (DBWTA), to make plans for the next two days. She had arranged interviews and invited me to stay at her and her husband's house the next night. "We're eating at five, so don't be late," Robert said as he let me out.

"I'm not a stray cat, you know," I answered, trying to sound jokey but feeling defensive.

"We're having a birthday party for Isaac," he said, "and it wouldn't be right if you're not there." Grinning, he added, "You figure you can find your way back to the campsite? Not too far a walk, is it?"

Joan was dressed in her eighteenth-century garb to greet visitors, although none were around when I arrived. We discussed plans and chatted until a young couple came by, when I returned to the campsite.

Robert and Patty were sitting in the shade outside their camper, and I took the spare chair.

"You all set?" he asked.

All set.

Jason and Carrie Ann started to fix dinner, and Patty got up to help, first carrying an enormous chocolate cake to the picnic table.

"Your daughter's coming tonight, right?" Robert asked. Sarah and I had arranged for her to bring a few supplies and a replacement for my broken GPS tracking device. She would drive the distance in about an hour. My walk had taken five days.

Robert hoisted himself out of his folding chair and ducked into his camper, reemerging with a honey-colored walking stick about five feet tall, its top third naturally corkscrewed by a honeysuckle vine that once strangled it. A silver medallion was glued on the top.

"I want you to have this," he said, holding it out to me. "I know you can't carry it with you, but your daughter can take it home."

I was dumbstruck. He had mentioned in passing that he made walking sticks, but I hadn't given it much thought.

That night's dinner was as generous and tasty as the previous night, even before that great cake was served up with ice cream. Sarah arrived just as we sat down to eat, and the Bledsoe clan—now including Jason's parents, Ed and Teresa—immediately invited her to stay.

After we had eaten and oohed-and-aahed over Isaac's gifts, Jason, his father, and I talked beside the newly kindled fire. Ed, it turned out, laid most of the blame for the nation's ills squarely at the door the White House's current occupant, whom he suspected was not really an American. Robert sat with his grandson, looking at the boy's new video game, and Sarah joined the other women to clean up after dinner. After they finished, Sarah and I walked to Lover's Leap, where she oohed-and-aahed over the view, and then strolled back to camp. Sarah stowed the walking stick in the trunk of her Honda and walked around to say her goodbyes while I restocked a few packets of oatmeal from the small supply box she had brought with her. Then she and I stood behind her car and hugged tightly. This, I realized, was likely the last in our unplanned series of goodbyes, a thought that sent a shiver of sadness and thrill through me: sadness at yet another parting, thrill at an intuition that tomorrow would begin a new phase in the journey, with places less familiar and less accessible. Maybe this was how sailors of old felt, standing on the pier just before they boarded their ships.

6

THE DEVIL'S RACETRACK

Memories need to be shared.

—LOIS LOWRY

The morning was bright and a touch chilly. I broke camp at just past nine o'clock, after a final cup of coffee with Robert and Patty. We exchanged small talk but did not say much. I was caught between my eagerness to get back on the road and my reluctance to say goodbye to these folks. From one second to the next, I would shift between feeling like I was wasting time—*Let's go already!*—and wanting to ask for another refill of coffee if only to spend a few more minutes with my new friends. We talked about staying in touch, but you just never know if that will happen. But at last I stood and stretched and said something like, "Well, I'd better get moving." A hug from Patty and a handshake from Robert, and I was off.

A few minutes later I arrived at the replica of John Anderson's blockhouse, a full-scale wooden building about twenty-foot-square at its base, its upper story overhanging about two feet on all sides. It was built by the DBWTA, which was founded in 1995 "to identify, preserve and promote historically significant sites along the Daniel Boone Wilderness Trail corridor from Long Island of the Holston to Cumberland Gap by creating historically accurate interpretative, educational and recreational opportunities which will foster regional tourism and economic development."

The association's early work focused on identifying the trail—or an approximation that makes allowances for driving—and signposting it between Kingsport and the Cumberland Gap. But the blockhouse, a decade old, was thus far the group's most prominent project and was a good landmark. Primarily it serves as home base for the association's colonial

The replica of Anderson Blockhouse,
Natural Tunnel State Park, Duffield, Virginia

reenactments and other events. Because the land at the site of the original structure was not for sale, the group approached the state park. The
association collected donations and received $100,000 in grants, and
now the blockhouse sits on a grassy hilltop with a panoramic view of surrounding valleys and distant ridges. The organization has since added
other features around blockhouse grounds: a wood-burning oven made
of stone and terra cotta, a dogtrot barn and workshop, and a garden. The
state built a small visitor center a hundred yards away, which includes an
auditorium and a shop that sells frontier-themed gifts and books, mostly
self-published by local authors.

I followed a secluded gravel road out of the park to Natural Tunnel
Parkway, the same two-lane blacktop that Robert had driven the day
before. I turned toward Duffield.

Just before a bridge over Stock Creek, an abandoned service station
was sagging into a cracked concrete apron. Two rectangular stumps of
concrete stood in front, where gas pumps used to be. A fading metal sign
tacked next to the roofless one-car garage warned "No tresp." The shell
of what was once an office had no front wall, and the remains of the roof

looked near to collapse. Pigeons perched on exposed beams. Plant life was taking over the whole place. Weeds pushed up through the concrete apron and the dirt-covered floor of the building, vines embraced the chalky walls, and small trees and clumps of grass had taken root in the dark rafters. In western deserts, buildings and cars forsaken decades ago can be preserved by the arid climate. But in lush Appalachia, the vegetation asserts itself constantly, inexorably, and it will overgrow anything unless it's pruned or worn down.

This service station was once part of a small community, probably a landmark on the main road (*Turn right by the gas station, just before the bridge . . .*). Then came the new highway. The service station closed, the humans vacated, and the overgrowth and all that comes with it—the dampness, the insects, the molds, the fungi, the birds—started their reclamation project. One day the building will collapse. A few years more and its remains will be broken up and sunken, difficult to find. This part of the world does not maintain manmade objects when we abandon them; it consumes them.

Farther down the road, dogs came after me for the first time. Just after I had passed a house on a small hill overlooking the road, four dogs raced down the driveway like a squadron of barking fighter jets swooping in from five o'clock. I instinctively turned to face them, swinging my trek poles to keep them at bay, walking backwards. My small can of dog Mace was useless because I had stupidly zipped it in a pocket of my hiking pants. But the dogs were wary of the trek poles, and, about thirty yards past their property, three of them barked a last time for good measure and turned and trotted home. The fourth, some brand of Schnauzer and by far the least intimidating of the gang, kept after me—compensating for his size, maybe—yipping and then looking back, apparently wondering where his wingmen went. He gradually fell behind but kept tracking me for another quarter-mile before issuing a final bark (. . . *and stay out!*) and turning around. I moved the Mace to the open pants pocket, where it stayed for the rest of the trip, and started thinking about tactics.

The morning had grown hot and sticky by the time I came across a one-story brick ranch-style house, unremarkable except for the small cemetery in its front yard. Nine stone grave markers of varying ages sat under a maple tree on a rise in the front corner of the lawn. The oldest-looking marker bore the name Panell. Another with a variant spelling—Pannell—stood next to a Bishop and a Bledsoe. Just then a blue pickup truck pulled into the driveway. A collie jumped out, followed by a middle-aged man who moved gingerly.

"Can I help you?" he called out.

"Just passing through," I said but then thought better of it. "Actually, I'm supposed to meet Jean Brown at her house. Do you know where she lives?" I had a good idea where her house was—Joan had set up an interview and provided directions—but this exchange let me start a conversation.

"Sure, you're almost there," he answered. "Just around that bend and you'll see a blue house on the right. You can't miss it."

We introduced ourselves. Shannon Bishop was a friendly, 47-year-old local whose ancestors came from New York in the late 1700s and settled in this valley. He said his family once owned much of the surrounding land, an area once known as Little Flat Lick, after a nearby salt spring. The Bishop buried in his front yard was his grandfather—their family name was not English, as I had assumed, but was corrupted from a Persian name—and the Pannell was his great-great-aunt whose house used to sit next door. From her, Shannon had learned about "the goat man," a hillbilly who wandered around the area for a few months in the 1940s or '50s, selling odds and ends out of a small cart pulled by six goats. When he disappeared, the locals assumed he had simply moved on. A few weeks later, however, agents from the Federal Bureau of Investigation (FBI) tore up a bunch of moonshine stills, and several people were thrown in jail. The goat man was an undercover agent, or so the story went.

"Something like that happened again in the 1970s," Shannon concluded. "They need to do the same thing again now, but more for drugs than alcohol."

When I asked what he did for a living, Shannon looked at his feet and shook his head. "I'm on disability," he said. Years of construction work had permanently damaged his back, and he now lived with a portable pump strapped under his shirt that injected pain medicine directly into his spine. "I expect to be in a wheelchair one day," he said simply. On good days, like this one, he ran errands or worked around the house as much as he could. Other days he couldn't get out of bed.

As we said goodbye, he wished me well.

"Are you carrying a gun?" he asked.

"No, I'm not."

"Well, you'd better watch out for dogs on Wallens Creek Road."

Shannon was right: I couldn't miss the blue house. I walked up its driveway to find a tiny, bronzed, white-haired woman and a tall man with wispy white hair sitting under a carport, eating from McDonald's bags.

"You must be Jim," she said in high-pitched voice.

"I am. Are you Jean?"

"I am. And this is Benny Bloomer. He's a friend of mine, and I'm helping him with some paperwork today." He stood and offered me a limp handshake and a quiet "hello." Lean and doe-eyed, Benny carried a naturally elegant air, though he was dressed plainly in a blue Henley, jeans, and old running shoes.

Jean struggled to her feet and grabbed her walker. "Let's move into the house," she said. "Are you hungry? I've got an extra coupon for McDonald's. Why don't you use it and go get something to eat?" McDonald's was within sight, at the single major intersection in Duffield. At her insistence, I left my gear by her door and walked to the restaurant, which was attached to a convenience store. Inside, the wall separating store from restaurant featured a mural in a style that could generously be described as amateur American primitive, portraying an imaginary scene of pioneers gazing over a vast valley that exists nowhere on the Wilderness Road. (A polite Southern critique might be, "They meant well, bless their hearts.") The central figure of the mural was a tall man in buckskin and a coonskin cap. Nearby stood a rack of "Dan'l Boone Coonskin Caps," selling for $9.99 each.

Jean and Benny were waiting for me in her small, paneled living room. A mandolin, a guitar, and a set of three sepia portraits of girls from the nineteenth century hung on a wall. (They were no relation; Jean had bought the pictures at an auction.) Stacks of magazines, pamphlets, and books took up all the table space, so I balanced my meal on the edge of a spare chair while we talked.

I had been told by Joan Short that I should talk to Jean. She had written a couple of books, one a local history and the other a collection of stories she had heard and repeated through the decades. "Some people are interested only in today," she explained. "I wanted to create an interest in their past, in their own backyard. Do you have a copy of my book?"

Jean Brown and Benny Bloomer

I confessed that I didn't. She took this as a cue to ensure that I walked away with more than a superficial knowledge of the area.

Jean, somewhere north of eighty years old, knew she was a character, and she breathed deeply of the blustery atmosphere she created. Her family roots were in Duffield, but she was born in Dryden, ten miles away as the crow flies, almost twice that by road. Being on the other side of Powell Mountain, Dryden was a completely different place. (Mountain communities tend to be determined by topography rather than by distance. High ridges separated hollers, effectively isolating families or entire towns from those literally just over the hill.) Jean and her husband moved to Duffield more than sixty years ago so he'd be closer to his job at Holston Munitions Company, and they had reared three children. But they divorced when she was fifty-five, courtesy of his attraction to a young secretary.

She did not regret the split because it "liberated" her. She went on to become a successful real estate broker and traveler, visiting such far-flung places as Hong Kong, Korea, Poland, Germany, Scotland, and England. Her wayfaring days over, she felt content to live out the rest of her years in Duffield. "I'm satisfied with my life," she said. "There's no pressure." Even so, she considered herself an "outsider," although she did not say why. Maybe because of her long-past divorce. Or maybe because she was born over the mountain, which still counted for something even after six decades.

Jean asked if I had noticed the Devil's Racetrack. I had no idea what she was talking about.

"Go look out my door, up at the mountain on the other side of the highway." I did as I was told, and indeed saw the faint trace of a road curving into the trees.

The Devil's Racetrack, she informed me, was part of the Wilderness Road before it was bypassed and cut off by newer roads. It earned its name from two attributes. First, even by Appalachian standards the track is steep and windy, especially treacherous in winter as it climbs Purchase Ridge with endless switchbacks. By the time white travelers reached the crest, often hauling their possessions, they were exhausted, and the second reason would then become apparent: Native Americans would often be waiting to ambush them at the top. So, settlers made a point of traveling that section of road as quickly as possible—hence, the "racetrack." The once-perilous track, however, had long been demoted to side-road status.

"[Pioneers] would sight from the top of one mountain to see the low places to cross, and they'd go in that direction," Jean continued, shifting topics smoothly. "In valleys, they'd look for rivers and shoals where they would cross. They built mills at natural drop-offs of rivers to power the mills. You can still see pillars in rivers. Those were the mills' foundations, like at Pattonsville. It's all in my book. Do you have a copy of my book?"

No book, I said, but I had visited Pattonsville the day before. She nodded in approval and plunged ahead.

"It was the gathering place. It had the post office, and there was an inn," she explained. "Pattonsville was at the base of Powell Mountain, and when a stagecoach reached the top of the mountain, they'd shoot a volley to alert the innkeepers that people were coming. You can read all about it in my book."

Jean filled in other blanks with historical details, such as the state of Kane Gap a century ago, when the timber industry cleared the old forests and left the mountain virtually bald, as photos from the day vividly illustrate. She continued on to talk about the importance of salt licks. They were absolutely essential, she declared, to animal and human survival on the frontier.

She was not exaggerating. It is almost impossible to overstate the importance of salt in the days before refrigeration. Salt was used to preserve meat, to make food palatable, especially if it had begun to rot; to make medicines; to store fresh pelts being hauled back east, thus preserving the valuable assets of long hunters; and to tan hides to sell and barter. Practically every aspect of daily life and commerce was affected by the presence or absence of salt—and it was certainly present on the western side of the Appalachians. The springs proved so mineral-rich that many local economies in the early 1800s were based on salt making, producing enough not only for local use but also for shipping back east.

Nineteenth-century historian Jackson Frederick Turner went so far as to credit the discovery of salt springs in the frontier with freeing the West from dependence on the East Coast. "It was in part the effect of finding these salt springs that enabled settlement to cross the mountains," he wrote in 1893. Until then, he argued, settlers were compelled to travel back east annually to buy enough salt for a year.

"[T]he discovery of salt springs . . . was a strong inducement to settlement," agreed John C. Campbell when he published a groundbreaking study of Appalachia in 1921. "These 'licks,' so called from the fact that the spring basins incrusted [*sic*] with salt were the rest of buffalo, elk, deer, and other wild game, had long been familiar to the Indians, who had manufactured salt in early times. The lack of this commodity was keenly felt by the first settlers, and even now there are in the mountains those who tell of the long annual journey to the east, made by their great-grandparents in search of salt."

Producing salt, however, required enormous amounts of raw materials, starting with water from salty springs or the soil from salt licks normally found along rivers. One early salt producer said that eighty gallons of water were required to render a bushel of salt. A family or small community could get adequate amounts of salt by boiling down water in kettles, but large-scale production had immense environmental costs. Depleting the natural salt reserves on which deer, elk, buffalo, and other big game depended was only the beginning. In his 2003 book on the environmental history of the Appalachians, Donald Edward Davis said, "Of greatest consequence to the local environment were the

large amounts of coal and timber needed to fuel the saltworks' continu-
ously burning fires. The mining of coal seams precipitated acid runoff
in mountain streams, and the cutting of cordwood aided in the further
clearing of mountain woodlands, intensifying soil erosion and the silta-
tion of creeks and rivers." The path to civilization always creates a large
footprint.

Benny sat silently while Jean talked. The two had met at a craft show two
decades ago and had been friends ever since. Now in his seventies and a
retired social worker, Benny was by all accounts a skilled woodworker.
He had built several pieces of furniture for the reconstructed blockhouse
and for Jean's house, including the coffee table next to me, which I had
been admiring for its elegant, simple lines and honey-hued finish.

Benny came to Jean's house that day so she could help him get his
affairs in order, before he lost his memory. To Jean it had become clear
in the past twelve months that Benny's memory was not slowly wan-
ing, but disappearing as if in chunks—more like computer files being
deleted than like old ink fading. Sometimes he forgot his own address.
He could not tell me how long he had been retired. During a lull in our
conversation, Jean phoned a Gate City lawyer for an appointment. She
and Benny would drive there that afternoon to draw up the power-of-
attorney documents before visiting the driver's license bureau to see if
he could still pass a driving test. Jean seemed to think he would.

Jean, Benny, and I said our goodbyes after almost two hours, and
I walked west. At the main Duffield intersection (where McDonald's
stands), Natural Tunnel Parkway intersects with US Highway 23, which
bears north to Big Stone Gap and beyond, and US 58, which heads west
over Powell Mountain and on to Cumberland Gap. Duffield reported
a population of 91 in the 2010 census, making it the second smallest
incorporated town in the commonwealth. (It was the smallest a decade
earlier, but redrawn boundaries had given the title to nearby Clinchport,
population 70).

A small, old-fashioned, mint green train depot stood incongruously
on the southwest corner of the intersection. A dozen train-station signs
hung on its wall or leaned against it: Clinchport, Glenita, Norton,
Pocket, Sunbright, Church Hill. A red Norfolk and Western caboose
rested alongside the station. I walked to the brick rancher next door to

see if the people there knew anything about the building, and a tall, thin, old man, shirtless and sweaty, answered the door. Kenny Fannon owned the depot, the showpiece of his own railroad museum.

"I'll be glad to show you around, but I can't stay long because I have a veterans' meeting in Norton in an hour," he told me. "I just finished weed eating and was just about to get in the shower." Kenny disappeared for a minute and came back with a shirt on and invited me into what might once have been his garage. The room, however, had been converted into a museum annex, crowded from its caboose-red shag carpet to its low ceiling with train lights, identification plates, signs, esoteric tools, photographs, timetables, books, badges, and other memorabilia. One wall was completely given over to five long wooden shelves, each neatly crammed with railroad signal lights and handbells. The opposite wall was covered by framed photos and clocks. A pegboard covered the short wall abutting the house and was festooned with scores of ancient padlocks and chains, their keys dangling below. File cabinets and display cases filled all remaining nooks.

One back corner, however, was not dedicated to trains. There, a large wooden display box held an assortment of items: a half-dozen photos, most black and white, a pack of Beechnut gum, a dog tag. This was a shrine dedicated to Kenny's older brother, Jack, who was killed in Korea in 1953, only weeks before the shooting stopped. Near the pack of Beechnut gum he was carrying when he died lay a Purple Heart and a Bronze Star for valor, both awarded posthumously. Jack featured in each of the family photos—one taken at the scrap-metal business their father started, one with him standing in front of a railroad car, another with his arm draped around his kid brother's shoulder. Kenny looked about ten in that picture.

We walked across the yard to the depot, which, it turns out, was a prop in *Coal Miner's Daughter*, the 1980 biopic starring Sissy Spacek as Loretta Lynn and filmed in nearby Wise, Virginia, the stunt double for Lynn's eastern Kentucky hometown. The depot was only a shell for the movie but was saved from postproduction destruction when a railroad supervisor planned to take it home. His wife objected, however, so he offered Kenny the chance to buy it. A few of Kenny's employees at the family scrap-metal business dismantled the building, hauled it to Duffield, and reassembled it. After Kenny finished the interior, he stuffed the depot with relics he had collected over five decades: ticket dispensers from the early 1900s, logbooks, coal buckets stamped with railroad company names, pigeonhole shelves stuffed with timetables. As we walked around, at least a half-dozen times Kenny randomly picked up an item and said something like, "Oh, I remember when I got this. . . . It was at an auction in 1958." One of his prize possessions was a framed and mounted wall chart: a work schedule for engineers and conductors on the Illinois Central Line in 1895, including the scrawled name of Casey Jones.

After a ten-minute tour, Kenny said, "I'm sorry I have to break this off, but I need to go." Several times before I left, he invited me to return to spend more time looking around.

The road west—US Highway 58—passes a spread-out string of grocery stores, fast-food joints, and auto-parts dealers, all fronted by broad parking lots. But Duffield seemingly has no center. The town, Jean Brown had told me, barely existed before the railroad came in the late nineteenth century to take advantage of a fortunate convergence of mountain gaps to haul out coal and timber. The remnants of the old town still remained, but only as a quiet side street with a few houses and abandoned storefronts. The low, flat ground where I walked, dominated by a shopping center and an industrial park, was a reedy swamp until the 1960s, when a regional planning commission tagged the site for an industrial park. (The commission adopted the bulky name of LENOWISCO, one of those acronyms that sounds like a fake Native American name but actually refers to Lee County, the city of Norton, Wise County, and Scott County.) The industrial park attracted a few small factories, but Duffield did not evolve into a charming country town or a bustling economic center. Instead, people came to earn or to spend money, but not, it seemed, to live. Residency was relegated mostly to a small suburban-style subdivision tucked between the industrial park and the base of Powell Mountain.

That's where I ended up in the late afternoon, hot and tired, sitting on a curb under a tree in front of a brown split-level house. Powell Mountain began its ascent directly across the street, as near as a neighbor's driveway. A steep, gravel trail suitable for four-wheel-drive trucks started there, blocked from the suburban street by a single steel beam painted a faded Pepto-Bismol pink. The road was mainly used by maintenance workers for the giant water tank on the hillside, but it also led toward Kane Gap. This was where Joan Boyd Short would pick me up today and then drop me off in the morning, when Robert and I would start hiking up Powell Mountain. After phoning Joan, I pulled out my canteen and almost drained it in one long gulp.

Waiting for Joan to arrive, I reviewed the day. Even after three good conversations, I still felt an inexplicable disappointment. Maybe I was spending too much time around Duffield. I had arrived at the state park on Sunday and would not depart the area until Thursday. Jean Brown was charming and fun, but I left wanting to know more about Benny, whom I found more intriguing in his quietness. He spoke just a few times and then only to answer direct questions. His expression showed calm resignation, not depression. Knowing full well what awaited him, he was methodically preparing for the day when his memory evaporated altogether, and I was sorry I didn't have the chance to talk with him alone. I wanted to know what he was thinking. I wanted to know what motivated him to keep working at his life, what memory he would hang onto if he could keep just one, and what devils he was racing before time ran out.

----- **7** -----

THE ASSOCIATION

If you don't know history, then you don't know anything.
You are a leaf that doesn't know it is part of a tree.

—MICHAEL CRICHTON

oan arrived in her maroon Honda Element about twenty minutes after I phoned. Her white hair, almond-shaped eyes, and smooth tanned skin lent her a patrician air enhanced by a soft Southern accent that was more rounded than the local mountain dialect. Her hands were large and looked strong, with short fingernails. The first time we had met, at a reenactment the previous October, she was dressed as an eighteenth-century frontierswoman and had shown me how settlers turned flax into linen thread. Now she was dressed in jeans and a button-down shirt pulled over a T-shirt.

She and her husband, Ron, live on the south side of Powell Mountain, in a two-story cottage at the end of an unpaved cul-de-sac off the two-lane highway that climbs steeply from Duffield. When Joan and I drove onto their property, Ron was riding around on a bright-orange riding mower—a new purchase—with his shoulder-length gray hair flowing behind him and an open-mouthed grin on his bearded face. The whine of cars straining up the mountain filtered faintly through the trees from the highway.

The cottage is set on a cleared acre that overlooks the Clinch River valley, with Purchase Ridge and Clinch Mountain rising in the distance. (I recognized a tiny white church tucked into a low hill on the far side of the valley as Patty Bledsoe's church in Red Hill.) Inside, small watercolors from Cape Breton, the Shorts' favorite vacation spot, dotted the earth-tone walls. A colorful but surreal Zuni warrior figure, a gift from

Ron Short and Joan Boyd Short

a friend, stood like a three-foot-tall sentry in a corner of the enclosed side porch. Musical instruments and pieces of folk art occupied nooks and tabletops throughout the house. The ambience was rustic and tasteful, but not primitive. None of the artwork and probably none of the furniture was mass produced. A flintlock rifle, its stock burnished to a chestnut glow, was mounted over the double doors leading to the porch.

Ron and Joan had been involved in the DBWTA for five years, and their interest came honestly, the latest iteration in a lifetime of concern for Appalachian culture and history. Growing up in southwest Virginia, Ron expected to follow his father into the coal mines. He was as surprised as anyone when he instead carved out a career as a grant writer, publicist, actor and, for thirty-four years, the artistic director of the Roadside Theater, an Appalachia-centric touring company. As a professional singer, he's played in several bands—traditional mountain music, rock, blues—including Ron Short and the Possum Playboys. Joan grew up in what was then the rural outskirts of Chattanooga, where Hamilton Place Mall now sprawls. After college she worked in Nashville as a publicist for the Grand Ol' Opry and Jack Daniels and—a fact I discovered later—was a civil-rights activist in the 1960s. "Jack Daniels by day and a hippy three-chord folk singer by night," she said, chuckling.

She and Ron met in the early 1970s in Nashville and were married in 1975. (They had recently figured out, however, that their first brief encounter occurred at a music festival in Norton, Virginia, in 1971. Ron's loud electric guitar playing nearby had annoyed Joan. "'Could you turn that thing down?' Those were the first words I ever spoke to Ron Short," she recalled with a wry grin.) A few years after marrying, they moved to Big Stone Gap, Virginia, where Ron supervised a nutrition program at an agency for elderly people and Joan taught English at Powell Valley High School. When she realized that her students knew virtually nothing about their own heritage, she used her English classes to launch a program that encouraged students to learn and write about their family histories, old tales, and local traditions. (Joan said it was reminiscent of Foxfire, a program launched in a rural Georgia school in the 1960s that led to a magazine, a series of anthologies, and a heritage center.) The high school eventually merged with another regional school, but the English teachers at the new high school continue guiding students in creating an oral history magazine by interviewing relatives and other local folks.

"Other teachers are doing their own versions," Joan said. "The teachers have a high consciousness of Appalachian upbringing, and how turning the spoken word into the written word is very valuable, especially for kids in a rural area to listen to their elders and see how things have changed, how language has changed."

When Joan retired in 2008, she and Ron decided that reenacting would give them a chance to work together and live out their shared passion for Appalachian culture, music, literature, and history. They immersed themselves in the work of the DBWTA, and Joan became president in 2012.

The group is composed of local individuals who work with a budget patched together from membership dues, donations, and grants. Even so, the association has posted signs along a drivable approximation of the original route, built the replica blockhouse, bought property to preserve on Powell Mountain, and was helping to build a heritage center in Duffield.

The association's biggest regular activities are reenactments staged each April and October at the blockhouse at Natural Tunnel State Park. Presiding over an association board meeting in March 2013, Joan announced in a deadpan voice that nobody would try to kill anyone else at the following month's reenactment; the scenario was changing. Until then, the April event was called the "Blockhouse Siege," which dramatized a Cherokee attack on white settlers. The action could seem fierce, aiming to give visitors a sense of how dangerous life on the frontier had been. Reenactors used props made to late-eighteenth-century standards—real blades in the knives, real powder in the guns. Daniel Boone and his comrades could have used the weapons. The two main accommodations of reenactment are that the participants do not fire real ammunition and the action is choreographed. There can be no surprises, lest someone gets hurt. Injuries are rare at reenactments, but not unheard of. If a "victim" misses a subtle visual cue from an "attacker," she could get brained by a tomahawk. If a faux frontiersman pours slightly too much black powder into a rifle, it can burn his face. If he forgets to remove the ramrod from the barrel, he can fire a potentially lethal spear, as Joan and Ron saw happen at a reenactment in Canada.

"We were visiting the Highland Games in Nova Scotia," she later recalled. "They had some sort of precision rifle drill team, reenactors, doing a presentation on the field—flipping them in the air and all that. Then they fired, and one of the reenactors forgot to take his ramrod out. Fortunately, it went between two people, but it flew almost the width of the field and stuck in the ground."

There's never been a serious mishap at a DBWTA event, but Joan's droll announcement at the board meeting signaled a change in direction: The association decided to downplay battle scenes to focus more on educational settings. ("Although we might allow a fistfight or two," Ron interjected, prompting laughter around the table.) So, goodbye to the "Blockhouse Siege" and hello to the "Frontier Muster and Trade Fair."

Thus, the following month's fair featured, for example, a local African-American woman who played the part of a frontier slave, telling stories from an often-neglected perspective. A full-blooded Cherokee man who teaches his native language at a reservation school in North Carolina offered a workshop in basic Cherokee vocabulary. ("`O-si`yo elisi" is "Hello, grandmother," he told his audience, for example.) A few reenactors stirred boiling saline water in an enormous iron kettle to render salt. Others cooked frontier food. (The bear stew drew mixed reviews, but I thought it was delicious. The apple turnovers were an unqualified hit.) Ron entertained visitors with old Scots-Irish tunes on his fiddle.

Reenacting has spawned an elaborate subculture, with careful distinctions drawn between scripted "historical reenactment" and unscripted "living history." Like many groups, the DBWTA practices both. A weekend event may include workshops, demonstrations, and informal conversations about frontier life but could also include reenactments of actual historical events, such as a specific attack on a fort. Depending on the level of authenticity, participants are categorized as "farbs," mainstreams, or progressives (also known as "hard core," as Tony Horwitz explains in his wonderful *Confederates in the Attic*). No one is sure what farb stands for, but it is not a compliment. One theory is that the word is short for "Far be it from me to be authentic." Farbs are more likely to mix modern and period materials—say, by using Velcro to hold a dress together or lighting up a Marlboro instead of rolling their own or smoking a clay pipe.

The so-called mainstream reenactors—such as those in the DBWTA— strive for more authenticity, but they break out of character when audiences are not around. They may not play a role at all when dispensing information and answering questions, serving more like guides at a living museum. Their clothing might look authentic on the outside but use internal stitching or construction that didn't exist in the period. One man I met who was dressed as a simple eighteenth-century hunter carried a cell phone in his leather pouch.

A hard-core reenactor, on the other hand, would throw a chamber pot in exasperation at such accommodations. The self-described progressives immerse themselves in the period, spending an entire reenactment event in character, trying to live as close to the original conditions as possible, and insisting on authenticity down to the fabric they wear and how it is sewn—thus the unflattering nickname of "stitch Nazis."

While there's no way to tally the number of active reenacting groups or individuals, it is clear that the American Civil War is the most popular period for reenactors, followed by World War II. The colonial and Revolutionary eras fall fairly far down the list.

Reenacting can be an expensive commitment. The clothing alone for a man in Revolutionary garb can cost upwards of $500 from a specialty outfitter like Smoke and Fire or James Townsend and Co., not to mention the price of a gun, knives, cooking gear, tent, blankets, and accessories. And reenactors go to extraordinary lengths for authenticity. That flintlock rifle mounted in Ron and Joan's living room, for instance, was handmade by Billy Heck, a historical interpreter at Virginia's Wilderness Road State Park and an expert in Revolutionary-era weaponry. Billy, a native of southwest Virginia, regularly reenacts the role of an early settler, Captain Joseph Martin, and he led the effort to build a true replica of Martin's Station at the state park where he works. (The original Martin's Station stood twenty miles farther east, at present-day Rose Hill.) After securing a waiver from Virginia's modern building codes, Billy and a crew of volunteers constructed the full-scale wooden picket fort by living on the grounds, off and on, for six months. As they did, they wore period garb and used only materials, tools, and methods that were available on the frontier in 1769.

All this effort, money, and time raise the obvious question: Why?

"The reenactment takes the storytelling to a new level," Joan told me. "I'm not an actress; I consider myself an interpreter. When I show someone how to process flax and can tell them, 'And from that came everything I have on,' and when I can say the settlers made linen from flax and then show them the linen—that's a powerful teaching tool. It's not 'dress up and come out to play.' The idea for me is to translate that idea of human expression, to put a human face on history, to help people see the human connection."

Joan was aware of the artifice. No one will confuse reenactment with the real experience. "I doubt I could do what they did," she said with admiration. But she regarded reenacting as a way to link real people of today with real people of the past by providing at least a semblance of common experience, "to help people see what it took to create a life of dignity out of their circumstances."

And why, I asked, was making that connection so important? The past is past. Why not just respectfully nod to the ancestors and move on?

"For me it comes from a sense that I'm more connected than I can ever understand," Joan replied. "The idea that this place was found by people like that. We need that sense of continuity. Knowing other people's stories defines our own destiny, to help us see that it's not just birth to death. Everyone should have the chance to lead the best life they can—and I don't mean monetarily—and having those connections to the past is part of that."

Ron later told me that he believed in what he called personal history. "History is a collection of personal story," he said. "Like soil, there's layer on layer, the product of the local environment. We choose certain stories to tell as public history, but there's all that personal history—of soil, of land. Culture is the product of all those stories. But in education, we get generic history. Generic culture is pop culture. Like *Seinfeld*, it's about nothing. It's generic. You don't dig into the local culture. But, really, there is no generic history."

Ron saw his work with the Roadside Theater as part of the effort to explore that local, personal history. "We wanted to connect with elements that make us all human. Telling this story about myself connects with you. The best critical review we got was in the Czech Republic. They had not been able to tell their stories under communism. But they saw a celebration of the story. We performed Jack tales—as in Jack and the giants—and a play about religion, politics, economics. An old man was fighting the power company that wanted to take his property and home. What would he do? They—the Czechs—had the same problems. We all experience the same problems and issues. We were using tools to tell the story from our local environment to reach them."

Before dinner I showered, changed, and, at Joan's invitation, laundered my hiking clothes. As she tossed a salad and grilled chicken, I retreated to the front porch to write notes, take in the expansive view and cooling air, and phone Robert to arrange tomorrow's hike. At length, Ron emerged with a tray of crackers and salsa, which I devoured as he described the lay of the land and the sunlight shifted across the valley below us.

Various owners, individual and corporate, held acreage around Kane Gap, including a member of the association. The US Forest Service administered other land to the northeast. The association owned a parcel of the top. Ron and a few other men had spent part of the fall and spring trying to precisely locate the route of the Wilderness Road over Powell Mountain.

"The problem with determining the land is that it started changing immediately: cutting, putting in fields, and all that," Ron explained. "There are a lot of rocks, and it's hard on the feet. There was all this logging done very early. None of the trees that Boone would have seen survived very long."

The evening wore down and eventually so did I. We said good night and, as I climbed the stairs, I considered an offer from Joan to ferry my pack the next day in her car so I wouldn't need to lug it over Kane Gap. She could bring it to the guest house where I would stay that night. It was a thoughtful suggestion, but we gently debated about it because I was determined to carry my belongings, after all. Somehow her idea seemed like cheating.

I settled into the plush bed, intending to read a passage from *Walden*, but was distracted by a thought that had been percolating throughout the evening, about the futility of trying to relive the experiences of pioneers. After more than two centuries of mitigating the very hardships that molded them—the rough and muddy roads, the attacks by Native Americans, the isolation, the unreliable food supplies, the occasionally violent land disputes—more than the land had changed. We had. It did not seem likely that we could understand our ancestors, much less claim a measure of their spirit, when we had systematically eliminated the conditions they faced and changed the very contours of the world they walked through. Ron and Joan were clear-eyed about the limitations. They understood that even the most hardcore re-creations and reenactments could go only so far. Until time machines are invented, however, this might be the best we could do. Reenactments were better than nothing and much better than forgetting.

And who was I to question such efforts? There I was, lying in a comfortable bed, reading Thoreau's ode to rustic simplicity on a Nook reader and debating with myself about how much weight I should carry to ensure that my hike was somehow legitimate, an option that pioneers never enjoyed.

I shut down my e-book and closed my eyes. Wednesday morning suddenly arrived, cool and bright.

— 8 —

OVER POWELL MOUNTAIN

*The journey I'm taking is inside me. Just like blood travels
down veins, what I'm seeing is my inner self and what seems
threatening is just the echo of the fear in my heart.*

—HARUKI MURAKAMI

ven as late as half past eight, a morning glow tinted gold and diffused by mist filled the valley as Joan and I climbed into her SUV and rode down the mountain. She and I had compromised on her offer from the previous night: I stowed a bag of food and a few other items in the back of her vehicle, lightening my pack by about ten pounds for the day's hike over Powell Mountain. She would drop them off at the farmhouse on the other side of the mountain where I would spend the night.

Robert was waiting at the trailhead's faded pink gate, and he and I set off. Robert wore jeans, a T-shirt, and the familiar trucker's cap and was carrying only a small disposable water bottle. By contrast I looked ridiculously overdressed and outfitted. As usual, he was chewing tobacco.

I wasn't sure what to expect, either from the terrain or from Robert. He used to hike and hunt on the mountain, but this morning he offhandedly mentioned that it had been at least twenty years since he had been up here. The path was about ten feet wide and served mostly as a track for utility trucks. We often walked in tire ruts. Grass and weeds crept from the edges and sometimes overgrew the path. We frequently stepped around low, muddy spots, dank pools where tadpoles swam, with rivulets running parallel to the path. Robert pointed toward a small pile of brush gathered around a fallen tree and said, "That's a good place for snakes"—and we stepped carefully. Ron's words from the previous night came back, full force: Kane Gap was "one of the snakiest places" he knew. The notion of meeting a rattler kept my mind off the sharp rocks that pressed into my feet with each step on the narrowing trail.

Robert and I hiked silently, walking side by side or with me following as he looked around to get his bearings. I could not imagine how he hoped to recognize anything after two decades, but now and then he would stop, look around, announce something like, "Yeah, I know where we are," and plunge ahead. But when we reached a fork in the trail, we both stopped, bewildered. Nailed to a tree was a sheet of white paper tucked inside a clear plastic sleeve: "Kane Gap," it read, with a hand-drawn arrow below it, pointing roughly, ambiguously to the left. Another crude sign was tacked to a nearby tree, but the ink was smeared beyond reading. We agreed to take the ascending trail to our left. We walked by faith for another ten minutes, until Robert recognized a path fading off to the left into an ankle-deep sea of bright, spring-green flora speckled by sunlight. He was sure that this trail led to Kane Gap. I followed him, silent and nervous: Joan and Ron had emphasized that the old road was the way to go.

"Be careful about snakes," Robert said casually as we stepped over the trunk of a fallen tree. That single sentence changed the scene. In a rush of adrenaline, I saw the welcoming forest transform into a potential lair where rattlers bided their time, waiting for me to put down a foot in the wrong spot. I knew my reaction was ridiculous. I had read enough to know that snakes normally don't attack; with a little advance warning, they'll slither away rather than confront. But it was the advance warning part that made me anxious. We were likely among the first humans to have walked this way since last autumn, so I thought we might come upon a snake actually napping. While snakes cannot hear, they can feel vibration, so as we walked I tapped every exposed log and rock with a trek pole. I stayed just behind Robert, literally following in his footsteps.

Ten minutes down the path and suddenly Robert didn't recognize the place anymore. We paused as he looked around, assessed our surroundings, and then agreed to return to the main trail. My nervousness faded with every step—surely, we had scattered any snakes—and by the time we rejoined the main path, I felt positively stupid about my fear. "Never again," I muttered. Yes, I had kept going, but I winced at how easily some small, unchecked anxiety had threatened to explode into panic.

Until then Robert and I had not talked much, maybe because we were focused on finding our way. Back on the main trail, though, we chatted freely. He mentioned coon-hunting tournaments, which I had never heard of before. I thought guys just headed into the woods to track and trap raccoons. In fact, there are competitions all over the country, and Robert had won a few in years past. He recalled some particular hunts with relish, featuring long rides in trucks with friends and nights out in the woods, trying to keep up with the hounds. When he mentioned his best dog, Red Bandit, his voice grew soft and lost its crispness. There had been an accident. During a summer tournament, he and some friends were in a hurry, and a couple of their dogs, including Red Bandit, died after riding in a closed truck, probably the victims of heat stroke. Robert got another dog, but it just wasn't the same, and he soon gave up coon hunting for good. He fell quiet for a few minutes.

Most owners treated their dogs well, he finally said, but some could be cruel. One hunter he knew fitted his young dog with a shock collar and then put out scent of a buck—almost irresistible to a dog—and shocked the hound whenever he went for it. Another man, disgusted with his dog's performance at a tournament, literally threw the animal out of the truck as he drove home.

Robert asked about my background. I told him about growing up in New York City and in Florida, and how I came to this region in the late seventies to attend college. When he heard that I had been a minister for a few years, he asked what my church believed. He couldn't understand all the divisions within the church and thought that God probably doesn't make too much of them either. "What I think is that if someone really believes, is really convinced, then that's okay," he said. "Nothing really crazy, but someone who believes." I assumed he meant someone who believes in Jesus, but he did not specify.

Robert and Patty grew up across the hill from each other and started dating after he returned from a two-year hitch in the army, marrying a few years later. Their forty-sixth anniversary was coming up. He had held down two jobs in Kingsport for a few years—a common practice at the time—but started working Virginia coal mines because they paid much, much better. He had worked in the mines thirty-two years.

"How did you like it?" I asked, expecting a typical tale of backbreaking, sunless labor. He surprised me.

"I loved it," he said. "It was adventurous."

Southwestern Virginia and eastern Kentucky have been defined by coal. I came to understand that it is not merely a commodity. The very word—*coal*—invokes a universe of identity and community. Men do not simply work in coal mines; they are coal miners. Vehicles throughout the region sport bumper stickers and specialty license plates featuring the "Friends of Coal" logo which, I realized, are like pledges of allegiance—and occasionally declarations of hostilities—rendered in black-and-blue badges, a reaction to the real and perceived threats to the industry and all it has stood for.

And the threats *were* real. Coal had always been subject to booms and busts, to the inevitable ups and downs and to the just-as-inevitable advances in technology. Miners and mining communities had typically been able to adapt for most of the twentieth century, but over the last generation other changes had piled up. Hundreds of mines were shut down, thousands of miners became unemployed, and dozens of old communities evaporated from the Appalachian coalfields. Most easy-to-reach and therefore cheap-to-extract coal seams finally tapped out. The price of coal dropped as global coal supplies surged and natural gas emerged as a cleaner, favored energy source. The government passed new environmental regulations or started enforcing existing regulations more stringently. And there was the advent of a cheaper method of extracting coal, one that required mammoth machines and microscopic numbers of workers: the hellishly efficient innovation known as mountaintop removal. As the name implies, mountaintop removal involves scalping a mountain to get at the coal. In the short run, it creates blackened moonscapes, clogged streams, and displaced communities. In the long run, it leaves behind a flattened, irrevocably altered landscape, perhaps replanted with grass or given over to the construction of an office park. Environmentalists hate mountaintop removal. Local communities endure it. Coal miners accept it, sometimes reluctantly but always with a sense of inevitability, a price that must be paid for jobs. As they say, coal keeps the lights on.

None of these facts should be surprising, and yet this was the first time during my hike when I began to comprehend the reverence—I can think of no better word—for coal in the region. Coal seemed like another deity. Entire communities, the coal camps, were literally built around the mines: houses, company stores (think Tennessee Ernie Ford's "Sixteen Tons"), schools, churches. This was no accident. Well past the mid-twentieth century, coal companies did all they could to encourage people to think of coal as their lifeline, their only imaginable basis for survival.

The community's devotion to coal is perfectly understandable from this perspective. Why should it be startling when not only a job or even an industry is under threat, but an entire way of life, with no apparent alternatives at hand?

Attitudes about coal mining, as with so much else in American public life, became polarized during the early 2000s. A person could be "a friend of coal" or "a tree hugger," but not both. Any coal-country politician who suggested there was value in any but the most rudimentary safety regulations committed political suicide, even after April 2010, when the Upper Big Branch mining disaster in Montcoal, West Virginia, killed twenty-nine miners.

Robert was not opposed to regulations, but the way he saw it, the US Environmental Protection Agency (EPA) during Obama's presidency was killing the industry. The changes should be implemented gradually, he said, to give people and the local economies time to adjust, to train for other jobs, and to change the region's economic base.

Maybe, I wanted to say, but coal companies had years to invest in emerging technologies, bring their equipment up to federal standards, and invest in new energy sources and job training—if they had chosen to do so. But they had not. They had, however, garnered profits, invested heavily in lobbying—more than $18.5 million in 2010 alone—and often cut corners on safety, as the Upper Big Branch investigation had shown. In a sweep of inspections following that disaster, the US Mine Safety and Health Administration (MSHA) issued nearly 1,500 citations and other more serious enforcement orders in West Virginia, Kentucky, Alabama, Colorado, Illinois, Indiana, Pennsylvania, Utah, and Virginia. MSHA found almost three hundred violations in just six Kentucky mines, and another five hundred violations in twenty-three West Virginia mines. Inspectors considered forty-four of the enforcement actions around the nation to be "significant and substantial."

I did not say any of this to Robert. Miners were caught in the middle. They felt more connected to the mines—and therefore to the mine owners—than to a federal agency in Washington, DC. The owners and local politicians had the advantage in the battle for hearts and minds.

Instead, I asked Robert about mountaintop removal. "You mean strip mining?" he asked. Sort of, except that mountaintop removal is like old-style strip mining on steroids. The worst damage comes with the runoff into the water, Robert said. He claimed the mines were required by law to restore the land to 90 percent of its original condition, but he considered that requirement overkill. (This is actually a common misconception about the regulations. See the endnotes for further explanation.) To make his point, Robert named a few places built on swaths of reclaimed land in nearby Norton and Wise, Virginia. "It won't be the same, but it won't be bad," he said.

I wondered what he would think if a profitable coal deposit was discovered on rugged Powell Mountain—the place we were walking, on his old hunting ground. Its top would be sheared off, turning the mountain into a desolate wasteland crawling with gargantuan earthmovers for years, before being "restored" as a domesticated slope suitable only for office buildings or golf courses.

Robert carried himself through the woods with a balance of alertness and tranquility I've seen in only a few men. Yes, I told myself, he had grown up with forests and mountains in a way that I had not. I admired his ease and wished I had possessed it a few days earlier when I bypassed the Clinch River. As we tramped through the thickening trees, he was neither reckless nor anxious. After about two hours of hiking, we reached Kane Gap.

The place looked like just another clearing, about the size of a baseball diamond, carpeted by broad-leafed plants I didn't recognize. But Robert suddenly stopped, looked around, and said, "Well, here we are. Here's the gap." Even then, it took a moment for me to register that the trail descended from this spot in both directions and that the light was subtly, suddenly brighter.

Kane Gap is a wind gap, formed over millennia as air currents found their way through the small opening between peaks—a chink in the topographical armor—and carved it wider and deeper. Water gaps were formed by streams and rivers that flowed through low elevations and eroded the land even as prehistoric tectonics were uplifting the mountains. Water gaps, like Moccasin Gap and Cumberland Gap, are often more dramatic.

The trail before us forked. Robert was inclined to bear left onto a wisp of trail that quickly disappeared under the green carpet. That route, he said, would take us west along the high, long ridge of Powell Mountain, parallel to Wallen Creek and its valley. He had gone that way many times while hunting.

I hesitated. Ron and Joan had said we should walk to the right. If they were correct, this would bring us down at the head of the valley, where we would pick up the road that ran beside the creek. The trail to the right was overgrown, too—not many people would have been up here since winter to tamp down the spring growth—but not as much as the other trail. Robert left the decision to me.

I mentioned snakes: Weren't they more likely to be hidden in the taller grass? That settled it. We bore to the right, Robert leading the way. We had taken only a few steps when he abruptly stopped. "Well, now what," he said, more a statement than a question.

A massive tree had fallen across the trail, its thick branches randomly woven into a seven-foot-tall fence. Even if the space underneath had not been too small to crawl through, the ground below the fallen tree, where the trail should have been, was all mud and tall weeds and thick limbs—which I, of course, immediately saw as yet another good hiding place for snakes.

If Robert thought about that, he didn't show it. "I believe I can climb through," he said simply. He paused a moment to consider his route and then started climbing up and in and through the limbs. I hesitated long enough to absorb a jolt of fear. I could not let phantom serpents paralyze me. Besides, I had no options. Sucking in a quick breath, I traced Robert's path through the fallen tree, my pack scraping the underside of a branch as I ducked under.

Another twenty yards down the trail, we easily clambered over a smaller downed tree, only to be faced with yet another large tree with limbs even more tightly bunched than the first. Robert scampered over, but I lost my footing on the slippery bark, and my feet crashed into the thick, soggy weeds underneath. My head told me that any snakes surely had fled by now, but my heart was pounding. I hoisted myself up and crawled through. Robert was waiting patiently. "You all right?" he asked. I couldn't tell what he was thinking. *Maybe concerned . . . maybe amused?*

"I'm fine," I answered, sounding more sharp than I intended. "Let's go."

Those were our biggest obstacles on Powell Mountain. The trail was drier and rockier on the northwestern side of the gap, its edges better defined by grass and weeds. We passed a salt lick, a bare spot of ground hardly a foot in diameter. The surrounding earth was trampled and damp. No trees grew within five feet of the lick, but deer had recently left behind tracks and the striated marks of their tongues. Robert used to bury bricks of salt while hunting, and deer would dig knee deep or more without licking the salt itself, only the soil around it where the salt had leached.

As we walked, Robert occasionally paused to investigate some slightly disturbed ground or a small pile of leaves. "I always look for where the ground or things have been turned up, and I wonder what did it," he explained. He pointed out the signs of animals: the tracks of deer, dog (*or maybe fox or coyote—he wasn't sure*), and raccoon. Bear scat. A torn-up patch of ground that he figured was the work of a wild hog. But the only wildlife we saw all day were five wild turkeys strutting through a clearing near a hunter's empty trailer. We saw not a single snake.

We passed through the gate of an electric fence, a coiled wire flagged with a few florescent orange strips. Robert grasped the handle, a cylindrical sheath at the gatepost, pulled it open, let me pass, and then latched it. We ignored the "No Trespassing" sign.

Finally, we descended into Wallen Creek Valley, that J-shaped glen between Powell Mountain to the south and Wallen Ridge to the north. Our path dumped us at the eastern end, onto Kane Gap Road, at the elbow of the J. A rusted metal gantry with "WRGC" spelled out in metal letters stood above a simple gate that had once led to the Wilderness Road Golf Club.

Robert and I rested by the gate. I desperately needed to take off my pack. With each step for the last quarter-mile, the familiar pain had shot down my right thigh. I drank some water and ate an apple while he chewed tobacco. Chewing creates saliva, he explained, which quenched his thirst. I offered him a bite of apple, and he offered me some tobacco; we both declined. We checked each other's necks and waists for ticks, each of us finding one, but neither bug had latched on. My leg took about ten minutes to stop hurting, and then we started walking west on Kane Gap Road.

Passing a freshly cut hayfield, I asked Robert about the business of hay. A bale of rolled hay—four feet long and four, five, or six feet in diameter—costs about fifteen dollars, he said, and is more efficient for farmers to produce, needing only two men to work the baler. But sold individually, square bales are more profitable. They cost about three dollars each, but a dozen squares equaled a single roll. Less prone to mold and rot, square bales were favored for horses because mold can cause potentially fatal colic. Cows, however, are able to digest moldy hay because they have two stomachs. Robert once owned six head of cattle, and ten rolls of hay per head would last from November to March. Thus, in about five minutes, he had just about doubled my miniscule knowledge of agricultural economics and livestock anatomy.

Three miles later, we arrived at a small, white farmhouse with red-and-white metal rockers on the railless front porch. Nancy Hobbs grew up in this house, but now she and her husband, Larry, rent it to people who want to live a few days on a quiet country road in a Virginia valley. Wallen Creek meandered just behind the house, a few hundred yards from the base of the great, green wall of Powell Mountain. Nancy and Larry, friends of the Shorts, had invited me to sleep there overnight, literally on the house. I phoned Joan to let her know we had arrived, and forty-five minutes later I was pulling my supplies from the back of her SUV. Joan, Robert, and I stood chatting a few minutes, and Robert and I agreed that we should get together again. Maybe we'd go out for dinner the next time he and Patty came to Johnson City. "And let me know when you finish your walk," he said. After a quick series of handshakes and goodbyes, he and Joan climbed into her vehicle and drove off; she would take Robert home on her way.

Alone, I went inside the house to unpack, shower, and get ready for Larry and Nancy, who were arriving in an hour to talk. They lived only a mile from where I sat, having moved into their newly built home that very week. I sat on the small couch with a cup of tea, a granola bar, and my maps laid out for studying.

The farmhouse was decorated simply. The living room featured modest furniture on a honey-colored wood floor with an oval braided rug—but it also offered a few upgrades such as wireless internet and an oversized TV with satellite service. Two short bookshelves were stuffed with books of all sorts: humor, religion, classics, local history. A guest book lay on the table near the front door. Each of the three bedrooms included a combination radio and iPod dock, iPods included and loaded with music ranging from bluegrass to progressive jazz. I could wash and dry my clothes in the new high-efficiency machines tucked into a nook of the back bedroom. The kitchen was spartan by comparison: All the appliances were clean and working, but old, including a massive electric range and a sixties-era Formica-topped table with matching chairs.

I suddenly startled awake on the couch, my tea cold and the granola bar untouched. Larry and Nancy arrived ten minutes later. The day was pleasant, and we sat on the matching porch rockers. Larry, a trim and neatly grizzled sixty-eight, was a retired economics teacher who had taught in high school and college, with degrees from the University of Virginia and Virginia Tech. (Hokie burnt orange and maroon were tastefully displayed around the house.) But in the late 1960s and early 1970s, he worked mostly for the Lonesome Pine Development Corporation (LPDC) in Lee and Wise counties, a local outpost in President Lyndon Johnson's War on Poverty.

"A lot of good was done by those programs," Larry said, "but a lot of money was wasted."

Larry left the LPDC in 1973 over "philosophical differences" with the executive director. The organization had formed a partnership with local businesses to develop tourism in the county, and a sticking point arose over funds that were designated to develop an old mill. LPDC had promised to give the income to the local board, but according to Larry the director had decided it would be wiser to use the money to supplement the LPDC budget. Larry, then twenty-eight, resigned over what he saw as a broken promise. Forty years later, he still believed in keeping promises, but he also thought his supervisor's practicality was probably wiser in the long run than his own idealism—"and pride," he added. Even more strongly in the present, Larry sometimes saw an attitude that fosters wastefulness, or at least carelessness, among local overseers of federal and state grants. "They figure 'It's not my money,' but I disagree," he said. "*We're* the government."

For all the good work that the War on Poverty did, said Larry, it often reinforced stereotypes of Appalachian poverty, and older residents of Lee County still feel a twinge of resentment at the images that were broadcast to the world in the 1960s—pictures of people who were uneducated, lazy, and, more than anything, poor and helpless. Enough examples of that image existed to sear it into the national mind. Indeed, a

Nancy and Larry Hobbs

combination of long-term economic factors came to a head in the early twentieth century, leaving the region depleted in almost every way by the time John F. Kennedy toured West Virginia during his 1960 presidential campaign and LBJ visited Kentucky four years later: The boom-and-bust economics of coal and timber. The stubborn soil, full of clay and rocks and difficult to farm. The advent of coal camps, which left a once-sufficient mountain people dependent on coal companies for their jobs, their houses, their food, their church buildings, and their schools. In the meantime, investors commonly sent the profits from the mines and timberlands back to New York and England.

In reality, people in Appalachia grew up with a robust work ethic. "People worked hard out of necessity," Larry said, "and then kept working. The strong work ethic was instilled and eventually led to prosperity, or at least financial stability."

The War on Poverty, waged directly from Washington and through area "offices of economic opportunity" like LPDC, was conducted with lofty goals: better roads, better schools, more diversified industries and jobs that were boom-and-bust resistant. But along the way, something profound changed. Larry was blunt: "We got addicted to grants. We may revel in work, but our choices may reveal the opposite. We don't like to admit we're dependent, but in many ways we're takers." I was later surprised to learn that in 2010 the average Virginian received $575 more—about 19 percent more—in disability and retirement benefits from the federal government than the average American. Roll in other federal programs, and Virginia received more federal dollars per capita than any other state except Alaska. It was a long way from the pioneers, those icons of self-sufficiency.

The power of Appalachian stereotypes and the real cultural differences in the region grew painfully and sometimes humorously obvious to Larry when, as a college student in the mid-sixties, he transferred from a branch of the University of Virginia at nearby Wise to the main campus in Charlottesville. Many of his classmates came from the gentrified bloodlines of Richmond and Washington. Larry's father was a farmer and coal miner who cleared $2,500 a year, slightly more than his college roommate's allowance. Larry recalled his friends' joking about their surprise at his having shoes. At least he interpreted them as jokes.

"We got along at UVA," he told me. "We kidded around about the accents, but we were both being exposed to new cultures."

His accent changed enough at the university to mark him when he moved back to his native southwest Virginia after graduation. "People would say I 'came back above my raising.' That had more to do with language than anything: my speech had changed." Maybe so, but speech signified a gap bigger than the three hundred miles between Big Stone Gap and Charlottesville.

Despite these striking regional differences, Larry didn't consider Appalachia to be a closed culture.

Nancy disagreed. She had a broad, square, friendly face, and short brown hair combed back to reveal a devil's peak. Her almost-constant smile was intelligent and kindly; it was easy to believe she was a pastor. She wore a sky-blue polo shirt with the familiar cruciform logo of the United Methodist Church.

Nancy had earned an undergraduate degree from Virginia Tech in "clothing, textiles and related arts"—it was the sixties, after all—with hopes for a career in fashion merchandising. She instead returned to Lee

County—not a fashion-merchandising center—and taught elementary and high school before eventually finding herself drawn to church work. She left to study at United Seminary in Dayton, Ohio, and was ordained as a deacon. She had returned home as the pastoral care minister at the Methodist Church in Pennington Gap, about ten miles away.

She was also a member of the denomination's Appalachian Ministry Network, an association stretching from upstate New York to Georgia, and it was obvious to her and to people from outside her area that East Tennessee, eastern Kentucky, southwest Virginia, and West Virginia were different from the rest of the region.

"You can still hear the sense of being apart in Lee County when people say, 'You're not from around here, are you?' or they ask, 'Who's your daddy?'" Nancy said. "Since we've been back here from Big Stone Gap, I've been asked several times, 'How is it coming home?' We lived just ten miles away!"

Larry laughed. "Well, yeah. People ask me if I think Nancy will be happy back here, but that may have more to do with their perception of our lifestyle than our location."

Just then a young man rumbled by on a green tractor, hauling a small load of hay, and waved. We all waved back. That was Adam, Nancy said, a farmer in his twenties who rented some land down the road. He was the exception here. All the other farmers up and down the road were at least fifty-three, and most of them much older. Several families along Wallen Creek have lived on their land for generations, but the younger generations are not staying, scared away by the high risks and the high costs of farming. Replacing the equipment on a farm in the valley would cost well over a quarter-million dollars, Larry supposed.

He and Nancy were worried about the future. The topic of development had come up at a community meeting the previous week. Tourism was high on the agenda, but Larry was skeptical. He reckoned it to be the latest chapter in a history of economic fizzles in Lee County. For starters, there was the problem of lodging for visitors: There was none. "We want people to drive through and see the poor people," Nancy said with a note of sarcasm.

Larry continued his impromptu inventory. "People thought the federal prison would be our ticket to growth when it opened in Jonesville—but most of the employees commute from Kingsport. We want to attract retirees—but there are no medical facilities." (After the county's last hospital closed, in Pennington Gap, the Hobbses were left with a forty-five-minute drive to the nearest medical center.)

"The leaders are not facing reality," Larry said. "They think the tax base needs to be on the land. But why would someone want to come here? We don't give a good reason. We haven't invested the money or put pressure on Richmond [the state capital]. Our best reasons to come are land and beauty, but there's been no effort to grow produce for the prison, which seems like an obvious move." Instead, many landowners are selling to developers, turning the farmland into more subdivisions to be inhabited by people who drive to work in neighboring Scott County or in Kingsport. Eight or nine new houses were just built on a former farm down the road from where we sat.

And yet.

And yet Larry and Nancy still sounded hopeful. I couldn't tell if they were trying to find a silver lining in the clouds, stoking a never-say-die fire, or summoning up their authentic love of the land as they sat talking with a journalist holding a notebook. Maybe all three.

"But maybe we don't have a problem," Larry said in the voice of a clear-eyed economist, rather than a wistful idealist. "Maybe increased income is not what we should be looking for. Economics is about using resources in the most efficient means." Then he told me what happened when Nancy's brother died in 2007, exactly at hay-mowing time. Larry had recently retired from teaching and, by his own admission, knew almost nothing about farming. Even so, the hay had to come in, and three of his neighbors took to the fields in their tractors immediately after the funeral. "It's just what they do here," he said. The solution for regions like Lee County, he seemed to be saying, would not be found in the usual means and the usual grand plans.

"We don't recognize what we have here," Nancy said. "Many people who live within the sound of my voice have never been to Natural Tunnel State Park. Not to Wilderness Road State Park. Not to Carter's Fold. Not to Cumberland Gap Park."

She recalled her childhood, when she rode horses with her father on the land he owned at the head of the creek, near Kane Gap—the very land Robert and I had traversed that day. "He'd tell me Daniel Boone rode through here, and whenever I drive in Lee County I see the White Rocks and Cumberland Gap and wonder what it would have been like." Her voice trailed off.

"We're all part of our past," Larry said, reminding me of William Faulkner's dictum about the past not being past. Faulkner meant it darkly, but Larry said it hopefully.

We sat talking on the porch more than an hour. The day grew humid as the sun gradually started throwing long shadows with a silvery light. We said our goodbyes, and I retreated inside to doze in the cozy living room.

Anything in the kitchen was fair game, Larry had told me, and so I patched together a dinner of penne pasta and an unopened jar of spaghetti sauce, followed by hot tea, two little cups of peaches, a granola bar, and shards of the dark chocolate bar I carried. A mix of fifties rock 'n' roll, classical, and bluegrass wafted through the house from a bedroom iPod. By nine o'clock, I climbed into a cushy bed, eager to read. I don't think I lasted five minutes.

9

NATIVE LAND

People are always moving, even those standing still
because the world keeps changing around them, changing them. . . .
But the old world exists under the present world
the way an original painting exists under a newer one.

—KURT BROWN, "Road Trip"

I woke up thinking about Middle Wallens Creek Road and about dogs. Once I packed up and locked the door of the farmhouse behind me, I tested the Mace by shooting a couple of yellow-brown streams into the front yard. I jammed the small can in my left front pocket and walked west on Kane Gap Road. A herd of about two dozen Angus grazed in a small, fenced field between the road and the creek. They're a popular breed because they have good marbling—or so I had learned from Robert the day before.

Kane Gap Road ends where the main highway, US 58, levels off after a curving mile-long drop down the southern flank of Powell Mountain into Stickleyville, an unincorporated village with at least one out-of-business video store and a diner. The single-story elementary school across the road, I later found out, would also be shuttered that summer. The main road ascended and looped around another small gap, but I crossed the highway and continued onto Middle Wallens Creek Road, a two-lane blacktop that follows the route of the early Wilderness Road more closely. Before the new highway was built, this winding country lane was the primary route between Stickleyville and Jonesville, the seat of Lee County, some fifteen miles distant. Within a quarter-mile of the intersection, the landscape opened up as fields of hay and tobacco defined the properties.

The road rolled and curled and rose and fell, its namesake creek sometimes running only a few feet below the asphalt and other times barely visible down a thirty-foot bank. The creek and its neighboring ridge were named for Elisha Wallen (or Walden or Wallin or any of several other variations), a mid-eighteenth-century hunter who was likely the first white man to explore the area, a decade before Boone came through. "A pure hunter," one present-day local man described him with admiration. Wallens still live in the region.

The day was pleasant when I started—temperature in the low seventies, clear sky, low humidity—and today I hoped to make it halfway to Jonesville. Tonight, I expected to camp, but I was nervous about that. Before setting off, friends and relatives had joked about how I'd hear banjos, *Deliverance*-style. I mostly laughed off such talk, but I had wondered about Wallens Creek Road after I drove it the previous October and noticed more than a few untethered dogs and long, empty stretches between farms. Free-ranging dogs and isolation felt like a risky combination, especially after Larry had warned me about this specific road.

The idea of a dog attack spooked me. On a level stretch of road, I practiced estimating and then pacing off ten feet, so I would know when a dog would be in range of the Mace. I was lousy at guessing the distance, so I gave up and settled on a more concrete measurement: If a dog got close enough to bite my four-foot trek poles and kept coming, I'd shoot. I had already noticed that dogs usually started barking as I approached their territory; that would be my signal to switch both poles to my right hand, pull the Mace out of my pocket with my left, and keep moving, on guard.

As I walked beside Wallen Creek, however, I was met by birdsong, the sweet smell of freshly mown hay, and the sight of a lane winding between patchwork fields, drawing my eyes up past two grazing horses to wooded foothills and the long, dark green ridge of Powell Mountain. The road was quiet and almost litter free. On an old gray shed beside an old gray trailer, white-spray graffiti proclaimed to the world that Chris "hearts" Briana. A gang of four dogs half-heartedly came at me once, but they backed off when I waved my poles in their general direction.

At a particularly picturesque curve in the road, the creek widened to fifteen or twenty feet between steep banks, splashing over rocks in front of a broad, level, freshly mown lawn. A white gingerbread farmhouse with a green metal roof rose primly on the far side of the lawn, an American flag fluttering on the porch—all set against a backdrop of a forested hillside. The home was a photo shoot waiting to happen: quaint, civilized, tasteful, patriotic, cozy. It was the last place on earth one would expect a massacre.

Somewhere between this house and where Wallen Creek emptied into Powell River, a party of Native Americans—fifteen Delawares, two Shawnees, and at least three Cherokees—ambushed eight white settlers, killing five—including seventeen-year-old James Boone, Daniel's oldest son. A roadside marker in Stickleyville describes the slaughter, but there are no such signs along Wallens Creek Road. The historical marker has been moved at least twice, as a few locals informed me, bothered that some agency in Richmond apparently decided the killings didn't happen closer to their own backyards.

In September 1773, a full year and a half before Daniel Boone cut the Wilderness Road, he gathered his family and about forty other settlers to move from North Carolina to Kentucky. They stopped for a while at Castle Wood on the Clinch River—not far from where Gate City is now—and split into two groups. Boone took the first, larger group ahead, soon to be joined by the others, led by William Russell, a wealthy Virginian who was eager for land in Kentucky. The going was rough, and by the time Boone and his group reached the Powell River in early October, their supplies were running low. Boone dispatched his oldest son back to Castle Wood to retrieve more provisions and livestock, accompanied by two brothers, John and Richard Mendinhall.

As the young men prepared to return from Castle Wood, Russell provided a few men to accompany them: a guide named Isaac Crabtree, a young hired hand named Drake, two slaves named Adam and Charles, and Russell's oldest son, Henry. Tired and in danger of getting lost in the dark, they camped along Wallen Creek on the night of October 9, not realizing they were only three miles behind the main party.

The attack came just before dawn. The Native Americans were traveling from a gathering of tribes that had discussed the white incursion, which must have fueled their anger. They fired into the sleeping group of white men, immediately killing both Mendinhall boys. Crabtree and Drake were wounded but were able to flee into the forest. Charles, frozen in fear, was taken captive. (His body was later found forty miles away, his skull split by a tomahawk.) Shot in the hips, James and Henry couldn't run. Adam hid in some brush by the creek and witnessed what followed.

While most of the attackers plundered the supplies, a few started slash-
ing at the boys with their knives. "Maybe it was the sight of blood on
their mangled hands that incited the braves to greater cruelty," writes
Robert Morgan in his biography of Daniel Boone.

"James recognized one of the torturing Indians as a Shawnee named
Big Jim, whom he had met before. In fact, Big Jim had been befriended
by the Boone family," Nathan Boone, Daniel's youngest son, told historian Lyman Draper years later. "James pleaded with Big Jim to spare
him, but the Shawnee's response was to begin pulling out James's
fingernails."

Eventually James and Henry stopped begging for their lives and
started begging for a mercy killing. "Finally, the boys' skulls were beaten
in with tomahawks and their bodies shot full of arrows," according to
Morgan. "The arrows were not just a ritual but also a warning, a calling card, to show who had killed them and a sign of the fate of any who
trespassed on Indian territory."

William Russell's group came upon the scene first, and they hurriedly
buried the bodies in a shallow grave, topping them with logs to keep
out wolves. The entire grieving band of would-be settlers returned to
Castle Wood. As word of the killings spread, Lord John Dunmore, the
colonial governor of Virginia, demanded that the Cherokees punish the
attackers. Young braves resisted, but after much argument, two Cherokees were found responsible and executed. Big Jim, however, escaped
north to the Shawnees. He was killed in 1786 during a skirmish with a
group of militiamen led by Boone himself, who apparently was surprised
to find Big Jim. One of Boone's fellow rangers, Simon Kenton, killed
the Shawnee fugitive, "one of the most notorious murderers among the
Indians." Dunmore pronounced himself satisfied with the Cherokee
outcome—"a remarkable instance of their good faith and strict regard for
justice," he said—and branded the Shawnees as the instigators. In any
event, warriors of all the tribes were furious with whites and, as Morgan
summarizes, "The murder of the Boone and Russell boys seemed to set
off a chain reaction of killings on both sides." The exchange of attacks,
now known as Dunmore's War, lasted a full year and stalled any further
settlements.

During a hunting trip the following May, Boone stealthily returned
to the scene of the killings. Wolves had tried to dig beneath the logs, so
he dug deeper graves and reburied the remains of the victims, who were

still recognizable. James had blond hair and Henry Russell's was dark. Blood was still visible on their heads.

According to Nathan Boone, while Daniel was still at the site, "having barely refilled the holes and replaced the logs, a sudden storm came up and lasted some time. During this time, the melancholy of his feelings mingled with the howling of the storm and the gloominess of the place made him feel worse than ever in his life." For the rest of his long life, Daniel "would be noticeably affected when he described this incident."

The previous night at the farmhouse I had leafed through a book that described accounts of other "massacres," including that of an entire family scalped within a mile from where I sat. That word—*massacre*—is a given, I thought as I walked, but then I considered how other words might apply. Somewhere near where I stood, Native Americans killed five people, including two teenage boys whom they first tortured. They were sending a political message, and so in today's argot they might be called terrorists—or they might be considered freedom fighters defending their native land. Whatever labels might apply, hundreds more whites and Native Americans would be killed along the Wilderness Road in the decades that followed, a precursor of even greater slaughters to come as white settlers pushed west. So, did the Native Americans viciously attack—or were they desperately defending their homeland and their way of life? Such questions, with their loaded adverbs, make me wonder why the settlers' descendants squabble over the placement of a historical marker. What piece of the history are they so eager to possess? Those questions also make me wonder who can justifiably claim the land as their own after more than two centuries.

A year and a half after Boone's son was killed, as the Transylvania Purchase was being settled at Sycamore Shoals, a Cherokee chief pulled Boone to one side and warned him that the whites would find their acquisition to be "a dark and bloody ground." By then, Boone already knew.

I hadn't talked to anyone all morning. Houses were set far apart and far off the road, and I didn't see anyone outside. As the road made a hairpin turn and ascended slightly, I paused to look back from where I had come. It was a grand view: undulating bottomland following the course of the creek, with green-and-fawn checkerboard hills rising on my right toward Powell Mountain. The fields and cattle gradually gave way to trees

that created a line of solid forest about two-thirds up the mountain, all
the way to the topmost ridge, which stretched into the distance, marking a clear, jagged border between land and cloudless sky to the horizon.

The road offered small sensory gifts as it meandered down the valley.
Next to a barn half-full of rolled hay bales, the smell of kerosene from
a spill on the gravel pull-off mingled sharply with the scent of hay and
cattle. Cemeteries punctuated the landscape, two of them in clear view
of one crest in the road—a small one near the road and a large one spread
over a hillside on the far side of the valley. Farther on, my eye was drawn
up to the top of a high, grassy knob, up to a great square house dominat-
ing the view. The home looked like it was built from giant Lincoln Logs
with its orange–brown timbers, bright green metal roof gabled on all
four sides, and a porch that wrapped around the entire house. At a tight
bend in the road, I came upon Livingston Chapel Farm, a small house
overlooking the creek. A white horse trailer was parked there, black sil-
houette figures adorning its side: a man and woman in cowboy garb of
chaps and hats kneeling on either side of a Christian cross. Black-and-
white spotted horses stood behind them, their equine heads devoutly
lowered. Soon thereafter, I chuckled at the name of a private road: Many
Daughters Trail. I wondered how many daughters and if a house on that
road was numbered "two."

The heat was building as the canopies of trees started to thin out, so
I was grateful for shade at the crest of a small hill, which also offered
enough shelter to let me pee freely into a cluster of goldenrod and daisy
fleabane as I looked down on the creek thirty feet below. After a mile-
long series of sun-drenched ascents and descents, I came down into a
hollow with a cluster of houses, the remnants of a general store, a roofless and lifeless garage, and two or three other shuttered businesses. Not
many years ago a community existed here.

Then near the crest of a hill just beyond the village remnants, next to a
hay field, I noticed an elderly man and woman sitting on the small porch
of a brick house. I stopped at a tree at the road side, took off my pack, dug
out my green canteen, and lifted it in salute. They waved me over.

"Is it okay if I catch my breath?" I asked as I approached.

"Sure," said the woman, who then invited me to sit on the porch steps
and offered to fill my canteen. She disappeared with it, emerging a few
minutes later with it dripping condensation and a glass full of ice water

Edna Mae Ward and Millard Hall

besides. Then she retrieved a wooden chair. A small black dog with a
cloudy left eye sniffed around my feet.

"You made good time," the man said. He had a full head of wavy
white hair, wide-set gray eyes that narrowed into slits when he smiled,
and a slightly bulbous chin that must have been impressive before the
waddle of his neck fleshed out. He had passed me earlier on the road,
he explained. Millard Hall was eighty-two years old, and Edna Mae
Ward, age unknown but I guessed about the same, was his friend. (*"Just
friends,"* he emphasized.) At first, he seemed reticent, even wary, but he
soon warmed up. In short order, I learned that he was originally from
Blackwater, a community only five miles southwest that, being on the
other side of Powell Mountain, seemed more distant. Millard had moved
around a lot: Dayton, Ohio; Spartanburg, South Carolina; Johnson
City—part of the postwar migration from Appalachia, when millions
of men left for jobs in the cities of the Old North and the New South—
before boomeranging back. He had bought this property in 1955, moved

here in the 1960s, and began raising hay and cattle on his ninety-five acres. He was now retired from farming, but he leased his land. His wife had died four years earlier.

Millard peppered his conversation with jokes and stories. His father was a Baptist preacher who had a reputation for performing marriages for anyone who asked—something not often done in those days, he said with a hint of pride. He recalled one local woman engaged to a fellow from somewhere else, and she suggested they ask the Rev. Hall to do the ceremony. She phoned him and asked, "Will you marry me on Saturday?"

"No, thanks," the reverend answered. "I'm already married." Millard laughed hard at the memory. Edna Mae had surely heard the story before, but we all laughed.

Most of Millard's jokes had a moral point, like the one about how simple life was when he was a child: A boy (*Was it him? I wondered*) walks into the general store wearing one shoe, and the shopkeeper asks if he'd lost a shoe. "Nope, I found one," the boy said.

When I mentioned the remains of a village I just passed, his demeanor abruptly turned serious.

"We don't have any real community here anymore," he said, surprising me. I told him I had assumed there were good neighbors and family around, like I had seen in Duffield. He nodded.

"Yes, there's that. There was the teacher, the preacher, the blacksmith. But we used to have a midwife. If my wife were expecting, I'd be careful how I'd treat her husband, because I'd have to call on her for my wife. We treated each other better."

The grand-scale industrialization that started with World War II led to the domino-fall of changes, he said, surprising me again. Most people I had talked to had pinpointed the genesis of the revolution in the 1950s and 60s. Parts of Millard's conversation sounded like prepared remarks, which in a sense they were. He had written a poem about all this, he said. In fact, he told me, he'd written several poems, and he asked whether I would like to see a couple. He retreated into his house to find copies.

Edna Mae sat quietly as Millard spoke, but when he went inside to fetch his poems, she told me they became acquainted when she worked for his electrical company, a detail he hadn't mentioned. A short woman with a square, friendly face, Edna Mae's blue eyes darkened behind her oval wire-rim glasses when I asked about her family. Her husband committed suicide back in 1981, when their son was four years old. She didn't say how he did it—I suspected a gun—but he killed himself at his mother's house, leaving an enigmatic note: "I did this myself. Take me home so I can rest in peace." She wasn't sure what he meant, but she brought his body back to their house. Three times, near tears, she told me, "Our son kept asking, 'When will my daddy wake up?'" Edna Mae never remarried.

Millard came back with papers, which he handed me: a used business-reply envelope with his address on it, and two of his poems. He recited the first few lines of one: "The barber lived just down the road / The blacksmith shop just over the hill / The medicine doctor was in walking distance / If one of the family became ill. / Your neighbor was your insurance and caregiver. / Today you don't borrow sugar next door / We have improved some and lost a lot / But there's no community anymore."

When I asked Millard how we could regain community, he shrugged. "That's just the way it is," he said. He didn't oppose innovation or sound like a Luddite. He talked at length, for instance, about one of his medicines that fights "hydropsy," a condition now known as edema, that caused him to break out in painful sores. The condition could have proven fatal in the past, as it did for one of his uncles. But with progress, he said, has come important tradeoffs.

"We've seen so many changes," he added, sounding like he was wrapping up. He leaned over and pointed to the small sheaf in my hand. "There's another poem I wrote in there." I couldn't help smiling at his neat segue.

"Fourscore and two years ago I was born / And I've seen many earthly sights / I realize there is more in my rear view mirror / Than there is in my headlights. . . . If you've passed fifty years in life / You've see many wrongs and rights. / Now there's more in your rear view mirror / Than you have in your headlights."

I asked Millard about the white clapboard church across the road, at the fork with Rollers Chapel Road, surrounded by mown hay. It turned out that it was Rollers Chapel itself, a Methodist church building before it closed. Now he owned it. He had bought it and the surrounding acre of ground after it sat empty several years. He didn't like the idea that a trailer park might move there.

We said our goodbyes and, as I turned west and took the right fork at the church, I found myself mentally gnawing over Millard's poem about headlights and rearview mirrors. I was solidly past fifty.

Roller Chapel, a retired Methodist church building near Jonesville, Virginia

----

A menagerie stood in a sloping yard a half-mile from the church—surreal sculptures of birds and horses and an elephant the size of a Shetland pony, all overseen by a scrap-metal seven-member bluegrass group lined up against a white detached garage. Two houses sat on the property, one behind the other. Passing a pickup truck with its doors swung wide open, I went to the tidy double-wide in back and knocked. The goateed man who answered the door sighed when I asked about the statues. "You want to talk to my dad. He's down in the other house."

The screened and shaded front porch of the second house was claustrophobic, crowded with a jumble of pictures and lamps and statuettes and all sorts of bric-a-brac with only a narrow path to the front door. Peering in the window, I could see more of the same inside.

One ring of the doorbell brought forth Eddie Rutherford, a stocky man with bushy black hair, beard, and eyebrows. Eddie, who resembled Ernest Borgnine, eagerly stepped out to show me around his property, talking nonstop. He had worked as a power company lineman for thirty-four years but retired early after bypass surgery in 2006. Soon

"Heavy Metal Bluegrass Band," sculpture by Eddie Rutherford

afterwards he started collecting scrap metal and other castoffs to create his whimsical sculptures. At least two dozen pieces populated his
yard: peacocks, chickens, a miniature elephant with DirectTV dishes
for ears, and a "horsefly," a Pegasus-like horse with ceiling-fan blades
for wings—not to mention his "heavy metal bluegrass band." His newest
creations were a half-dozen fanciful birds with bowling balls for stomachs. Eddie said his works aren't for sale, but people stop and look. "I'm
just enjoying myself," he told me. "I like being creative."

Eddie walked to the pickup and climbed in the cab. "Let me show you
something," he said, and I sat in the passenger seat. He pulled out a thick
photo album. "Here are a few things you should see on this trip," he said,
flipping through a score of pages before stopping at a strangely colored
photo of a mountain stream; the water looked like it had been covered
with gold leaf. I assumed the picture was altered, but no, he assured me,
this was a natural phenomenon to be found at Pennington Gap, near
Keokee Lake. He took the photo himself. When the sunlight hits the
cliffs over the stream at a certain angle, the reflection turns the water

golden. He kept flipping through the album, mostly of shots he took in the area. Here's a nearby waterfall. There's a mountain with a jagged man's profile, like Abe Lincoln's if you look at it the right way. "I love taking photos," he said, which was confirmed by three or four more albums stacked on the bench seat of the truck. But at the end of the first album, he snapped the book shut, said he needed to get moving, thanked me for stopping by, and told me to be careful out there. *And no, he'd rather not have his picture taken. Just take pictures of his work.*

The asphalt wound uphill until meeting State Road 70, which descended toward a wide-open valley defined by Powell River. Rolling hills were given over to hay. It was midafternoon when I reached the river and, after six hours on the road, the day seemed long and lonely. The heat and humidity had peaked, and there was neither shade nor breeze. I felt myself tiring with each step. My feet hurt. Even so, somewhere around Millard Hall's house, I had changed my plan to camp along the way, figuring I was close enough to make Jonesville that same day. That decision seemed stupid now, but I was only a few miles from town.

As I crossed the wide, concrete bridge over Powell River, a pickup truck headed toward Jonesville stopped next to me. "You already made it this far," Eddie Rutherford observed. "You want a ride?"

"Thanks," I said, "but I need to walk it." He nodded in understanding and with a quick wave drove on without another word. I paused mid-bridge to look down on the Powell, once an important landmark and major obstacle to early travelers. At other places the river is a dark green snake meandering between deep and impressive banks. Here, it was a broad, shallow, gray–brown stream, and not so impressive. Trees snagged on a sandbar in the middle of the river had collected into a brushpile eight or ten feet tall. Even so, the water looked inviting. I couldn't see an obvious way to reach the river from the bridge until I got to the other side and looked back to see an opening on the opposite bank. Going back didn't seem worth the trouble.

A few steps later, I saw for the first time the jagged green wall of the Cumberland Mountains rising in the far distance. In a flash of gut-level realization, I understood—maybe for the first time—the mythic importance of the Cumberland Gap. The gap was the highest point on the Wilderness Road, but yet more than six hundred feet below the surrounding mountains. Thanks to that low anomaly, forty miles from where I stood,

neither I nor the thousands of settlers who preceded me needed to scale
the saw-toothed Cumberland chain.

I can't remember what time I arrived in Jonesville. I was beyond caring.
Ted and Kristen Booth were renting an old house on the eastern edge of
the town, across the road from the county courthouse and sheriff's office.
I couldn't miss their place, Ted had told me on the phone, because the
sheriff department's bus—an old school bus painted white—was parked
in front. The two-story red-brick house, built in 1840, was trimmed in
black and white. As instructed, I straggled in the side door, stepping into
a spacious, light-filled, cluttered kitchen. Ted—mid-forties, balding, a
little on the stocky side, with a wide, welcoming face—ushered me into
the living room, where two little girls were playing dress-up.

The whole house seemed built for a larger species of human. As far
as I could tell, there were four main rooms downstairs, all with twelve-
foot ceilings and each wide enough to fit two cars. I counted two stair-
cases (the main one up front and a service staircase leading up from the
kitchen), three fireplaces, and four bedrooms upstairs, each the size of
a frontier cabin. The only exception to this scale was the tiny bathroom
wedged next to the main staircase.

Ted, Kristen, and I had met several years earlier, when we were all
working at Milligan College, he as an adjunct history instructor while
finishing his doctorate at the University of Tennessee, and she in the
student life department. They had since moved on: Ted now supervised
the career counseling center at Lincoln Memorial University, a private
university in view of the Cumberland Gap, and Kristen was an occupational therapist at a nursing home in Pennington Gap. Her previous job
was at the nursing home in Johnson City where my wife had lived.

Now Ted and Kristen had two daughters, four-year-old Eliza and
three-year-old Daisy, and, they learned that very week, another on the
way. They were also buying a new house on the other side of town and
had started packing.

I felt self-conscious of my grime and sweat as I gingerly perched on
the edge of a couch in the living room, where a tall fireplace was flanked
by even taller double-hung windows. Play furniture and girlie-girl dress-
up clothes were nestled between couches, and a few braided rugs lay on

the wood floor that had a honey finish so deep it might have been a pool of gold. The girls' toys were confined to the living room, kitchen, downstairs bathroom, and their bedroom upstairs—which meant that things were relatively well contained in a building that size. Even though their house had a vibe of fun chaos, Ted and Kristen were keeping the bedlam at bay in this humongous home.

The girls were shy at first, but within a few minutes they were asking questions and showing me their toys and modeling their purple and green boas. Their eyes bugged a little when Ted told them I had walked all the way from where they used to live in Johnson City, but when Eliza asked, "Why did you do that?" I went blank: Why *did* I do this? I don't remember what I said, but my answer didn't feel coherent enough to satisfy an adult, much less a preschooler. After the long, hot day, I was struck dumb by the most obvious question a four-year-old could ask.

Kristen, a dozen years younger than Ted, got home from work a half-hour after I arrived. She had endured various health problems in recent years, but she looked healthy now: straight auburn hair, wide-set brown eyes, a luminous smile, and a slight plumpness befitting a woman expecting a child. The plan was to eat at Ruby's Steakhouse, a cafeteria-style restaurant in Pennington Gap. I showered and changed into my relatively clean clothes, and we climbed into their black Jeep Commander.

Jonesville, Kristen's hometown, has always been a small town, and it's getting smaller. Her family has deep roots here, a fact that became obvious when I saw her maiden name, Speak, on various signs and churches. As we drove, Kristen pointed out local landmarks: the nursing home where she worked, next to the regional hospital that was on its way to shutting down. One of her childhood schools. The church her ancestors built. She was born in a cabin outside of town, and we drove there after dinner, a big brown house set among a grove of trees on a hilltop at the end of Calamity Hill Road. Ted, the historian, laughed as he told us that "calamity" used to be a euphemism for syphilis. ("How do you think Calamity Jane got her nickname?" he slyly asked.)

At the restaurant Kristen met an old high school friend, Sarah, whom she hadn't seen for at least five years. Sarah lived in Rose Hill, about fifteen miles west, but practiced law in Wise, about twenty miles in the opposite direction. Kristen later told me that most of her high school friends had earned master's or doctoral degrees, as she had, and most had moved back to the area. "We want to give something back," she explained.

Ted and Kristen agreed that the community is in trouble. The most noticeable problem is drug abuse among middle-aged people—meth, prescription drugs, bath salts. (Pennington Gap was known locally as Pill Hill.) "I can kind of understand teens," Ted said, "but people who are my age? That's just baffling." He and Kristen theorized that boredom is at the root of the problem; without anything to do and no steady employment, people self-medicate. There wasn't much to do when Kristen was young, she said, but instead of turning to drugs she and her peers were forced to study and do homework if they weren't working on farm chores. "We were able to hold onto that fifties ethos a little longer," she said.

The fifties are long gone even in Jonesville, but Ted and Kristen moved here because Kristen wanted her children to grow up in the environment she enjoyed as a child. The family had arrived the previous autumn, even before they had jobs lined up. "Desperately wanting to get back into academia," Ted searched outward from Jonesville for a university job, landing at LMU.

"I wanted my children to be around my family, to know who they are," Kristen explained. "There's an expectation of a certain amount of respect for authority, for hard work. Here, you're just as respected if you work and provide for your family if you're a coal miner or an OT."

Kristen talked at length about the importance of the community. For instance, there was Rufus, "the can man." He's "slow," she said, but he spends his days picking up cans along the road and trades them for money. Everyone in town knows Rufus, and "the community takes care of him."

One day, when Kristen was in high school, she fell down in the street on her way to her job at a bank. By the time she got home, her mother had heard about it from three people. "It's like that old song, 'Everybody Dies Famous in a Small Town,'" she said. "I appreciate where I grew up. Everyone's my cousin somehow. You can't run from who you are here."

We drove through the country on the way back to their house, dropping into a wooded hollow that followed a creek. We passed an old mill—the first commercial venture in the county, according to Kristen, which had been started by the Wynn family, who later founded the Powell Valley Bank. "Sarah, my friend you just met, she's a Wynn," Kristen added, almost as an afterthought. The Wynn family, I later learned, was one of the most prominent landowning families in Lee County.

Mill Hollow Road brought us onto the main road through Jonesville, west of town. Before we turned toward home, Kristen pointed to a small, steepled church building and a pavilion on a broad lawn. "That's where the Methodist campground is," she said. "The church is still there, of course, and they still have big meetings every summer. That's how my family settled here. My ancestors, Reverend Nicholas Speak and his wife, came as Methodist missionaries and started a camp meeting. It was early—around 1810—and it's been going ever since."

10

FEELING LIKE A KING

You see how little nature requires to be satisfied. Felicity,
the companion of content, is rather found in our own breasts
than in the enjoyment of external things: And I firmly
believe it requires but a little philosophy to make
a man happy in whatsoever state he is.

—JOHN FILSON, attributed to Daniel Boone

In the morning, Ted and Kristen gathered the girls for preschool and left in a flurry of lunchboxes and frilly hats while I was packing up. I needed to stay in town until the post office opened at nine o'clock so I could forward the resupply box I had mailed to myself in care of the Booths. I was eating more oatmeal than expected, my sunflower seeds were almost untouched (too much trouble to shell while walking), and I had overestimated the number of notebooks I would need. So, I refilled my oatmeal and trail mix, packed the leftovers in the box and addressed it to my daughter, Rachael. She and I planned to rendezvous in nine days, when I would restock again.

I walked around downtown Jonesville until the post office opened, carrying a cardboard box the size of a small TV. The town center essentially consisted of six blocks—three on each side of Main Street—dominated by the pale-yellow brick colonial Lee County Courthouse at the crest of a hill. There was a NAPA auto parts store, four attorney offices, a pharmacy-cum-home-health-care office, a consignment shop, and a real estate agent. Three retailers were open for business. Nine other storefronts looked abandoned. Three planters, barrels cut in half, dotted the sidewalk in front of the offices, but weeds had overrun two of them, and a sickly shrub barely clung to life in the third. American flags flew from power poles, and the sign in front of Powell Valley National Bank, which sat alone on the easternmost block, read eighty degrees at quarter to nine.

In the post office lobby, three people were waiting for the service desk to open. A short, dark-haired man and an ash-blonde woman chatted. He was asking if the county school board had hired any teachers at the previous night's meeting.

"There were no personnel changes that I'm aware of," she said stiffly.

"We can only hope for the best," he replied genially, and on that they agreed.

A computer printout pinned to the community bulletin board reported 4,477 registered voters in Lee County. Next to the array of post office boxes were two mail slots. One was for "Out of Town." A hand-lettered sign taped over the other said "NETFLIX." This, apparently, was how twenty-first-century Jonesvillians spent their time.

Several more customers had arrived by the time a woman in a USPS polo shirt emerged at precisely nine o'clock to unlock the counter area. The two female clerks chatted amiably with the other customers as the room suddenly filled with about a dozen people. Several were asking for money orders. Today, I realized, was the last day of the month and a Friday. I assumed government checks had arrived.

The clerk's computer froze during our transaction, which translated into a half-hour of tinkering. As the clerk booted and then rebooted her machine, I tamped down my frustration by reminding myself that I was still tired from yesterday's walk and, after all, I was in no hurry. By the time I had mailed the box, returned to the Booths' house to get my gear, and walked out the door, it was just past ten o'clock. The next town of any size was Rose Hill. I would need to sprout wings to reach it today, so I planned a ten-mile day, which would let me reach Rose Hill the next morning.

West of Jonesville, I turned southwest off the main highway onto Curt Russell Road, a relatively level and straight stretch passing open fields. (Kristen had known Curt Russell, a local farmer.) Opposite a broad hayfield where a blue tractor gathered round bales, a subdivision of single-story and split-level houses spread from the road over undulating hills. Three dozen homes were planned for the development, according to a sign erected at the entry road. (*Ted and Kristen's new neighborhood, no doubt.*)

Within an hour, I reached the site of a small natural stone bridge where settlers would have crossed a creek called Town Branch. The road went over a nondescript modern bridge, but a narrow path to the side wound through thick weeds down to the creek to give a view of a natural bridge, a stone arch three or four feet thick, fifteen feet above the water.

Back on the main road, less than a quarter-mile past the arch, stood a two-story rough log cabin with a foundation of hewn limestone and a porch. Local lore claims that Gen. Robert E. Lee hid in a cabin around here during the Civil War. *This may have been it!*

Cars were passing only about every five to ten minutes on this lovely, lonely road—including, to my surprise, a silver Smart car, a motorized gnat compared to the Ford F-150s and Dodge Rams. The road passed open, rolling hills, running for a while along the southern edge of the Cedars Natural Area Preserve, named for the native red cedars. Here was an uninterrupted view down and across a wide, shallow valley to hayfields bisected by trees and hedges, and then up toward foothills to an arc of trees in the distance. The Cumberland Mountains barely poked up from the horizon. An isolated cabin stood on a faraway hill, its bright red roof easily visible through the humid haze. After days of walking between high, steep mountain walls, I was enjoying the wide-open countryside.

Boone and the other early travelers would have seen this place much differently. In their time, these hills were dominated by enormous virgin woods, not hundreds of open acres punctuated by dozens of rolled hay bales. The pioneers would have needed to climb a hill and peer through trees to see the mountains ahead of them and get their bearings. But they would not have complained: The forest offered more shelter from the elements and from potential attackers. The landscape has changed, and our perceptions with it.

By noon the heat had settled in, and I stopped in the shade of a tree crowding the edge of the road. A brown Chevy pickup truck whistled past, close enough to brush me with a wake of air. I would not want to trade places with the early explorers, but I wondered how they would contend with cars and trucks and asphalt. I'm softer than they were, without a doubt. I had spent the past three nights in houses, and two nights before that in a modern state park next to friendly neighbors who shared a lot of good food. But if a time machine dropped Daniel Boone here now, how would he cope? This was a silly thought experiment, I decided. He would need some time to adjust, but adjust he would, even to cars and fences and hayfields, although he might choke at the requirement of a hunting license. And if that same machine transported me to 1775? I'd like to think I could also adjust, but my learning curve would need to be far steeper just to survive.

A small herd of cattle was doing all they could to keep cool on a hot day, standing in the shade of a tree or the barn. A few stood almost shoulder deep in the middle of a muddy pond, including a handsome white bull who watched me, Zen-like, as the few cows wading with him got spooked and ran away. *Poor beasts,* I thought, as I walked under a full sun in the middle of the same hot day, carrying forty-odd pounds on my back.

Curt Russell Road ends at Flannary Bridge Road and turns into Tobacco Road on the other side. There the terrain abruptly changes into a ravine defined by steep hills and banks plunging down to the meandering Powell River. Tidy fields give way to wild, weedy vegetation that encroaches on the road. Kudzu climbs here. After a brief descent, the road rises again into rolling hills. The fields were smaller and the houses closer, more modest and older than the ones I saw earlier in the day. Next to one hayfield, shielded from the road by a row of pine trees and barbed wire, is a blond wall made of dressed limestone blocks, laid out like an unfinished right triangle with its hypotenuse cut short. The wall is five feet thick and three feet high, and its longest side stretches a hundred feet or more. It could have been the remains of an old city wall, but it was probably the base of a barn or holding pen.

I had walked almost four hours, probably close to my ten-mile goal, and fatigue was setting in. I was struck with the sad realization that I might not talk to anyone today. I knocked on the door of a brick farmhouse, hoping for water and a chat. Two pickup trucks were parked in the gravel driveway, but no one answered. Next to the house, a rugged stone chimney—the final remnant of an early cabin?—stood like a lone sentry.

I turned left on Flatwoods Road, which looked recently repaved, and paused for a drink. My hip and leg were starting to burn. I gave myself another hour to walk, and then I would find a place to camp.

Silver Leaf was the name of this scattered community, and a white, two-story farmhouse featured a simple, elegant silver maple leaf motif centered on its single gable. Silver Leaf was the only place along the Wilderness Road that Daniel Boone had named himself.

Soon an open grassy space appeared to my left. On a power pole, I saw a sign from the state Department of Conservation and Recreation indicating that this was a natural area preserve, followed by a long list of prohibitions: no fires, ATVs, horses, unleashed dogs, public use of alcohol, hunting without permit, unauthorized discharge of firearms, removal or destruction of plants, animals, minerals and artifacts. And no camping. My first question was where I might camp, if not here. But my second question involved conservation—or maybe the better word was *curation*, as in a museum.

People obviously consider some things worth preserving, but in a controlled way. This region began as wilderness, dotted with remote outposts. Now it's mostly settled with farms, houses, and towns, and it is nature that is fenced off. We've tamed the place or at least made it manageable, and any semblance of wilderness exists only with our permission.

Maybe it's this reversal that defines the difference between wilderness and civilization. In wilderness, so called, humans are the minority, the weaker partners. But in civilization, so called, we are ascendant. In wilderness, "nature" calls the shots. In anti-wilderness, humans do. In wilderness, we survive with skill, luck, or good timing—but always tentatively. Once we gain a toehold, however, we aim to create order out of the seeming chaos and decide how much wilderness to permit. We curate.

- - - - - - - - - - - - - - -

I need shade.

After a long stretch of flat road, I turned up Wilson Hill Road, which offered none. The road led past hayfields and large farms to several houses grouped together. At the first one, a tidy brick gabled house, a woman was sunbathing in the side yard. I did not want to approach a stranger in her bathing suit, so I knocked on the front door. A small hound and a German shepherd peeked around the corner of the house. The windows and doors were open, and I could see a TV in the living room blaring Country Music Television. Children were playfully yelling somewhere and a boy in glasses—maybe ten years old—raced into the living room and spotted me. He went out the side door, and I could hear him talking to his mom. Walking around to the side of the house, I saw two boys in the yard with water guns. The woman sat up. I held up my almost-empty canteen and asked if I could fill it up. "No problem," she said politely. The two boys hovered near the side door, keeping watch, as she went inside and came back with my canteen full to the brim, heavily iced. The cold weight in my hand felt wonderful. The woman and I chatted a few minutes—she asked where I was going and, understandably, offered no information about herself—and I mentioned, as casually as I could, that I was looking for a place to camp. Did she have any suggestions?

"There are some folks up the road with fields, and maybe you'll find a place—but be sure to ask." I thanked her, picked up my pack, and left.

I started to approach a double-wide at the crest of the hill until a big, barking, loose dog bolted from under the deck and sent me backpedaling into the road. After another half-mile or so, I stopped to talk to an angular old man working an overgrown six-foot-high bank with a gas-powered trimmer. Beyond him spread a level, freshly mowed, inviting hayfield, directly across the narrow road from a small, gray, fraying house with an ample side yard. It's hot, we agreed. I asked him where I might camp. He mentioned Rose Hill, "only five or six miles." I explained—no doubt sounding pitiful—that I had already walked from Jonesville after a long, hard day yesterday. He paused. "Well, someone up ahead might help you out," he said before turning back to his work.

My head had been swimming a little before I stopped to talk, and now mallets thumped my knees with each step on a steep downhill stretch. I wanted to stop walking, but I had no choice except to continue. It was a little past three o'clock but felt later.

The road descended into a shady hollow, past a clutch of houses that fit the stereotypes of down-and-out Appalachia, including hounds that barked as they sprinted to the edge of their property, halting abruptly at the road. A brick ranch-style house stood near a creek, with two cars in the driveway and several flat spots in the yard. It looked promising. On the narrow, concrete front porch, I rang the doorbell and waited. The curtains were drawn. Maybe the owners were on vacation. I pulled out my water bottle and a granola bar, pausing to psyche myself up for a possible walk into Rose Hill. Suddenly the front door opened slightly with a pop of vinyl weather stripping, and a man with a thin face peered through the crack he opened. He sat in a wheelchair and spoke with a severe twang. "Can I help you?" he asked.

I told him I was hiking through and looking for a place to camp.

"What's your name?" he asked. I told him.

"Where you from?" Johnson City.

"Where'd you come from today?" The other side of Jonesville.

"You didn't come very far." His tone felt like a police interrogation. It was a hot day, I said, and felt a little worn down after yesterday. *Why did I feel the need to explain myself?* I outlined my back-roads route, showed him my driver's license and a business card, and told him that I was writing a book about the Wilderness Road.

"Well, that's fine," he said, clearly unimpressed.

"I'm just looking for a flat spot to put my tent."

"I don't have any flat ground." I looked around at an extremely suitable flat spot next to a dogwood tree in his front yard, not fifteen feet away.

"I just need enough space to pitch a tent."

"I don't have any flat ground," he repeated.

Bullshit, I thought but did not say. I pointed toward the tree and said if it was good enough for him, it was good enough for me.

"What do you mean by that?" he asked, sounding testy—or maybe I was feeling testy. He obviously did not want to say yes but was running out of reasons to say no, and I was pushing him. After a long silence I finally said, "I'll just go on. No problem. Sorry to bother you." I turned toward my pack, hearing the door close and the deadbolt latch behind me.

It took me about a quarter-mile to realize that I was as angry with my-self as I was with the man at the door. Something in the encounter made me realize that I was too picky. I caught myself wanting a camping spot next to a nice house with a generous side yard, with access to a bathroom and maybe even a shower. A controlled setting, that is. Not wilderness. When I would glance at ravines or creek-side spots and think, *What a great place to camp,* in the next instant I knew there would be snakes and bears and coyotes close by. In truth, I was succumbing not to mere pickiness but to fear. The reality was scarier than the romance.

The first travelers did not have the luxury of such choices. Their environment was not sanitized or controlled. I also thought about people like Robert. They are not "one with nature," but neither are they intimidated or paralyzed by it.

There were real dangers, of course, and I was not going to crash down a creek bank and put out a "Come and get it" sign to the beasts of the field. But after all these miles, I did not yet feel at ease with wilderness or with wildness.

Up and down two more hills, pushing five o'clock—the sunlight was beaming obliquely through late-afternoon humidity—and I came to a brick rancher with a spacious front yard. A rough cattle barn stood to the side, separated from the house and driveway by a barbed-wire fence and a metal gate. A few cows grazed on the hill that rose behind the house and barn.

I hesitated before walking up the drive and knocking on the front door. A matronly woman in a floral dress and upswept dark hair opened the door. Her slight smile and her raised eyebrows showed bafflement. I introduced myself and explained my situation. She said softly, "You can talk to Chester. He's at the side of the house." I turned and sure enough, standing at the corner of the house, near the garage, was her husband—probably in his late seventies—with thinning salt-and-pepper hair, double-knit trousers and a button-down shirt. I introduced myself and extended my hand. He shook it tentatively and introduced himself as Chester Montgomery. The woman at the door was his wife, Rosemary. Chester seemed wary as we spoke, and when I asked about camping I steeled myself for another rejection. Instead, he hesitated only a moment before asking if I'd like a place in the shade. A sixty-foot-tall red maple tree dominated the center of his front lawn, and I asked if I could pitch my tent between the tree and his front porch.

"I won't be any trouble," I said, sounding like an eager-to-please schoolboy. "I won't need anything else, except maybe a refill of my water bottles."

"Well, sure," he said in a flat tone, neither pleased nor annoyed. But he nodded slightly, which I took as a sign of approval. I felt like I had passed some kind of secret test.

A wave of relief washed through me, stronger than I expected. Relieved because I did not need to walk anymore today. Relieved to find a place to stay. Relieved to meet someone that day who was not indifferent or surly.

As I set up my tent and arranged my gear, Chester came to check it out. He had never seen a tent like mine before and asked a few questions in a quiet voice: how much it weighed, how well it held up in weather. He offered to fill my canteen and returned with it full of ice, and a cold can of Pepsi.

"You probably don't have a chair, do you?" he asked. He disappeared into the house and returned in a few minutes with a green resin patio chair. He told me I could use their bathroom if needed. This was a surprise. Among the few instructions he had given me only minutes before was that I should go behind the barn. He obviously had not wanted me in the house—but now this. Chester retreated inside.

I finished arranging my gear, sat shirtless inside my tent and wiped my face, torso, and legs with a damp cloth to get rid of the worst of the sweat and grime, and changed into shorts and a fresh T-shirt. I knocked on the front door, and Chester led me down the hall to the bathroom. The house was tidy, solid, middle-America in the Sears mode, with furniture and decor that looked as new as the day it might have arrived in the 1980s. Several framed watercolors hung on the walls, country landscapes painted by Rosemary years before. She was nowhere in sight.

A few minutes later, Chester escorted me to the front door.

"We're going to have hamburgers about five-thirty," he said. "Would you like a hamburger?"

I would never have predicted that one day I would experience a burst of gratitude so potent that for a moment I felt dizzy, simply because someone offered me a hamburger. Sure enough, just before five-thirty, as I basked in the green resin chair, drinking Pepsi, Chester came bearing a paper plate with a hamburger between slices of plain white bread, with mayo and pickle and, on the side, a slice of American cheese. He excused himself—he and Rosemary were going to Friday-night prayer meeting—and I sat watching sunlight filter through maple leafs, eating my burger and feeling like royalty.

A few minutes later Chester and Rosemary pulled out in their red 1990s-era Oldsmobile. (A bronze-toned Chevy pickup truck also sat in the driveway with a Christian cross decal and a "Choose Life" sticker on the back.) As dusk started to settle, a long, high-pitched voice called from somewhere—a human voice, to be sure, but it sounded unearthly. Then came the faint clank of cowbells. Across the road, a herd of about

Chester and Rosemary Montgomery

two dozen cattle was walking across a hill, single file, heading home like workers at the end of their shift.

After Chester and Rosemary returned, long after dark, he came out to ask if I needed to use the bathroom. (I did: I had tried to go behind the barn while they were gone, but my plastic trowel couldn't break the hard ground.) Inside, Rosemary sat dreamily at the kitchen table, eating a bowl of canned peaches. As I came back through the house, Chester offered me a bowl of peaches. We sat at the table, Rosemary to my right and Chester to my left. She smiled sweetly and occasionally chuckled softly while Chester and I talked.

Both Chester and Rosemary were raised in this area, and it took a two-year hitch in the Army to first dislodge him from his home. But then he left in the mid-1950s to find work in the North. Chester eventually landed at the General Electric aircraft engine factory in Cincinnati, where he worked for twenty-seven years before retiring and returning to Lee County in the early 1990s to build their house on land he had bought years earlier. (He and Rosemary married in 1992, a second marriage for both.) They farmed for a while but gradually gave that up and now rented most of their thirty-nine acres to another farmer for grazing cattle. His two sons still live in Cincinnati, and there's a granddaughter, so Chester tries to visit a few times a year. Their families don't visit here very often.

"A lot of people left to find work in the northern factories," he said. "Some came back; it's a good place to retire. But there's no good economy here now."

Chester thought the county population was much smaller than in the 1950s, but US census data show that Lee County's population in 2010 was almost the same as in 1960, just under 26,000. The population did plummet to 20,000 by 1970, however, and I suspected that the impression of decline had stayed with Chester. Not that his worries about the long-term future were unfounded: Compared to the 1990s, the county's birthrate is down and its death rate is up. The population is shrinking again, and communities are feeling the impact. The regional hospital in Pennington Gap, taken over by the Wellmont Health System only six years earlier, had been reduced to provide only emergency triage, sending most patients, including Rosemary and Chester, to the system's facilities in Kingsport. A few months after I walked through, Wellmont closed the hospital altogether.

On the other hand, Chester noted, a number of Amish and Mennonite people had moved into the area. I knew of an Amish food store along the main highway, east of Rose Hill, and Chester said there was another store that sold boots.

I asked Rosemary a question—something about her upbringing—but she just looked at me with a kindly, blank expression and chuckled softly.

"Sometimes she has trouble getting her thoughts out," Chester said and continued the story. Rosemary's father was a coal miner who worked in Harlan County, Kentucky—one of the many Lee County miners who would walk over two Cumberland peaks to get to work. The miners would leave home before dawn, work underground for eight hours and then walk home after dark. They might not see the sun for days. Chester's father, by contrast, was a farmer.

A few minutes after we said good night and I returned to my tent, Chester came out and sat on the porch. He wanted to talk about De-Royal Industries, a local manufacturer of medical supplies. The founder, owner, and chairman, Autry "Pete" DeBusk, was raised in Lee County and graduated from the local high school and Lincoln Memorial

University. (DeBusk was also chairman of the university's board.) For
years the company did much of its manufacturing in Rose Hill and
nearby Dryden, but almost all of that work had moved elsewhere—
Guatemala, Estonia, Ireland, a few other countries as well as other
places in the United States—putting a few hundred employees out of
work and devastating the local economy, according to Chester.

"Rose Hill was doing good until he took it out," he said, an edge in his
voice. It was the closest thing to anger I had seen or heard from him.

The morning was warm and clear, and without prompting I woke around
six. (My body's rhythms were changing, aligning more with the sun: I
woke at dawn and felt ready for bed within an hour of sunset.) About an
hour later, after breakfast, I started to pack, and Chester came out on
the porch.

"I have a book here that might interest you," he said as he gently laid a
big brown volume on the porch and then walked back inside. I picked it
up a few minutes later, intending to skim it, just to be polite. But soon I
moved to the porch rocker, thumbing through the enormous, decorative
hardback produced for the Lee County bicentennial in 1992. Predictably,
the illustrious history of Lee County included details about Boone and
other early explorers and settlers. Then came the pages of family histories contributed by local residents, including entries about Montgomerys
who had emigrated from Ireland in 1730. A Montgomery traveled with
Daniel Boone in 1775. Benjamin Logan had married a Montgomery, the
same Logan who traveled with Boone before starting his own settlement a little farther west in Kentucky. Logan later rose to prominence
in Kentucky and was almost elected governor. He was also a severe critic
of Daniel Boone. *Any relation?* I wondered.

Yes, Chester said when he returned. These were his ancestors—some
direct, some not. Then he invited me in for a bowl of cereal, and I accepted even though I'd already eaten. Rosemary, her slight smile always
present, poured me an enormous bowl of raisin bran. We sat eating, not
saying much. Rosemary, I concluded, was showing signs of dementia.
Chester, no doubt, spent much of his time and energy caring for her, worrying about her, and wondering about his future, not alone and yet more
alone each day. Maybe this strange, creeping isolation explained why he

quickly, surprisingly warmed up to a hiker who camped for a night in his front yard. Maybe it explained why I felt a kinship with him.

Chester came out and watched me pack the last few pieces of gear and roll my tent, and we chatted quietly. Then we walked to the road together—he to retrieve the newspaper—and shook hands and said goodbye. I turned north while Chester stood in the road, watching me go. "Stay in touch," he called. I nodded. A minute later, just before cresting a small hill, I turned around to wave once more, but he had already returned to his house.

—— **11** ——

WHERE THE BUFFALO ROAM . . . A LITTLE

*[We] are by no means divided, or readily divisible, into
environmental saints and sinners. But there are legitimate
distinctions that need to be made. These are distinctions of
degree and of consciousness. Some people are less destructive
than others, and some are more conscious of their
destructiveness than others.*

—WENDELL BERRY

About an hour after leaving Chester in the road with his newspaper, I came to the end of the narrow country road and reached US Highway 58, passing the remains of two flattened snakes on the way. A small, decrepit trailer park stood on the opposite side of the four-lane highway. Beyond, in complete contrast, emerald hills glowed in the morning sun: the foothills of the Cumberland Mountains.

Now on the northern side of Wallen Ridge, US Highway 58 runs more than twenty miles through the center of Poor Valley all the way to the Cumberland Gap. The valley is wide, level, and straight enough to provide expansive views of farms and fields that spread like picnic blankets before steeply banking up toward the great, green wall separating Virginia from Kentucky. That wall would have separated pioneers from the West were it not for the famous gap that served as a migratory funnel for bison, elk, hunters, and settlers. The Cumberland Mountains run from central East Tennessee (not far from Oak Ridge) to southern West Virginia, but this valley is among its most impressive points. The mountain wall rises hundreds of feet above the valley floor, its ocean-wave profile softened by open farmlands at the base that yield to forests on the way up. About halfway along the valley, a long section of limestone cliffs—the obviously nicknamed White Rocks—breaks out from the trees in the top tenth of the mountain face, like a recessed fortress wall. Scores of pioneers described these rocks in their journals as notable landmarks. Poor Valley is simply a quintessential rural scene—rolling meadows, farmhouses, silos, grazing cattle, country stores, tiny towns, dramatic mountains as a backdrop—all laid out along a wide-open road. From what I can tell, travelers need about three or four trips through this area before they stop instinctively craning their necks to gawk.

I followed the highway west for a half-mile, a slight breeze in my face, before turning left onto Thomas Walker Road, a loop running parallel to the highway through Rose Hill and, ten miles beyond, Ewing.

In Rose Hill, immediately after the NAPA sign for Bacon's Auto Parts and 24-Hour Wrecker Service, stands a historical marker sketching the story of Martin's Station. Virginia militia Capt. Joseph Martin built the outpost on the site in 1769 as a vanguard of white settlement, offering shelter for hunters and early travelers, only to be abandoned a few months later. Martin tried again in 1775 but eventually was driven out in June 1776 by Cherokee raids. Any settlement would need a water source and, sure enough, Martin's Creek, a brook that could be spanned by a Volkswagen Beetle, ran alongside the road for several hundred yards before turning south and out of sight, flowing toward Powell River.

At an abandoned gas station sat an old man ostensibly selling second-hand toys, tools, and clothes out of cardboard boxes laid out in front of him. There was no sign or anything else to attract potential customers. He was seventy years old, a retired farmer, and his history was the fourth or fifth variation of what had become a familiar story of necessary departure and optimistic homecoming. He grew up near Rose Hill until he was eighteen, left to work construction in Indianapolis for thirty-five years, and moved back about fifteen years ago. His wife wanted a trailer—which he could not understand—so he bought an acre of land from his mother and parked a trailer there. His tone of voice led me to think that (a) he was not happy either about the trailer or the land or both, and (b) his secondhand selling was less about pulling in a few extra bucks and more about getting away from his wife on a Saturday morning. I imagined a weekly routine, with him shouting as he walks out the kitchen door and pulls on his yellow trucker's cap: "I'm going down to sell some stuff. See you later!"

Rose Hill mostly hugs the two-lane road. Mixed among the compact, tidy houses is the community library, located in a repurposed farmhouse. A metal book-return bin stands like a husky bouncer on a corner of the porch. Three churches—Christian Church, Methodist, and Baptist—press close to the road. In front of a store on the western edge of town, the Trinity Tabernacle youth group was running a bake sale to raise money for summer camp. I bought an Amish-made apple-cinnamon muffin (only $1.50) and struck up a conversation with a few of the kids. A fresh-faced sixteen-year-old boy named Dylan was especially curious and talkative. He considered my hike "very cool" and advised me to stop at the IGA next door for a bottle of water, since it was ice cold and only fifty cents. Walking in, I was transported back to the cozy neighborhood grocery of my boyhood in Tampa, circa 1968—low ceiling, narrow aisles choc-a-block with boxes and cans—and felt a rush of nostalgia. As promised, the half-liter bottle of Cumberland Gap Mountain Spring Water ("Uncap the Gap," the label urged) felt frosty and cost fifty cents.

Rose Hill was a hopping place on a Saturday morning, and the traffic picked up on the west end of town. The parking lot of Lou's Deli was full, several vehicles waited in line at the car wash, and a half-dozen cars were parked at the bank, with another seven or eight at the pharmacy next door. The homes on this side of town were bigger and newer and had more land than those on the eastern fringes.

Meanwhile, across the valley, trees reached farther down the slopes of the mountains. The forest seemed to suck up the fields as it crept down the mountain wall.

A couple of miles out of town, a wiry old man came whipping down a long driveway from a brick ranch-style house, steering a red Honda ATV. He scooted across the road, briskly checked the mailbox, and then buzzed past me, heading east. A moment later he pulled alongside me and held out an eight-ounce bottle of water.

"I thought you might be getting thirsty," he said. This Samaritan's name was Joe Crockett, a farmer who owned several hundred acres and, down the road a few miles, the Indian Mound Farms. (A nearby historical marker noted that the Indian mound was constructed from 1200 to 1650 and had been discovered during an excavation in 1877.) Joe had lived here all of his eighty-two years, except for a two-year stint in the army. His family, he said, settled in this valley hundreds of years ago, a claim borne out by Crockett Cemetery and Crockett Ridge Road.

Another mile, and there stood Thomas Walker High School, a neo-classical brick building featuring two prominent gables and tall, white-framed casement windows. The school and the road were named for a Virginia physician who passed this way in the spring of 1750 on a scouting mission for the Loyal Land Company, which he had helped found the year before. Walker came thirteen years before that British treaty restricted settlement west of the Alleghenies (and a full quarter-century before Boone cut the Wilderness Road), and so Walker and five companions went in search of a promised land described by long hunters, where plenteous game roamed over fertile hills. It was a paradise that Walker's land company hoped to obtain, section, and then sell to eager settlers—the first in a line of speculators. Walker kept a detailed journal during the trip and along the way named every other natural feature, or so it might seem, after Prince William, the Duke of Cumberland.

The duke (1721–1765) was made famous when he crushed the Jacobite Rising at the Battle of Culloden on April 16, 1746—four years, almost to the day, before Walker wrote about his discovery of the gap. Walker named it and the surrounding mountains in the duke's honor, as well as a river they crossed about fifteen miles later. (Among his Whig supporters, the duke was "Sweet William," the victorious hero of Culloden. Among his Tory and Scottish opponents, he was the vicious "Butcher Cumberland" who had torched "rebellious" settlements, ordered wounded prisoners shot, hanged noncombatants, and confiscated land and livestock.) Walker also named another major waterway the Louisa River, in honor of the duke's wife, but that name did not stick. It is now called the Kentucky River.

Once past the gap and into Kentucky, Walker and his crew traced the newly dubbed Cumberland River deeper into the interior for twenty hard, exhausting miles. One of the number fell ill, so they built a tiny cabin as a temporary base, the first known non-Indian house in Kentucky, about five miles south of present-day Barbourville. (A state park, including a reproduction of the cabin, stands on the site now.) Walker and two men set out in search of the fabled fertile ground only to circle back a few weeks later, foiled and frustrated by the high, daunting mountains and thick canebrakes. They returned to Virginia where, at home in Albemarle County, Walker grew prosperous and influential. He died in 1794, aged seventy-nine, after a lifetime of exploration and surveying. The high school named in his honor chose its slogan well: Welcome to Pioneer Country.

On the eastern edge of Ewing stood the Boone Trail Drive-In, a substantial two-story, white house with an extension on the side. This must have once been a hub of Ewing's social life, but it was closed now. Then came a couple of trailer parks, one with a four-foot-tall statue of the Virgin Mary standing by the driveway offering a demure welcome in a robe more purple than blue. Across the road, next door to Kim's Klassy Styles Salon, stood the remains of Uncle Joe's, another defunct drive-in. Next was a tiny, one-story brick gas station probably dating to the 1920s. Two rusty gas pumps stood in front, each two feet square and four feet tall. They had long ago pumped Gulf Super No Nox and Good Gulf gas, trademarks I recalled from my youth. Surprisingly, the antique gas station sported a new red metal roof.

In what passed for downtown, just west of Indian Creek Outdoor and Farm Supply and a one-screen theater, People's Bank Road provided access to four-lane US Highway 58. Next to the bank building, two men were unloading a riding mower from a trailer. Josh Short, a burly man in his twenties with a bushy black beard, was helping Bill Martin, a tall man in his sixties who wore a checked button-down shirt, glasses, and the obligatory trucker's cap. Josh planned to leave the area soon because there was no work. He was set up to interview at a General Motors plant in North Carolina in a few weeks, for a job picking parts. Bill said he might be related to the Joseph Martin who built the station in 1769, but he admitted this was only what another relative had told him. Family trees often twist around on each other here. When as a young man Bill started dating a certain girl, his father asked who she was. When Bill told him her name, his father said, "Do you know that's your third cousin?" Bill did not say how the relationship had turned out.

Straight across US Highway 58 is Sand Cave Road, which leads to Civic Park, a small nook of grass and picnic shelters tucked into the base of Cumberland Mountain. I hoped to camp there that night. From the highway to the Civic Park the walk is almost a mile and a half, gradually uphill. The day had grown hot and humid—rain was on the way—and I was sweating hard by the time I reached the park. A wedding was in progress. Cars, pickup trucks, and vans lined both sides of the narrow road into the small park. A "No Camping" sign stood at the park entrance. After the ceremony ended and while guests milled around, I surreptitiously scouted around for a place I might pitch a tent without attracting attention. No such luck. Returning to the entrance, I dropped my pack and drank some water, considering my options. Just then a white-and-green National Park Service cruiser drove in. I flagged it down, told the two rangers my predicament, and asked if I could camp here despite the sign. They deferred the question to the office at the Cumberland Gap National Historical Park, which leased Civic Park, and gave me the phone number. They wished me luck and drove away. When I phoned, a recording told me the number had been changed or disconnected. Now that I had alerted a couple of rangers to my presence, I dismissed any thoughts about bedding down in the park. Besides, there was the matter of my own "no trespassing" rule. I briefly thought about ignoring that for one night, but it somehow felt like cheating. Only later did it occur to me that the rangers might have been giving me a kind of wink-and-nod: *"We can't tell you it's okay to camp, but . . ."* I felt appropriately naïve.

By then the afternoon had begun its long fade, and I had no idea where to stay. I was mentally kicking myself. I could have been pitching my tent in the replica of Martin's Station at Wilderness Road State Park. I had recently met Billy Heck, the park's historical interpreter who had overseen the fort reconstruction, and he offered to let me camp in the fort, if I were to contact him a few days before I arrived. But the days blurred together as I hiked and by the time I thought about Billy's offer, it was too late. So I returned to the highway from the park, considering my options. A gravel hike-and-bike trail started about two miles west of Ewing, following the level route of an old railroad track. With farms and fields dotting both sides of the trail, I hoped someone might let me camp on their land. If worse came to worst, I could always bivouac under some trees along the trail.

At the eastern end of the trail, next to a small parking lot, stood a tidy ranch-style house with a handsome limestone block exterior. I started there.

A woman with short blonde-to-gray hair and a big smile answered the front door. I explained myself, and she said, "You should talk to my husband, Fred." She nodded to my left. "He just got back." I turned around and saw a man with mussed salt-and-pepper hair and matching goatee, a black sling on his right arm, and a rolling gait walking my way from his silver pickup truck parked in front of the two-car garage.

Fred McCurry, it turned out, was the foreman who oversaw the farms owned by the DeBusk family, of DeRoyal Medical Supply fame, which comprise about a thousand acres around the valley and another six hundred acres near Silver Leaf. Part of the McCurrys' compensation is this house, where Fred and his wife, Donna, had lived for the past fourteen years. Fred, garrulous and hospitable, readily offered the freshly mown hayfield next to the house. After my bollixing up the plans for Martin's Station, this generosity felt like a touch of grace.

In the hayfield, separated from the house by a hundred yards and a line of tall, thin pine trees perpendicular to the road, I found a level spot for my tent near the crown of the field. Tall clouds were rising in the east and a slight breeze stirred the trees. The McCurrys' dog, a border collie named Sadie, barked madly from the back patio at the house. Fred came out to my tent.

"My wife and I just finished dinner," he said, "and there's some food left on the counter if you want to come in and make yourself up a plate." He didn't need to offer twice. I tossed my gear into the tent and followed him into the house.

The spacious kitchen featured dark cabinets and new appliances. A broad table separated it from the living room, where Donna sat watching an enormous HD television mounted on a limestone wall. A gallery of thirty or more family photos filled one of the coffee-colored paneled walls.

Fred handed me a plate and pointed me toward the pork beans, cornbread, vegetables, and stewed apples warming on the stove. He and I sat at the kitchen table, and I plowed through the food as we talked. I devoured a second plate, feeling no shame, and then he offered me a plastic-wrapped raisin cake, which tasted delicious. It all tasted delicious.

Fred, fifty-three, wore a nylon sling and brace (manufactured by DeRoyal) for the rotator cuff he injured on the job, a post he came by partly because he grew up near Pete DeBusk's mother in Silver Leaf. He had supervised the grounds crew at Lincoln Memorial University before Pete DeBusk hired him. As we talked, Fred pointed out the picture windows to the pastures rolling up from the trail to the tree line of Cumberland Mountain. The landscape was dotted with a few houses and a few dozen cattle, a deep green pastoral scene aesthetically pleasing enough to qualify for a Turner landscape. It hadn't always looked like that, Fred told me. There used to be cliffs in the field, near the foothills, but some years back he had the cliffs and other rough spots scraped and contoured to create these more picturesque and profitable hills. Not only did it look better, he said, but it provided more grazing land.

As he walked me out, he told me that every morning, literally, he met some friends at "the diner" in Ewing, to drink coffee and talk. I'd be welcome to come along if I wanted. I hesitated a moment—I was tired—but this was a good opportunity to meet some other local men. We decided we'd leave about quarter past six in the morning.

The wind had picked up, and heavy clouds were churning from the west and the north. I hustled to my tent, Sadie barking after me.

The rain began just after dusk, around nine o'clock, a slow patter that soon turned into steady splats of heavy drops and then into a constant rumble on the thin fabric an inch above my head. The wind threw the rain hard from the west, against the broad side of the tent—which is to say that I had set up my tent facing the wrong direction. Had I turned it ninety degrees, perhaps the gentle misting inside would not have evolved into occasional drips and small puddles that gathered in the corners before breaking toward the middle. I shoved small washcloths in the corners to stanch the trickles and stacked my gear to minimize its contact with the floor. If I slept at all, I slept fitfully. What I remember clearly is wind and lightning and thunder echoing up and down the valley and rain so heavy and unceasing that I wondered how Noah had stayed sane, if indeed he did.

Faking alertness a little after six, I climbed into Fred's pickup truck, and we rode three miles east into a wet, overcast morning. Fred was steering and reaching over to shift with his left hand, his right arm riding in the sling. The Black Diamond No. 2 convenience store was locked, but an elderly man was already sitting at a booth inside. He waved when he saw Fred. A blonde, petite woman, her face hung with glasses and boredom, unlocked the door. The young clerk—maybe twenty years old—was named Angie, and the old man was David Crockett.

David, eighty-seven, was nursing a large Styrofoam cup of coffee. Fred and I pulled our own cups from the giant stainless-steel machine before sitting across from him in the small, yellow Formica booth. David owned about a hundred acres, mostly given over to farming hay. His family had deep roots in the valley, reaching as far back to his grandfather, who had fought in the Civil War. His grandfather "was a worker," as high a compliment as could be given, but his working days had ended in 1912 when a log rolled over him, and he spent the last twelve years of his life suffering. "They only had aspirin, not any real medical care," David explained. Gil, a tall, thin man in his late sixties, joined us for a while, and the conversation flowed around the table. David was clearly in charge of the chat, with Fred as his second.

The talk somehow moved on to kids and their cell phones these days, with the unsurprising consensus that youngsters are lost without them. Then David reminded Fred that "we don't go anywhere without ours now."

"I only carry mine because I work for the company," Fred protested. "If it rings at home, I let it go. If they want me that bad, they can come to the house."

For much of his life, David worked as a long-distance truck driver. Delivering chickens to Detroit was one of his regular routes.

"On one trip three niggers tried to steal some boxes of chickens," he recalled. *Did I just hear right?* Armed only with a baseball bat, he ran off two of them. ("They went down an alley, but I didn't follow them.") He came back to find the third man driving off with some boxes in his car. David pounced on the hood and smashed the windshield—"It looked like it got hit by a shotgun"—but had to jump off when the thief started to speed away with a half- dozen boxes. David claimed that when the police came they also tried to steal chickens, but he slammed a car door on a policeman's hand and drove away. David had personally signed for the chickens, and the load wasn't insured, but, he added with satisfaction, the shipper told him to take one box at a time until he got his six boxes back, which is exactly what he did.

David claimed he occasionally drove his rigs "half drunk"—a chilling thought—until one night ten years earlier when he pulled off near Corbin, Kentucky, after a close call. He finally realized he couldn't take those risks anymore and gave up trucking for good.

I asked if his grandfather owned slaves, but David was noncommittal. "They owned slaves here," was all he allowed before he gave the topic a course correction.

"The trouble with the niggers was they weren't interbreeding," he said matter-of-factly. "Once they started having kids with other people, they got better."

As the men around the table agreed no one was "pure"—nor should be—I felt a jolt of revulsion at the casual use of the n-word and what lay behind it. I silently weighed my options. *Should I say something?* I decided I was here to listen and learn and so swallowed a big dose of coffee and held my tongue.

"You don't want purebred cattle," David concluded. (Barack Obama, the world's most famous mixed-race American, was never mentioned.) Some of "them," the men granted, were all right—"good workers." I noticed Fred was uncharacteristically quiet during this part of the conversation.

Angie brought David a breakfast of fried eggs, biscuits, and bacon on a Styrofoam plate. Maybe he saw my eyes light up, because he told me that she would fix me a plate if I asked.

I went to the counter, where Angie was busily shelving cigarette packs and doodads, getting ready for the day. I asked if I could get scrambled eggs, bacon, and biscuits.

"You'll have to wait until I'm finished what I'm doing," she said, without pausing. That's fine, I told her. I expected to wait at least ten minutes, probably longer—but in less than five, she walked over with a plate stacked with eggs, an inch-deep stack of thin, crisp bacon, and a fist-sized biscuit. The total tab, including all the coffee I could drink, was $2.60, instantly turning me into a fan of convenience-store diners, at least before opening hours.

By the time Fred and I climbed back into his truck, the rain had stopped and the sky seemed slightly brighter. Back at his house, we said goodbye. He was going to hitch up some mules for a Sunday wagon ride if the rain stopped. I had no sooner crawled back into my tent when the rain returned, cycling three or four times through heavy rain, lighter rain, brightening skies, and back to rain.

Watching water run down the netting of the tent and occasionally drip from the spine of the roof, I resigned myself to dampness today, tomorrow, maybe the next day, and, for all I knew, the rest of the trip. I could feel frustration building, knowing how the weather would make conversations scarce. I silently coached myself: *I must wait on the weather and take my cues from it, like a farmer.* Distant thunder rumbled, and the rain fell harder. This was a forced pause, and I could not control anything beyond the basic decision of when to walk. I figured that I should pack out by noon if I wanted to reach the national park campground today. So, there was plenty of time; it was only half past nine. Frustration was pointless, and boredom was optional. I leaned on my pack and in the green-tinted light watched beads of water chase each other down the arc of the tent roof to the floor, where they disappeared into the carefully placed washcloths.

Then I thought of other reasons to feel frustrated. I had forgotten to take photos of Fred, David, or anyone on this stop, and I had failed to ask Fred for more details about DeRoyal. Most of all, I had not pushed David harder about what he thought of the Civil War, slavery, race, and the n-word. I could have asked questions without being combative or obnoxious. I was a journalist, after all, although at that moment I did not feel much like one.

After an hour the rain eased enough to let me quickly pack my tent and leave. I turned west onto the rail-to-trail, misjudged a puddle, and promptly submerged both my feet. Dry socks were stowed deep inside my pack. I kept walking. The rain returned, turning into a downpour that was still going strong when I reached Wilderness Road State Park, about two miles and an hour later.

The visitor center sat just off the trail, featuring a cathedral roof, log posts, exterior stonework, and rocking chairs on the front porch. I dropped my pack and poles on the porch, stripped off my rain jacket, and shook out my dripping hat. I sat in a rocker, took off my shoes and soaking socks. My feet looked pickled. Digging in my pack for the dry socks, I looked up to see four buffalo grazing unperturbed in a field fenced by split logs on the other side of the park's main road. I padded inside the visitor center in dry socks, where two young women in khaki Virginia state park uniforms were chatting, one at the counter and the other in the small office behind it.

The center included a small gift and snack shop, a theater for show-ing one of those earnest "dramamentaries" with stirring period music that are the staples of historical parks, and a room set up as a small frontier-era museum. Three large display cabinets in the middle of the floor contained a modest collection of rifles, powder horns, maps, hand tools, and other colonial-era artifacts. The room was dominated by a life-size diorama of the signing of the Transylvania Purchase at Sycamore Shoals, where I had started my walk. Mannequins stood in for five of the main characters, whites and Cherokee alike, with Richard Henderson and Chief Attakullaculla front and center. A mural backdrop included a crowd scene—the whites were painted with hopeful expressions, but the Cherokees looked skeptical—and a reasonable re-creation of the Watauga River and the surrounding hills as they appear in real life.

Ember Sutton (left) and Olivia Marcum

I had hoped to talk with Billy Heck, but he was gone. Outside, rain-drops exploded on the asphalt parking lot like tiny bombs. I decided to hang around a while.

According to her badge, the friendly, oval-faced brunette behind the counter was Olivia Marcum, "education support specialist." She had worked at the park for five years, presenting programs about the weather, birds, stargazing, and—one of her favorites—"critters in the creek," as well as leading hikes and bicycle rides. Olivia had grown up in Oklahoma hoping to be a storm chaser. Then her family moved to this area in 2001 and she attended LMU to major in wildlife and fisheries management.

Olivia's partner that day was Ember Sutton, a trim nineteen-year-old from the town of Cumberland Gap who was studying "parks and rec" at LMU. Her tag labeled her as an "administrative and office specialist"—a part-time "contact ranger," she explained. Public relations, that is. We were the only ones around—not surprising on a rainy Sunday morning—and the three of us stood talking at the counter.

"A lot of out-of-state people visit the park, history buffs especially," Olivia said. "A lot of locals use it. And there are people who stop randomly— they just see the sign and pull in."

The reenactments at the replica of Martin's Station were a big draw, sometimes attracting a thousand visitors or more. "They get kids interested in history, and it gets them outdoors," Olivia said. "Billy does an amazing job, and the reenactors try to be as authentic as possible and try not to be hokey. They know their stuff."

She loved her job, but her future at the park felt unsure. State budget cuts had scaled back the nature programming, and who knew how long the number crunchers in Richmond would fund the ten or fifteen programs that attracted a grand total of three hundred people each year?

The prospects for the wider area, including nearby Harrogate, Tennessee, and Middlesboro, Kentucky, seemed uncertain as well. Olivia and Ember agreed that jobs were scarce for young adults.

"Nothing except Wal-Mart," according to Ember, "and some in restaurants and social services."

"And nursing," Olivia added. "Especially if you're a man."

Ember gave a quick nod in agreement, and the two rangers smiled slightly as if sharing an inside joke, but they did not elaborate.

More than an hour after I had arrived, the rain finally let up and the sky slightly brightened. *I'd better go.* Reluctantly I reassembled myself: Soggy shoes pulled over dry socks. Jacket. Pack. Hat. Trekking poles.

The trail was laid with fine gravel, a wonderful walking surface when dry. In this drenching rain, however, puddles swelled into small ponds that spanned the trail, forcing a walker to negotiate its slippery edges or to hopscotch from one turtle-sized island to the next. Even so, the beauty was hard to miss when the trail skirted rolling pastures or ducked in and out of canopies of trees, causing the muted sunlight to play tricks. Farther along, the trail passed within fifty feet of the huge machinery of a rock quarry.

Less than an hour after leaving the park, fatigue started to creep up on me. To distract myself, I made a mental inventory of needs: I needed to get under cover. I needed to get dry. I needed a warm shower. I needed sleep. Instinctively I shook my head, trying to clear it. (I didn't need to remind myself that I'd barely slept the night before.) I needed to tell myself I was okay. Maybe I needed more bacon, eggs, and biscuits. I needed to focus on WWDD: *What Would Daniel Do? Daniel would not whine. I needed not to whine. Or was it too late for that?*

The trail eventually emerged at a small parking lot next to the four-lane highway. A steepled Missionary Baptist church dominated a nearby hill. Its sign advised, "Don't mistake God's patience for his absence." Duly noted. By then, mercifully, the rain had stopped.

At this section alongside the highway, the trail ascends and descends several hills in quick succession, roller-coaster-like, crossing driveways and small access roads that connect the highway to churches and homes. I had stopped at the edge of a driveway to unwrap a granola bar when a white pickup truck came zipping down toward the highway. Startled, the driver hit his brakes, skidding to a stop in front of me.

"You liked to scare the fire out of me," he said. "I thought I was going to run somebody over." I stood agape, stunned, holding the granola bar in front of me like a microphone, and apologized. "No, that's what the trail's there for," he said with a quick wave, and drove away. I had dodged a few close calls along the roads. How ironic it would be if I had gotten run over on a footpath.

By midafternoon the clouds had thinned enough to allow a hint of sun, and the temperature climbed sharply with the humidity. Sweat literally poured out of the sleeves of my rain jacket. When I took off the jacket, it was wetter on the inside than the outside.

Another collection of buffalo—maybe four or five—huddled against a backdrop of trees on the far side of a field bordering the trail and hemmed in by a tall chain-link fence. A BP convenience store directly across the highway was running a contest, according to the sign mounted on the side of the store: "Name the baby buffalo, win free tank of gas."

Popular imagination places the buffalo—the American bison, to be precise—west of the Mississippi River, from the Great Plains to the Rocky Mountains. But great herds once roamed farther east, from Pennsylvania and Ohio down to the Florida panhandle. Explorers and hunters in the mid-eighteenth century reported bison so numerous that anyone could hunt them. In a two-month period in 1767, a group of English hunters killed upwards of seven hundred head and rendered their tallow to sell at market. A long hunter named Isaac Bledsoe reported a salt lick near present-day Nashville in the early 1770s that was so congested with bison that he was afraid to dismount, much less fire a shot,

American bison—buffalo—at Wilderness Road State Park, Ewing, Virginia

lest he spook the herd. Likewise, when Boone and his companions arrived at their destination in central Kentucky in 1775, they crested a hill to see a herd of about three hundred of the animals. The impact of the bison remains: Migration routes, typically connecting salt spring to salt spring, formed the basis of road networks between the Atlantic coast and the Mississippi River. A local road less than a mile from my house began centuries ago as a buffalo trace. Interstate 81 through Virginia got its start the same way. So did the road I was walking.

The buffalo were central to Cherokee culture, providing essential meat, hides, and tallow. They also were part of the early trading when Europeans arrived. By the seventeenth century the Cherokees and Spanish had established a vibrant fur trade to supply the Dutch and Mexican leather markets. Early white settlers followed the example of the Native Americans, killing mainly for subsistence and a relatively modest fur trade. None of this at first disrupted the Cherokees' way of life or radically affected the herds.

But something changed by the late 1600s, when the British took control of the lands between the Atlantic coast and the mountains. The spreading settlements pushed the herds west, and long hunters started competing with the Cherokees for buffalo, elk, and deer hides. The fur trade reached its zenith in 1750, supplying a lucrative global market, especially through the ports of Charleston, Savannah, and Augusta. Cherokees and then long hunters brought their harvests for shipment up the coast or for export to Europe and China. In a single season a good hunter could harvest sixty to eighty skins—buffalo, deer, and bear. A great hunter could gather five times that many, which provided a good annual income, assuming he wasn't robbed on the way back to "civilization" or tempted to waste his proceeds on "high living." (The going rate for one male deer skin in the late eighteenth century was a dollar, which gave the currency its nickname—a buck.)

But buffalo were hunted not only for commerce or survival. Deerskins were more profitable than buffalo hides, but "it was tales of buffalo hunting that boys and men recounted." Dr. Thomas Walker of Virginia, he who loved the Cumberland name so much, observed that great herds of buffalo had been killed for "diversion." Another pioneer confessed, "Many a man killed a buffalo just for the sake of saying so."

Beginning a pattern that lasted a century and increasingly stretched westward, white hunters wasted the animals they killed, sometimes taking only the hide and a few pieces of meat, leaving hundreds of carcasses to rot. The devastation not only made game more scarce as the herds moved north and west; it inflamed Native American fury, making hunting more dangerous.

And so the bounty did not last. As historian Stephen Aron succinctly states, "Wherever backcountry hunters trod, depletion of game soon followed." When Isaac Bledsoe returned to the same salt lick he had discovered only a year before, the growth of cane was so thick and the absence of buffalo so striking that he momentarily thought he had gone to a different place by mistake. Then he found a mass of bleached bones surrounding the lick, the remains of indiscriminate killing.

Within a few weeks of arriving at Boonesborough in early April 1775, hunters had all but eliminated the local herd. The men were "almost starved" by mid-May as they waited for hunters to return from expeditions that took them thirty miles from the fort in search of big game, a pattern that other settlements would repeat. So fierce was the slaughter of buffalo that during the first and only convention of the House of Delegates of the Transylvania Colony, in May 1775, Boone put forward a bill to regulate hunting. Even so, less than ten years after the founding of

Boonesborough, the big animals had vanished from the entire region. The last wild buffalo in central Kentucky was killed in 1793, somewhere between Lexington and Louisville, in present-day Spencer County. In June 2013, approximately eight buffalo lived along the Wilderness Road, fenced in and helping to hawk gasoline.

I turned toward Cumberland Gap a half-mile past the buffalo, where a National Park Service road intersected with the highway. The gate was a simple, single metal bar. Just beyond, a narrow, rough path—the Colson Trail, according to a sign at the gate—led uphill into the woods. The footing was slippery, but I was glad to be off the asphalt and walking an honest-to-goodness trail, despite the drone of cars through the trees. The path wound through the woods for a mile, ending at a parking lot where a two-lane road curled around a big bend and up a long ascent to the Cumberland Gap National Historical Park Campground.

Two rangers—a tall, lanky man and an equally tall, matronly woman—were at the campground entrance. Dripping and tired, I entered the small log-veneered office to pay, wanting only to find a site quickly and get settled. A campfire would be nice, so I extravagantly sprung seven bucks for a small bundle of wood. Once my tent was up and gear stowed, the first order of business was a shower. As I soaked in the warm water, tentative patters of rain began hitting the bathhouse's metal roof. In another minute or two, the rainfall grew loud enough to drown out the shower. I dressed and waited inside until the cloudburst ended. Back at my site, my seven-dollar bundle of firewood lay exactly where I left it: out in the open, soaked like all the other wood in the park, the county, the state and, for all I reckoned, the world. Dinner was freeze-dried lasagna with cheese that, once out of its nifty cook-in bag, congealed to the consistency of old rubber cement.

The leaden sky brought a premature dark, and I zipped into my tent early. By the cool glow of my headlamp, I read a little of *Walden*, made notes in my journal, and again placed small cloths around the tent to absorb leaks before I felt myself nodding off to the sound of intermittent rainfall. As sleep came on, I wondered if it would be so terrible to cross the Cumberland Gap tomorrow and then stop all this foolishness.

12

THROUGH THE GAP

*Stand at Cumberland Gap and watch the procession of
civilization, marching single file—the buffalo following the
trail to the salt spring, the Indian, the fur trader and hunter, the
cattle-raiser, the pioneer farmer—and the frontier has passed
by. Stand at South Pass in the Rockies a century later and
see the same procession with wider intervals between.*

—FREDERICK JACKSON TURNER

In the morning, I knew I could not quit. This change of heart did not spring from sheer determination or a newly tapped vein of courage or even a good night's sleep. It was simply a matter of pride: I did not want to be the guy who *almost* walked the Wilderness Road or become the subject of conversations that began, "Whatever happened to . . .?"

Once I confessed that much, however, other reasons to keep walking leapt to mind—the adventure of a trip like this, the opportunities it offers, the choices I made. Hunched in my tent as I dressed, I spoke to myself out loud: "Okay, so the weather affects my moods—but I've got great gear. So, I'm a little damp for a few days? Big deal. Just be ready for it."

The simple act of getting dressed that morning reminded me how easy my life was. Compared to early travelers, I was living in luxury. Instead of soggy buckskin or tattered linen, I wore purpose-built, lightweight clothes made of high-tech fabric that dried quickly. Instead of needing to hunt and forage for food—to be cooked in heavy iron pots or eaten raw if a fire was out of the question—I carried snacks and virtually weightless freeze-dried meals that I could heat and eat in less than fifteen minutes on a tiny gas-powered stove.

My stomach knotted when a few brief showers fell, but by the time I started walking, the clouds were breaking up to reveal the first clear blue sky I had seen in two long days. My calves tightened on the first gentle hill I ascended, but as my body warmed and loosened, the aches sloughed away. A half-mile downhill from the campground, I turned off the paved road onto Boone Trail, a narrow westward path toward Cumberland Gap itself. I silently inventoried my state of mind. I missed my daughters. I missed my friends. I missed being dry. On the other hand—a second Tevye moment—I was out on my own, testing myself, doing something new. I was meeting people I never would have otherwise and even befriending a few. Living by a clock set by sun and weather rather than by some invisible atomic gizmo synched to the second. Learning gradually what was necessary and what was optional. In a meadow, a tiny flock of insects with black, mothlike bodies and pure white paired wings scattered upward, and my mood rose, too, as if I had just discovered an image hidden in an optical illusion. Crossing a tiny wooden footbridge spanning a meandering stream, I said out loud, "So, okay: go on. Finish the bloody thing!"

The path curled through small meadows. An early summer palette spread from the trail toward backdrops of beech and maple trees, with dainty purple-blue butterflies hovering around white daisies, yellow honeysuckle, and goldenrod. There was a centipede on the trail, striped black and yellow, two inches long and a half-inch thick. In a single elegant motion, it changed direction by rolling over onto itself to form a ball and then uncurling and righting itself to turn ninety degrees. Once walking, the movement of its feet looked like tractor treads edged with neon lights. It was easy to forget that the trail was a work of engineering until I came to a low spot where the gravel and top layers of soil were washed away to expose a concrete foundation.

A hiker approached from the opposite direction, the only other hiker I had seen on my trip. He was grinning mightily and clipping along with a walking stick and a daypack. We nodded to each other, but he obviously did not want to stop.

A small National Park Service visitor center perched on the eastern edge of the village of Cumberland Gap features interpretive signs, mounted trail maps, a parking lot, and restrooms. The Boone Trail intersects the Wilderness Road right behind the center, according to a wooden mock-rough sign. With noon approaching, I followed the Wilderness Road trail to a left-hand fork that descends into the village. I wanted to see people and drink a decent cup of coffee.

This fork, the Tennessee Road Trail, is broad and shaded and graded gently as it descends into the town. Within a few minutes, I stood in front of the Iron Furnace, the two-story-tall stone remnant of ironworks that fueled the local economy from the 1820s until the 1880s. With Gap Creek flowing next to it, everything needed for iron production was here—ore, limestone, wood, and water. The ironworks, according to the interpretive sign, had burnt ten square miles of forest in its sixty years. Now it looked like an unfinished pyramid made of impressively bulky, hewn stones. The entrance into the chamber is small enough to force a visitor into a crouch to step inside of what was, in effect, a great chimney.

The path ended at a small parking lot on the edge of town. Directly across the narrow street, the Cumberland Gap Tavern, established in 2012, looked promising but was already out of business. I walked past the Historic Olde Mill Inn Bed and Breakfast—the mill was built in 1890—and the smaller, older log house attached to it, the Civil War headquarters for the Sixty-third Tennessee Volunteers Regiment. On the short main street, the Pineapple Tea Room was closed on Mondays and Tuesdays. This was Monday.

A sign for The Old Country Kitchen hung over a building across the street, I walked over, dropped my pack near the door, and stepped inside to a tall room tinted by deep golden brown wooden floors and brick walls. One of the small group of women milling in the back broke from the circle to ask if she could help. I told her I just wanted a cup of coffee.

"We're not open yet," she said. "If you want a really good cup of coffee, there's a place in Middlesboro called Shades." A quick look around made it clear that renovations were in progress. Angelo's was coming soon—opening in only ten days, featuring an Italian menu, with live music two nights a week.

I was talking with the kitchen manager, Teresa Blanton, who offered a brief history of the building, which started as a bank and a hardware store. Angelo's will be the third incarnation in the last few years, after a tearoom and the Country Kitchen. She noticed that one of the new owners was trying to take care of some last-minute details, but a little girl was distracting her. Teresa excused herself to entertain the girl by showing her how much fun it is to use a broom.

Coffeeless, I retraced my route past the mill, past the furnace, up the Tennessee Road Trail, and back onto the Wilderness Road trail. The day was warm and the world was drying out, with scattered puffs of clouds sailing overhead. Less than ten minutes after rejoining the trail, I stood at "the saddle" of the gap, the low point of the Cumberland Mountains and the high point—topographically and emotionally—of the Wilderness Road.

I had reached the midpoint, more or less, of my trip and had crossed from Tennessee into Kentucky. The moment demanded some kind of celebration. All I could muster was a granola bar and a handful of almonds. I raised a private toast with a gulp of water from the canteen. The dirt-and-gravel footpath was twelve feet wide, a recognizable but far tamer version of what Daniel Boone and his crew hacked through more than two centuries earlier. That fact alone qualified it as an engineering marvel. In the past generation, the gap had undergone a complete transformation, or maybe a resurrection.

Starting early in the nineteenth century, the gap had been regularly graded and paved and modernized beyond recognition to accommodate wagons and then cars and trucks. US Highway 25E eventually ran over this ground, a curving two-lane road with severe switchbacks that made driving treacherous in the winter. Old photos show a time when stores and touristy kiosks lined the route here. But in the 1930s, groups ranging from local historical societies to the US Department of the Interior began calling for the gap to be reclaimed as a historic site.

"Someday a Homer or a Virgil will arise who will tell our descendants the story of our march across the continent not only in undying terms but so as to show the grandeur-filled prophetic visions of the time to come," extravagantly wrote Lucien Beckner, secretary of the Filson Historical Club. His letter to historian Robert Kincaid in 1946 surged with his era's belief in manifest destiny:

> When this is done the great Gap that was the threshold to such a vast part of the continent will loom as one of the moments of that epic more romantic and glamorous than the Statue of Liberty or anything that man can make. But for this Gap the history of our

nation would have been quite different and its development delayed so much that we may never have driven France and Spain and England and the Red Savage from what is now our national domain. It is depressing, painfully so, to imagine what would have been the status of liberty and civilization today if we should subtract the influence of Cumberland Gap. . . . [The Ohio River, the other main gateway to the West] finally became the more important, but for some years the gap's usefulness was greater and these were the years in which the Anglo Saxon made his foothold in the West unshakeable. Perhaps someday we will erect upon the Pinnacle a statue of Progress looking westward which will be greater than the Statue of Liberty, not because liberty is less important, but because the new statue will have to include both liberty and progress.

No statue was forthcoming, but in 1973 a federal law authorized the National Park Service to build a tunnel through Cumberland Mountain, reroute the federal highway, and restore the historic appearance of the gap. Within a dozen years, drilling began on a mile-long tunnel under the mountain and its four lanes opened to traffic in 1996. Five years later, work began to remove the road and return the gap to its previous state. Restoring the landscape to its original contours—as best as could be determined from descriptions and survey maps dating back to 1833—took more than two years. Altogether, the project cost about $265 million. This was not exactly the gap that Daniel Boone would have seen, but it was a lot closer than asphalt.

The Cumberland Gap has always been the most famous and recognized place on the Wilderness Road, an icon of early westward-ho America. The first white man known to have crossed the gap was Gabriel Arthur, a captive of the Shawnee in 1673. Dr. Thomas Walker traveled through it in 1750, and Boone traversed it nineteen years later. The saddle is 1,600 feet above sea level, between the Pinnacle Overlook (2,440 feet) and Tri-state Peak (1,990 feet), a seemingly arbitrary point where, as the name implies, Kentucky, Tennessee, and Virginia converge. (The exact spot is marked by a brass circle the size of a bread plate embedded in the ground and sheltered under a gazebo. A panoramic view overlooks Middlesboro, Kentucky, to the northwest.)

The peculiar topography of the gap also made it a strategic location for warriors. The Cherokees built a small fort at the northern base of the mountains, where Middlesboro now spreads, to guard against encroach-ing Shawnee. Union and Confederate troops fought over control of the gap, and it changed hands at least three times during the Civil War. Hik-ers can still see a reminder of that conflict on a side trail, where they will find what looks like a deep depression or sinkhole, overhung by a rock outcropping. This was the site of a Union ammunition magazine that detonated with an explosion massive enough to be seen and felt twenty miles away.

Maybe because of its place as a threshold between North and South or because of its role as a battleground, legend has it that in 1863 Presi-dent Abraham Lincoln suggested to General Oliver Otis Howard, com-mander the IV Corps of the Army of the Cumberland, that after the war he establish a university at the gap, for the people of Appalachia. The idea languished for about thirty years—understandable because after the war ended, Howard led the effort to start a school for African-American ministers in Washington, ultimately serving as the first presi-dent of Howard University. Then in 1888, a Congregationalist minister named A. A. Myers came to the area determined, as were many mis-sionaries of the day, to start an academy for mountain children. During a visit to the region to present a lecture series, Howard remembered his commitment to fulfill Lincoln's request. He, Myers, and a small group of local leaders—including a Confederate veteran—joined forces to launch a new university. They purchased property within sight of the gap—a re-sort hotel and surrounding buildings in Harrogate, Tennessee, that had gone bust two years earlier. And, so, Lincoln Memorial University was chartered on what would have been Lincoln's birthday in 1897.

The trail over Cumberland Gap forks at a clearing a half-mile into the Kentucky side of the saddle. To the right lay the path of the Object Les-son Road, named for a short stretch of road that was improved in the 1930s as an "object lesson" to show locals the value of paving. I bore to the left, following the Wilderness Road. On the other side of the clearing, just before entering a canopy of trees, stands a twelve-foot-tall rock with a bronze plaque bolted onto the side. This is "Indian Rock," according to yet another DAR marker from 1915. "This rock," according to the 1835 diary of General Robert Patterson of Philadelphia, "was selected by the savages as a favorite position to waylay the unsuspecting woodsman on his journey across the mountain. Many are said to have fallen victim by that fatal rock, and it was not until the country became cleared and a

Cumberland Gap

road opened exposing the ground around this death pass, that the spot ceased to be an object of dread. Its singular formation being cleft in the center, rendered the position peculiarly favorable for the purpose for which the natives had selected it." I saw no cleft, but part of the rock had been blasted away when the Object Lesson Road was built, according to the historian Kincaid. *The "savages" were long gone by then anyway.*

Once past the rock and into the trees, the trail grew twisted and clogged with rocks and tree roots and tapered into a passage wide enough for only one person. The focus of a long-term restoration project, this mile-long section is intended to restore the Wilderness Road and its environment to its condition in Boone's day, a process that will take another century, according to an interpretive marker. A portion of the first roadbed was visible, a bit of the route widened and improved for wagons in 1796 by the four-year-old Commonwealth of Kentucky.

I recalled the first time I had walked this section, eleven months earlier. Unfamiliar and tightly enclosed in trees, it had felt long, and I had literally broken out into an anxious sweat, wondering if I was lost— until I reminded myself that I could hear the occasional rumble of a passing car. But on this day the trail felt short and easy. I imagined people—white people, that is—walking here for the first time, forced to trust their guides, like Boone. The anxiety, the tiredness, the exhilaration they must have felt. The faith they must have summoned, whether in God or in Boone. Likely both.

The Wilderness Road Trail ends at the Thomas Walker parking lot and intersects with the Thomas Walker Trail, which runs alongside the main two-lane road and leads to the visitor center. Where it finally levels, the asphalt sidewalk begins, crossing underneath the double flyover of US Highway 25E, where four men in Day-Glo orange vests trimmed the banks under the highway. The blacktop trail—really a sidewalk through the woods now—wound past an interpretive sign titled "Pinnacle of Perfection," which tells the story of the New South Brewery and Ice Company: Its grandiose limestone headquarters rose in this spot a century ago, part of a magnificent and short-lived civic vision for *fin de siècle* Middlesboro.

Past the visitor center and across its parking lot, the asphalt walkway leads to Middlesboro. A stylish, zaftig teenage girl was walking from that direction, decked out in a hot pink fitness top, black Lycra shorts, white running cap, earbuds and—despite the trees and an overcast sky—sunglasses. Enbubbled, she did not acknowledge me or anything as we passed.

The first thing that caught my eye as I emerged from the trees was a set of familiar golden arches soaring in the distance. But there's a restaurant at the end of the asphalt trail, where US Highway 25E meets Cumberland Avenue, the boulevard into old downtown. I decided that my first meal in Kentucky should be at a local place. So, feeling puckish, I walked into the KFC.

13

DREAMS AND HOPES

*The very least you can do in your life is figure out what you
hope for. And the most you can do is live inside that hope. Not
admire it from a distance but live right in it, under its roof.*

—BARBARA KINGSOLVER

Approaching Middlesboro, Kentucky, a traveler learns from a small,
green road sign that he has reached the hometown of Lee Majors,
the 1970s heartthrob who used to be the Six-Million-Dollar Man
and the husband of Farrah Fawcett. *Such a claim to fame.*

But in small print, almost modestly, the town's official welcome sign
notes another, more epochal fact, namely that the town sits in a crater. From ground level, the four-mile-wide scar looks like a broad but
unremarkable Appalachian valley. But this geological oddity—created
roughly 300 million years ago when a meteorite slammed into the then-
rising mountains—is plain in satellite images. The area looks as if someone set a hot oval iron in the middle of a very wrinkled bedsheet. This
is what made the location what it is and attracted Native Americans,
settlers, Civil War soldiers, ambitious Gilded-Age entrepreneurs, and
perhaps Lee Majors' parents.

Nestled under the northern shoulders of the Cumberland Mountains
and only a short walk from the gap, the crater site offered an obvious
location for any travelers to rest or rendezvous before crossing the mountains. Native Americans appreciated the unique character of the place
long before whites arrived. Hunting trails and the great Indian warrior
path known as Athawominee passed through here. The Cherokees built a
fort on the site before white settlers came through, and it served as both
a meeting place and a fighting place between Shawnees and Cherokees.

The earliest white settlement grew up around a tavern started by a Mrs. Davis in the early 1800s, no doubt spurred by the Wilderness Road.

The crater was only one of "four geologic elements" within a dozen miles of downtown Middlesboro that made this the obvious route for the Wilderness Road, according to the Planetary Science Institute (PSI). Besides the impact crater, there's the gap itself and the Yellow Creek valley, which runs northwest to meet the final element, a water gap in the Pine Mountain ridge. The Cumberland River flows through that breach, providing a natural ford. Without the impact crater or the creek valley, the route would probably not have been suitable for pack horses, much less the wagon trains that came later. So, according to the institute, without two mountain gaps only a dozen miles part, a stream to connect them, and that crater—which presumably made the whole combination possible in the first place—"the route would be non-existent." Geology became destiny.

And one more thing, the PSI pointed out almost as an aside: This is the only known meteor impact crater where there is coal mining. *Of course. Coal is always in the story.*

But Middlesboro's claims to fame, it turns out, were all lodged in the past. Even the most recent attraction has gone: a Lockheed P-38F Lightning. The fighter plane, part of a squadron forced down over Greenland during World War II, had been forgotten and buried under snow and ice for almost forty years. But its discovery in 1981 sparked the imagination of a Middlesboro businessman and retired Air Force pilot named Roy Shoffner. He financed the recovery effort, and the fighter was excavated from 268 feet of ice in 1992. He brought it back to his hometown and put it on display at the small regional airport, where thousands of visitors came to see "Glacier Girl" even during its decade-long restoration. The old plane flew again in 2002, including a trans-Atlantic trip to England, its original destination from sixty years earlier. But Shoffner died in 2005, and "Glacier Girl" was sold and moved to Texas. The tale might be an almost-perfect metaphor for the cycle of booms and busts that the town has endured.

Middlesboro was founded in 1890 with high hopes and great aspirations, conceived as a center of commerce and industry in anticipation of the coming twentieth century, born to be a provincial debutante. Alexander A. Arthur, an entrepreneurial Scotsman, was the midwife. By way of Canada, Boston, and Knoxville, he arrived in 1885 to prospect for ore. When he realized the abundance of coal and iron ore in the surrounding hills, he envisioned a major manufacturing and mining city to rival Birmingham, Alabama, in steel production. He launched a company to carry out his plans, the American Association, and named the new town after the then-prosperous steel center of Middlesbrough, England. Believing he was building a "Pittsburgh of the South," Arthur planned on a big scale—hence Cumberland Avenue, the wide, central boulevard through old downtown. He imagined a future metropolis of a quarter-million residents. (The population never reached even one-tenth of that number, peaking at 10,334 in the 2010 Census.) Arthur even had the cheek to plant another town on the Tennessee side of the gap as a suburb and resort for the affluent citizens who would undoubtedly migrate to his industrial mountain paradise. There in Harrogate—named after another northern English town, a spa resort popular in the 1800s—he constructed a lavish home for himself and his family while his American Association built a grand, 700-room hotel, the Four Seasons, reputed to be the largest in the country when it opened.

But working against Arthur was the remote location, which kept the would-be rich tourists at bay, and the rugged terrain, which made extracting and transporting ore and timber more difficult and expensive than anticipated. Because the planned railroad could not scale Cumberland Gap, for example, Arthur's company was forced to burrow a tunnel through the mountain. Nor did it help when the coal turned out to be an inferior grade.

Ironically, while Middlesboro was too isolated geographically, it was not isolated enough economically. A global economic earthquake, the Baring Brothers Bank Panic, struck the very year the town was founded, threatening Arthur's grand hopes from the start. The ensuing aftershocks prompted Arthur's British backers to begin pulling their investments, and the great Panic of 1893 finally finished off Arthur's company and his dreams. The Four Seasons in Harrogate was sold for a wretched $25,000 and dismantled. The property later became the site of Lincoln Memorial University, which is today probably the major remaining asset within a dozen miles of downtown Middlesboro, especially after the decline of coal mining (because coal is always in the story). The town turned from promising debutante into aging spinster, like some municipal Miss Havisham, left to clutch at what might have been. Or so it felt when I walked through in 2013.

In search of a motel and a laundry, I trekked west on Cumberland Avenue, still a broad boulevard lined with generous sidewalks and two- to five-story buildings dating back to the early years of Middlesboro. A small bridge crossed Yellow Creek, and the water indeed had a yellow-brown cast, perhaps caused by iron in the ground. Pioneers followed this stream about thirteen miles north to its confluence with the Cumberland River, near the site of present-day Pineville. A Coca-Cola bottling plant now stands across the avenue—the home, I recalled, of Cumberland Gap Spring Water. *But please,* I thought, *not from Yellow Creek.*

I stopped at the Days Inn, a forlorn façade of rooms separated from the street by an oversized parking lot of cracked asphalt. When I asked the desk clerk about laundry, his directions were lost on me. I was listening for street names and numbers; he was naming landmarks. Once in my second-floor room, I found a laundry in the phone book and called to make sure it was still in business. It was a mile and half from the motel, but I figured the walk would let me see downtown. I jammed my dirty clothes into my big yellow stuff sack and returned to Cumberland Avenue, passing under a narrow railroad bridge decorated with large photos of Middlesboro's brief days of 1890s glory and a sign proclaiming this to be "The Magic City," a nickname bestowed by Mr. Arthur.

Matching fountains stood on each of the four corners where the avenue crossed Twentieth Street, offering the hint of a vibrant town square. A block farther west was the terminus of an attractive canal-side walking path that meandered through town. Shades of Brown Coffee Shop, the café that Teresa in Cumberland Gap village had mentioned, stood across the road. It would be open until nine—plenty of time. I turned north at Twenty-fifth Street and in a mile came to Binghamton Baptist Church and Gateway Christian School. The school ("Home of the Royal Eagles") was housed in an old church building wedged on a triangle of property. Three flagpoles stood in front of the building. An American flag hung from the tall, central pole, flanked by Christian flags. I tried not to dwell on the theological implications.

A sizable circular church building rose on a nearby hill. It featured a curved arch that came to a point over the entrance, like an upside-down wishbone. The coppery roof curved like a Hershey's Kiss up to a brass coronet adorned with stained-glass windows and topped by a cupola with a cross. I pictured an ambitious wedding cake. A matched pair of three-foot-tall black stone tablets stood like sentries at the semicircular driveway, one engraved with the Ten Commandments and the other with Jesus' Beatitudes.

Washing and drying my meager load of stinking clothes took an hour at the laundry, which was connected to a convenience store within sight of the church. Then I followed a different road back downtown, through a quiet neighborhood and past a lush park with rolling green hills and tall, shady trees.

I stopped to eat at Shades of Brown, a cozy room with soft lighting, soothing music, and eight or ten bistro tables. The owner, Teresa Brown, was also the wife of John Brown, a local attorney whose face smiled down from billboards around the county. She had opened the café six years earlier as a side interest, and it had taken off. Teresa gave me her opinion of Middlesboro. She conceded that the "mall"—a collection of supermarkets, restaurants, and retailers strung along a mile of the US Highway 25E bypass—had almost killed downtown. Now the mall was dying, which she blamed on "poor leadership" in the town. Even so, she felt encouraged by a few signs of life, such as the full occupancy of a couple of downtown blocks, including the one where her café stood. A lot of people lived downtown, Teresa said, and many of the old buildings had been divided into apartments. The chamber of commerce was trying to figure out how to attract tourists based on its meteor crater. The town, she said, had been making steady progress until recent federal budget cuts hit.

My turkey sandwich came out just as a customer walked in, and Teresa excused herself. I enjoyed the quiet, the sitting, and the food in almost equal measures.

A dense fog blanketed the town the next morning as I walked out. Heavy fog was common, I was told, because the town does, after all, sit in a crater. I followed Nineteenth Street north, which ran parallel to railroad tracks, and came into a workaday district with pawnshops, farm supply stores, and auto repair shops. J. R. Hoe and Sons, in business since 1909, offers computer-aided machining. A gun shop. A white-sided Missionary Baptist Church, rising behind Spider and Sons Glass and Radiator Repair. Well before nine o'clock, the parking lot was full in front of the Kentucky Cabinet for Workforce Development, which provides employment services and rehabilitation: a one-stop jobs center. Next door was

"Self Refind," which offers services to help "get your life back." Last night I had noticed a few other mental health and counseling services, which seemed a lot for a small town.

Pineville Pike is a two-lane blacktop that curls out of town alongside Yellow Creek, tracing the original Wilderness Road. (*Rule no. 1: Take the older route when possible.*) The terrain opened up on the pike, with farmhouses and double-wide trailers set back from the road. The buzz of traffic filtered through the trees from US Highway 25E, the four-lane bypass only a few hundred yards to the east.

The temperature had warmed and the fog had lifted by the time I reached the purely rural stretch of road, a narrow stream with clear, ochre-tinted water running alongside. At a sharp bend on the pike, a shack sat tucked into the woods with half-dozen plastic garbage barrels lined up between house and road: a make-do fence. Tall weeds over-whelmed the front yard, and a couple of old trucks seemed to be put-ting down roots as well. The place might have been derelict, or someone might live there still. Several traumatized mailboxes lined the road, one split open as if cleaved with an ax. Come nightfall, I did not want to be on this road.

Pineville Pike ended at US Highway 25E, where I turned north—*or was it more westward now?* I could have continued on a country road along Yellow Creek, but I wanted to stop at Adkins Barber Shop.

Driving this route in the past, I had often noticed the small, gray, solitary building standing in front of a steep bank, beneath the gaze of a handful of houses. The shop's narrow, steep steps led to the front door and a short, wall-mounted red-white-and-blue striped pole. Inside, a hefty man with a neat white beard sat in the first of three barber chairs. He could have been St. Nick's stunt double, with biceps the circumfer-ence of small trees. "Demps" was a seventy-four-year-old retired coal miner who had descended more than five miles into the earth almost every day for forty-two years. "On my seventy-first birthday," he said, "I decided I'd had enough, and I quit right then."

The slim barber, who wore glasses and modeled a military-style haircut, was just finishing up, trimming his customer's eyebrows and vacuuming stray hairs with a hose stretching from a wall-mounted ma-chine. Charles Adkins, age fifty-three, had been cutting hair profession-ally for only eight years, his second career after administering medical records at nearby Pineville Hospital. Barbering had been his long-time

Charles Adkins

dream. To achieve it, he had maintained a grueling schedule for eighteen months, attending a barber college in Knoxville, Tennessee, Tuesdays through Saturdays, and then driving home—two hours in good weather—to work at the hospital Sundays and Mondays. He opened his shop in 2007, two years after earning his license.

His business was decidedly a barber shop, not a salon: compact, functional, and plain. The main decor was a simple mural of four deer that dominated the long, white wall opposite the chairs, joined by a mounted deer head to one side. Two of the painted deer had labels: "Adkins Buck 155 B.C." and "Carter Buck, 112." The numbers, Charles instructed me, referred to the "Boone-Crockett score," a relative measurement of a deer's value—some algorithm, I suppose, of size, antlers, and other factors. A score of 160 will get the hunter's name into a record book. Charles' score of 155 fell just short.

He originally planned to open his business in Pineville itself, his lifelong home, but another barber shop was already operating in the small town. His voice growing taut, Charles said that he was "frozen out." He blamed "endless foot-dragging" when he applied for permits, and he said he had been charged in the beginning an exorbitant $375 monthly rent for a small, unheated room with a leaky roof on the edge of town. He finally built his current shop by himself on his own land after he was told that the county would build a small road in front of his shop to connect it with US Highway 25E. The connection never came through, so customers must drive a quarter-mile past the shop and double back on a narrow access road. To top off his troubles, his original roadside sign was stolen.

And if his shop didn't make it, what was Plan B? He and his wife were talking about moving to Tennessee, but for the present they needed to stay and help care for his single daughter and four-year-old granddaughter. A framed eight-by-ten photo of a bright-eyed blonde preschooler hung above the wall of mirrors behind the barber chairs.

As requested, he cropped my hair short, shorter than it had been since grade school, leaving my ears to jut out like satellite dishes. The haircut cost nine bucks, and it was a good one. Brushing my neck with talc shaken from a green Clubman bottle—old-style barbering, this—he said he was a little anxious about the future but had no regrets. Despite the problems, Charles loved barbering as much now as when he began. As we shook hands at his front door, he wished me well for my trip, and I wished him well for his life.

Back on US Highway 25E, I thought about Charles' story as a modern version of the Wilderness Road. Thousands of the pioneers had migrated from the East because they, too, had felt frozen out by powers-that-be. Frustrated, angry, and determined, the pioneers pulled up stakes and relocated to unclaimed territory. Charles was hatching a plan to do the same—except, of course, he would not find virgin territory in Tennessee. He would find other barbershops.

After passing three car dealerships in quick succession—one with Cadillac SUVs and Hummers on display—I came to an outpost of the Midwest Herb Company. Dozens of broad strips of tree bark, some as long as blankets, were spread out on black plastic sheets in front of a shed. Two thirty-something guys sat inside, munching on McDonald's and watching a small TV set, apparently waiting for local folks to walk in to sell them roots, herbs, bark, and other local flora to be shipped to the company's Missouri headquarters. They were not waiting for the likes of me. Other than saying that they were part of the "nutriceutical industry," the two men were not inclined to talk.

The great, green wall of Pine Mountain loomed ahead, a vast mono-lith. The sight was daunting, even knowing there was a gap where the Cumberland River cut between its ridges—the location of present-day Pineville. I tried to imagine the relief the first travelers must have felt, so soon after the Cumberland Gap, when they realized they would not need to scale this great wall.

I stopped for a water break at a sign advertising the Wasioto Winds Golf Course. Wasioto, or Ousiotto, was the Cherokee name for the Cumberland River. This was the only Indian name I had seen since Kingsport—that is, since starting the Wilderness Road—and it was only for a golf course. Go to Tennessee and find Unaka, Watauga, Etowah, Chattanooga, Catawba, and Chota. Go to Ohio and find Chillicothe, Miami, Wapakoneta, and Scioto. Go to Kentucky and find only a few Native American names, and none on the Wilderness Road. A nineteenth-century historian, Thomas Speed, concluded that early settlers were "intent only upon the business of occupying the country, and being filled with a rancorous antipathy to the Indians." The result, he said, were place names "destitute of beauty, romance or poetry. The musical Indian names found in the North, and Northwest, and in the South, are almost unknown in Kentucky. . . . The name Kentucky is an exception, so also is Ohio, but the exceptions are few."

I crossed the road to visit the Bert T. Combs Forestry Building, named for a governor from the early 1960s. State forestry service cars sat empty in the parking lot, and the lobby of the building—probably built not long after its namesake left office—was open and vacant. There were pamphlets, signs, restrooms, and a Coke machine with a sign on the front: "Do not use. Sodas out of date."

On a wooded embankment across the highway lies the small Wil-derness Road Cemetery, established in the late 1700s. The cemetery contained the graves of travelers who died while preparing to cross the Cumberland River. Later it was used as a Civil War cemetery, since both Union and Confederate armies camped on the same bottomland. Later yet, it found service as a poor farm cemetery. The earliest marker is carved: "A.C. D.C. Apr2225." There is also a commemorative marker for Pleasant North, who is buried nearby somewhere, in an unmarked grave. Here the stone reads: "Pvt, Co F. 49th Ky Infantry—1842–1923—Civil War veteran."

Less than a half-mile later, a woman and I passed each other on the wide shoulder of the road. Her short gray hair was crudely cropped. Her shimmery pantsuit, the color of spent charcoal, hung loosely on her gaunt frame, which reminded me of photos taken at Holocaust-era concentration camps. She moved slowly, determined but directionless. As we passed, her head bobbed almost imperceptibly, and I wasn't sure if that was a silent greeting or some kind of startle response. I was reminded of shock victims walking away from some sort of wreck.

Then came Pineville. Someone had set a hand-lettered sign at the town's southern gate, where a side street drops from the highway into the town: "Jimmy Rose—America's Got Talent—June 4 @ 9pm." I did not know who Jimmy Rose was, but I would miss his performance that very night.

Mention Pineville to people who have driven US Highway 25E in southeastern Kentucky, and they may well say something like, "What about those floodgates?" or "I wonder what it's like to live there."

Approaching the town, a driver will likely notice a pair of huge steel, battleship gray floodgates flanking the road like sentries. Each gate is about eight or ten feet tall, two feet thick, and long enough to block two lanes of traffic. The road itself curls around the town's perimeter, along the top of a dike that protects the town from the Cumberland River, and so most of the town sits on full display below road level, as if in a shallow bowl. The high school football field, for example, would almost abut the embankment of the highway were it not about thirty feet lower than the roadbed. Streets dead-end at the base of the embankment, so some homeowners must look out their bedroom windows and see only a grassy bank rising a few feet away.

A gray concrete wall, in some places more than twelve feet tall, encloses the entire perimeter, its bareness relieved by narrow vertical grooves, like seersucker. The only two gaps in the wall allow streets to cross bridges over the river and head out of town. It is a fortification against nature.

Pineville officially sits 1,014 feet above sea level, but some sections are below 990 feet. That would not be a particularly relevant fact, except for the presence of the Cumberland River. The river not only borders the town. It *defines* the town, whose original name was simply a description: Cumberland Ford. At this point in its 688-mile course, the river normally flows at around 980 feet above sea level and has a flood stage of 1,002 feet. That is to say, left as nature created it, the ground on which Pineville now sits would be regularly submerged.

But Pineville has its wall and its nine floodgates, some that swing open and shut like doors and others that slide in grooves embedded in the road. The Army Corps of Engineers finished the project in the 1980s to replace the previous flood protection system, which proved inadequate in April 1977. The Cumberland River crested at 1,021.8 feet that year, inundating more than two hundred homes.

The town grew up where the river wends through a natural gap in Pine Mountain, a 125-mile-long hogback spine between Jellico, Tennessee, and Pound, Virginia. This is the only water crossing for the entire length of the mountain. The place was a godsend to early explorers like Dr. Thomas Walker, who came through in 1750 and attached the Cumberland name to the river and to the gap and the mountain range it cuts through. It was here that he and his party of five men were able to cross the river, following an Indian and buffalo trail, a path later taken by Daniel Boone and the Wilderness Road.

Today we do not think much about such things. If not for the walls and gates at Pineville, it would be easy to ignore the river altogether.

Still, while a good river ford explains the traveling route, it does not explain the stopping: Why would people choose to settle and build a town in such a place? Perhaps, like several other communities along the Wilderness Road, Pineville may have sprouted from a house or tavern for tired, hungry, and cold travelers, and some of them might have decided to stay. About 2,000 people live in the 1.4-square-mile town now, almost half the population in 1950. It's hard to know how many more people live in the rough-hewn cabins, double-wide trailers, ranch houses, split levels, and rare McMansions scattered along the two-lane tentacular roads that trace the surrounding mountain streams into the hollers.

Pineville, with one-fifth the population of Middlesboro, is the seat of Bell County. The town square, dominated by an imposing courthouse, reminded me of Michael J. Fox's hometown in the Back to the Future movies, including the obvious fact that the town has seen better days. Several empty storefronts stood around the square, interspersed with a Mexican restaurant, a florist shop, a storefront church, and the like. The main façade of the courthouse was closed. A sign at the bottom of the staircase directed visitors to the three smaller entrances. Across the street, a drug store occupies the ground floor of what was originally a Masonic temple and hotel that took up an entire block.

There were hints of past prosperity, doubtlessly built on coal. On one end of town, a historical marker tells the story of the Wallsend Coal Mine, "the first to begin operations in Bell County," in 1889, the year after the Louisville & Nashville Railroad trundled into the area and "the beginning of a new industrial era." The marker notes that the mine did not make money until the Wallsend Coal and Coke Company purchased it in 1904. Wallsend was a Kentucky corporation, but its stock was "held mostly in England." (The company was named for Wallsend, England, once a major coal center in its own right.)

The company is gone, as is most of the coal. Three hundred and twenty mines once operated within a ten-mile radius of Pineville, according to the US Department of Labor. Only nine were still active in 2013, employing fewer than two hundred miners altogether. The Wallsend community is separate from the rest of the town, situated on a tongue of flat land on the opposite riverbank from Pineville. The community is bordered by the river on one side and a railroad track on the other, and the flood wall surrounding it makes it look and feel even more isolated. From what I could see in a quick walk-around, Wallsend is composed mostly of public housing, with an elementary school and a few churches. If the community had a grocery store, it was not obvious. If fortunes were made with the Wallsend coal mine a century ago, its namesake community has not shared in the wealth.

Evidence of a moneyed past can be found in the heart of Pineville, along Tennessee Street, right at the base of Pine Mountain. Great houses from the turn of the last century loom over other properties, above the floodplain. But even those once-grand houses are dingy now. One Victorian-style house with gingerbread details presented a turret and a wide set of steps leading to an impressive wraparound porch. But several of the porch's newel posts were missing or askew, and paint peeled around the eaves.

A visual joke hangs about a thousand feet above the town, where a jagged mass of bare rock pokes out of the trees, looking like it's ready to break loose and roll down to flatten Pineville. The only thing that's ever saved the town from that terrible fate, according to local storytellers, was a big chain that tethered the rock to the mountainside. The story, of course, was bogus. The rock is only an exposed outcropping of sandstone and shale that was never going to go anywhere. The hundred-foot-long, three-thousand-pound chain was hauled up and attached in 1933, thanks to the Civilian Conservation Corps and a local Boy Scout troop—"a master stroke of community promotion, gaining Pineville attention in hundreds of newspapers across the country," according to a Kentucky state parks website. Hikers can still walk to the "Chained Rock" on a trail in the Pine Mountain Resort State Park.

The rock was plainly visible from the patio at the Burger Hut, a white building with bright blue trim, where customers could sit at picnic tables in the shade. I studied my map while I ate a cheeseburger and onion rings. A matronly woman in a floral top sat at the next table, and we chatted while she waited for her order. The local economy had been bad ever since coal production dropped, she said. Just as she was called to pick up her food from the small window, she said the current president's policies was to blame for coal's decline. She gave me a final friendly wave and walked away.

I had just put on my pack when two men emerged from inside the restaurant, and we said hi all around. They asked about my trip, and I asked about places to camp.

"There's a nice fishing spot west of town, under a bridge," one of them said. "It might be good. Quiet. Near Four Mile." My heart dropped a notch. I had already come thirteen or more miles today and did not want to go farther.

I walked into the center of town, to the old courthouse. At one corner across the street was The Flocoe, which was advertising milkshakes and ice cream. Coffee and a bowl of butter pecan ice cream sounded good, so I walked inside and stepped back in time. The floor was black-and-white tile. The counter was oak polished to a deep sheen. The ceilings were twelve feet high. A framed newspaper clipping on the wall read, "Back from the past: Favorite town sweet shop reopens." More than a dozen flags were pinned high on the walls, encircling the room: Kentucky, both state and university flags. South Carolina. Union College Bulldogs. Morehead State. Auburn University. Pittsburgh Steelers. The Vatican.

Rosemary Combs—tall, thin, and white-haired—ran the place. The restaurant had started long ago as an old-fashioned drug store with a soda shop, she told me. Her late husband, Robert Mason Osborn Combs, was a pharmacist and artist who, after gaining a "wide reputation" in

New York's artistic circles, returned to his native town to buy The Flocoe. He later opened an art store next door. She nodded toward a black-and-white photo from the 1960s, showing Robert in a tux and Rosemary in a gown enjoying some gala in New York City. At some point the business closed, and the building was left to ruin. Then about ten years ago, Rosemary's daughter bought the husk of the building, refurbished it, and reopened the restaurant and soda shop. Rosemary was hopeful not just for The Flocoe but generally for the future of the town. Business was good, and this year's annual Mountain Laurel Festival had been a great success.

Tracy, who worked at The Flocoe, was not so optimistic. She loved the town, and she loved The Flocoe, and she was exuberantly proud of her nineteen-year-old daughter, a nurse who cared for children with disabilities, and her fifteen-year-old son who wanted to be a park ranger. She told me about Jimmy Rose, the first person ever from Bell County to appear on *America's Got Talent*, and how everyone in town was very excited. But, she said with a sigh, the drug problems were "tearing up families" in town, mainly bath salts and prescription drug abuse. She possessed firsthand knowledge: Her father- and mother-in-law were divorcing after forty-four years because of his addiction to prescription drugs.

Leaving The Flocoe feeling full, I walked through the center of town. At a grassy lot next to a church, a few teenage boys were tossing a football. They had just graduated from high school. One was bound for a small college in Kentucky on a football scholarship. The others were staying closer to home—community college for a couple of them, a fast-food job in Middlesboro for another. I asked about camping on this plot of ground for the night. They exchanged glances.

"Well, maybe," said the college-bound one. "But . . ." His voice trailed off. We said goodbye, and I kept moving.

It was pushing four o'clock, so I decided to try for the fishing spot near Four Mile. On the way out of town, just before another set of floodgates, I saw the large hospital where Charles Adkins once worked. The hospital stands next to the town cemetery, which spreads up the green hillside like a quilt. *A convenient location, if a hospital stay went poorly . . .*

As I left town I realized I didn't know which bridge the men at the Burger Hut meant—at least three of them cross the Cumberland River in that few miles. But by now the distance seemed impossible. My feet were tired, and my hip was sporadically shooting out electrical warnings.

I decided to try my luck at a cluster of houses that lined a looping side road about a mile west of Pineville. I caught up with a husky middle-aged woman and two young children just walking out of their house toward a detached garage, and I made my pitch. Their front lawn looked like a green plateau with its front dropping down a ten-foot-high bank to the road. The lawn offered ample room for my small tent. I had my eye on the farthest corner possible from the front door, but she had other ideas.

"You see those big rocks right there?" she asked, pointing to an outcrop of boulders near her long driveway—below the plateau but just above a shallow, grassy culvert only a few yards from the road. "You can camp there."

"Okay," I said, pointing to that distant, level corner of the yard, "but I was wondering if I could . . ."

"You can camp on the other side of those rocks," she repeated.

Beggars can't be choosers, they say, and after eight hours I was in no mood to return to the road. The sky was clear, so camping on the edge of a drainage ditch would not be a problem. I thanked my host and walked down to the spot while she, without another word, bundled the children into a red sedan and drove away. Dropping my gear by the rocks, I noticed a right-of-way marker on the other side of the driveway, almost hidden in a small stand of trees. That explained it. I pitched my tent about twenty feet from the shoulder of US Highway 25E.

The red sedan returned about three hours later, at dusk, cruising past me on the driveway without stopping. My host never came out to check on me or to talk. We never spoke again. I wondered what she or her neighbors would have thought if they had spotted me perching on one of those boulders to fire up my camp stove and cook dinner or discreetly peeing among that stand of trees after dark.

Cars and trucks rolled past all night long. Around two o'clock in the morning, I counted at least one vehicle passing every minute, including semitrucks that rumbled by every two and a half minutes. Headlights lit my tent for three or four seconds at a time, giving me occasional petrifying visions of wayward trucks plowing off the shoulder and into the tent. I didn't sleep much. Even so, except for the four-lane highway only a few yards away, it wasn't a bad spot.

14

BEWILDERED

I can't say as ever I was lost, but I was
bewildered once for three days.

—DANIEL BOONE

Wide awake by six, I crawled out of my tent into a clear, cool morning. The traffic was light. With less than a quart of water and not knowing where I might be able to refill, I looked toward my host's house. No movement. I settled on a cold breakfast without coffee. A convenience store with a diner lay ahead somewhere, but I couldn't reckon how far. With a final glance at the house, I hoisted my pack. "*Hasta,*" I said aloud and headed west.

For a while the Cumberland River was out of sight, since the road was built high above the river's course. But this stretch of US Highway 25E does not follow the river's meandering, and within a few miles I had crossed three wide, Spartan concrete bridges over the slow, brown, cloudy water. The broad and relatively straight highway was made possible by lopping off the ends of hills like pieces of cake, exposing bare cliffs of creamy limestone, gray coal, rusty iron, and clay the color of marmalade. On the other side of the road, just out of sight, the hill resumed as a steep, overgrown bank down to the river. Small businesses sprouted on the narrow strip of flat land between the road and bank. Standing alone side by side behind a chain-link fence, for instance, were the Vapor Shack and Gregory Fitness. An odd combination, maybe, but not out of place where small combo stores offer guns and vacuum cleaners or fishing bait and hair care.

At the county line, big green signs touted Knox County as home to the 2011 Petite Miss Kentucky, the 2012 Kentucky 11-year-old Little League Baseball Champions, the 2012 Kentucky Middle School Teacher of the

Year, and the 2012 Kentucky Middle School Social Studies Teacher of
the Year. Another two miles or so brought me at last to the Wildcat Market, which was either a small truck stop or a large convenience store with
a parking lot big enough to comfortably hold a football field or two. A
road sign pointed toward Flat Lick at the next access road.

Inside the market, three women were on duty. One of them, middle
aged and blonde, may have been the owner or manager, judging by how
the other two subtly deferred to her. I overheard the name of Sherry,
who was tall and looked exotic with olive skin, dark hair, and violet eyes.
A petite brunette in her early twenties, girl-next-door pretty, was working the diner. As I perched on a counter stool and shoveled through a
plate of scrambled eggs, sausage, biscuits, and gravy, I asked if she had
grown up here. Yeah, she said, she lived here as a child before moving to
Middletown, Ohio, with her family. She had returned after eleven years.

She kept moving from counter to stove to counter, not pausing and
making only brief eye contact. I silently wondered if she had learned to
avoid the gaze of men.

"Are you glad to be back?" I asked.

"Well, I'm married now, so I'm stuck," she said without missing a
beat, but then barked a quick laugh. "Just kidding," she said, apparently
in recovery mode. She did not want to chat, even as she quickly wiped
already-clean counters. Her defenses were up. She seemed a little sad.

Full of food, I paid and stepped outside, where Sherry was sweeping
the walk. I asked her about Flat Lick, where she had grown up. There
was really nothing there, she said. There used to be, I knew, but that
was long ago. It was once a notable place, almost chosen as the seat of
the newly formed Knox County in 1799. (The state legislature changed
its collective mind when James Barbour donated land for a county
courthouse near the junction of Richland Creek and Cumberland River,
the site of present-day Barbourville.) But long before white settlers arrived, the nearby salt springs—the "lick"—attracted big game and the
Native Americans who tracked them. The place was well known as an
important rendezvous point on the Great Warrior Path, "Athawominee,"
a woodland trail traversing hundreds of miles between the Ohio and
Tennessee rivers and connecting the Shawnee in the north with the
Cherokee in the south. White explorers, including Boone, had followed
and used the route, and much of Boone's original trace followed Athawominee. Boone, in fact, had headed more directly north at this point,

while the later state-sanctioned Wilderness Road slanted a little farther west to eventually link the Cumberland Gap with the Falls of the Ohio at Louisville.

Flat Lick was therefore important to white settlers as a meeting place, a landmark, and a hunting ground, which is what ultimately doomed the area to become a backwater. The whites' hunting grew so savage that a nearby stream had been nicknamed Stinking Creek because of the stench of rotting carcasses that piled up on the riverbank.

I followed the access road, a two-lane loop that passed through the remains of Flat Lick. From what I could see, Sherry was almost right about there being nothing here. Other than Concord Baptist Church—established in 1813 and claiming to be Kentucky's oldest ongoing congregation—Flat Lick contained a construction company, a furniture store, an auto mechanic, and a modern elementary school. It mainly consisted of scattered houses and ragtag trailer parks. A few people sat listlessly on front porches as I walked past and waved. No one waved back.

The two-lane loop rejoined the main highway on the western edge of the village, and I crossed to follow another two-lane country road into the community of Himyar ("HIM-year"), where I met Tom McCully. Skinny, tanned, and grizzled, he was forty-five, but his thin face looked older. He and a woman in a gray T-shirt were sitting on a rough plywood porch precariously pinned to the front of their trailer, just far enough from the edge of the road to park a small pickup truck in front. (Its front license plate read, "Thank God I'm a Christian boy.") Listing like a boat in his folding chair, Tom wore a blue T-shirt advertising Salt Run Church. "I [heart] Jesus," it said alongside a picture of the Statue of Liberty. He invited me to stop and offered a drink of water. The woman—we were never introduced—stepped inside without a word and returned with a tall glass of ice water before disappearing back into the trailer. Three small dogs pranced around the porch. A black-and-brown pug sat in Tom's lap.

I asked what he did for a living. "I'm a mechanic," he said, nodding toward a small collection of ratchet wrenches and other tools lying on the porch. "But I can't work no more. My knees are shot, and I've got four bad disks in my back."

Tom grew up in Himyar but had moved around—Pennsylvania, Maryland, Ohio—before returning to Kentucky and settling in Clay County for twenty-two years, a place even more rural and economically

Tom McCully

depressed than Knox County. He returned to Himyar in 2012, when he could no longer work. He didn't know many people in the community anymore—most of his family had died, and his friends moved away—but he was glad to be back. This was home.

A tattooed man hurtled past on an ATV. Tom said he liked to ride ATVs and horses when he could. "That's why I don't like big cities," he added. "You can't do anything there. You don't have any freedom there."

"Freedom" was not the word that came to mind as I looked around. His life, as far as I could see, was defined by limitations: health, money, place. I wanted to press him—*You have freedom here, now?*—but caught myself even as I opened my mouth to talk. Here was a man at home and, for all I knew, at peace. After his trade had finished with his body, why would he stay anywhere else if he didn't need to? All Tom had known of Himyar had changed or disappeared—a trailer park now spilled over the ground where his family's house once stood—but even so this place was home to him. I had trouble understanding how, but here he found some kind of freedom. I was the one on the road these days, wondering about home.

After saying goodbye to Tom, I started to think about where I might stop for the night. I did not want to repeat yesterday's near-debacle. Then I remembered Union College, a small Methodist school in Barbourville, the next sizable town ahead. So, standing on the edge of a two-lane blacktop next to a broad cattle pasture, I pulled out my iPhone, did a quick search, found a phone number on the Union College website, pressed the green call button, and wondered what Daniel Boone would have made of this little miracle.

A few moments later I was introducing myself to the assistant to the president, Margaret Senter, who spoke in a lilting, soft voice. (Her title was "chief of staff," and I tried to imagine *The West Wing*'s Leo McGarry as a Southern woman.) She was sure I'd be quite welcome—she just needed to make a few phone calls. The college kept a couple of guest rooms for visitors passing through and especially wanted to be hospitable to people from "our sister institutions." She would also try to arrange meetings and dinner with a few faculty members, if that would be all right with me. She was rolling out a red carpet. (Later I found out that one of her phone calls, understandably, was to the academic dean at Milligan College, to check my bona fides.)

A town of 3,155—that was Barbourville at the 2010 census—does not have suburbs, but after almost two more hours of walking, I could tell it was close. I came to a farming supply store east of town and stopped, thankful for a good resting place. It was only early afternoon, but the day had turned warm and humid, and I had already walked more than six and a half hours.

A short, wiry man with white muttonchops and stooped shoulders in a red-checked shirt stood outside the store. His two bottom front teeth were missing, and the remaining teeth were yellow and crooked. Tom Lawson, age seventy-three, worked part time at the farm supply, after retiring from a thirty-two-year career mining coal.

After a few minutes of small talk, I asked about coal. He repeated what I had heard time and again: Regulations were killing the industry. I asked which regulations he meant and, to my surprise, he rattled off three examples. First, he said, the coal companies are required to restore 90 percent of the landscaping, but that rule ignored the good that can come from reshaping the land. Besides, he said, "You can't put a mountain back." Then there was the regulation that said anyone who wanted to actually use the restored land must wait five years before doing anything with it. He did not bother to expand on this point, as obvious as it was. Finally, he thought the restrictions on gas levels—applying even above the water table—were pointless.

As Tom calmly talked I felt myself bristling and fighting the urge to interrupt. The economics of coal were complicated, and I had committed myself to listening more than talking. But with his measured, reasonable voice, Tom made me want to. . . . *Say something about the environmental impact! Maybe if they can't replace a mountain, they shouldn't butcher it in the first place!* But I felt out of my depth. He, like my friend Robert before him, had lived intimately with the culture of coal in ways I could barely imagine. I kept my mouth shut and hoped my face wasn't betraying my sudden swell of indignation.

Later, when I recorded audio notes about our conversation, I described Tom physically and then casually added, "Nice guy, though." Nice guy, *though?* Why wouldn't he have been a nice guy? Had I betrayed to myself some latent prejudice, maybe a bias against men with bad teeth or bushy sideburns? Or was he a nice guy even though his assumptions and arguments about coal had tested my own? In one way or another and in the friendliest way possible, the old retired coal miner had left me unsettled.

Unsettling in a different way was a familiar billboard on the edge of Barbourville, looming across the street from the town's expansive cemetery: A posterized, comic-bookish image of a bald infant who must be laughing but looks more like he's screaming. These billboards, ubiquitous in southeast Kentucky, are the handiwork of Surplus Sales of Corbin. Whether the company is pushing lumber, ceramic tile, or, in this case, mulch, the same image of the bald, washed-out, wide-mouthed baby is there. These billboards have adorned Kentucky roads for well over a decade, and the iconic child must be an adult now. I imagine him as some innocent relation to the owner—maybe a grandson—who now pleads at birthday parties or Thanksgiving dinner: "Please, Grandpa! Take them down!" But maybe not. Maybe no one could be prouder than the older version of the screaming child himself. Maybe he mimics his famous infant face on request, especially if he works for the family business. In any case, the billboards are eye-catching and so, by some standard of marketing, they must be effective.

Union College dominates the north side of Barbourville, just beyond the six or eight blocks of old downtown. For that matter, with coal mining all but gone, the college dominates the entire town.

It is ironic that southern Appalachia suffers a reputation for lacking in higher education when the region is home to campuses of every size, from massive universities and their city-sized enrollments—some thirty thousand or more each at University of Tennessee and at the University of Kentucky—to midsize regionals such as Appalachian State and East Tennessee State universities, to community and technical colleges, to small and even tiny colleges whose entire student body can fit in a decent-sized auditorium. With fewer than 1,200 students, Union is an example of the last category. It is also one of the scores of church-based educational institutions planted in the South after the Civil War, started in 1879 by local Methodists.

Typical for these small schools, Union College attracts most of its students from the area. More than half of their students come from the Appalachian region; three-quarters of them are from Kentucky.

On my chosen route through southern Appalachia, I could visit Milligan College (where I teach), Lincoln Memorial University, Union College, Berea College, and Eastern Kentucky University. (A twenty-mile detour here and there could add Centre College, King University, University of the Cumberlands, University of Virginia at Wise, and at least four community colleges.) Based on census data from the ten counties where I walked, in 2010 there was one college or university for every 121,077 people—a statistic that compares favorably with the educational mecca of Boston, which has a college or university for every 125,984 people.

Despite any arguments about quality or size of endowments, southern Appalachia is not a higher educational desert. Even so, the area perennially lags behind the nation in income, employment, literacy rates, educational funding, and high school graduation rates. Which leads to an obvious question for which I had no clear answer: Why?

When I was about two blocks from Union's tidy campus of dark red-brick buildings, a sedan slowed beside me. The front passenger window slid down and the driver, a petite woman wearing glasses and a slight smile, leaned over.

"You must be Mr. Dahlman," she said in an equable Southern voice. And she must be Margaret Senter, the college chief of staff, my host and guide. She offered me a ride, but when I said I needed to walk, she nodded and directed me to her office in the Speed Academic Center, a refurbished old building connected to a modern addition by an atrium. A few minutes later, when I looked up through its tall windows and skylights, I noticed how cloudy the sky had grown.

From there Margaret led me to the northwestern edge of campus, to a row of one-story apartments. My room, near the end of the row, held the ambiance of a mom-and-pop motel room circa 1980, including a small microwave oven and cable TV. She handed me a key and politely excused herself to finish her workday. I unpacked, draped my tent over the table and chairs to dry, showered, and then lay down for a nap, roused only when Margaret called to ask what I would like for dinner, from Pizza Hut. A half-hour later she arrived with a feast: spaghetti, bread, a quart of sweet iced tea, granola bars, apples, grapes, peanut butter-filled crackers, and a couple of water bottles: enough food to pack me full that night, nibble on fruit and snacks for the next day or so, and still have a few things to carry on the road. Later that evening, I strolled around Barbourville feeling grateful. Not knowing what to expect when I phoned from the open road only hours earlier, I had stumbled into a suburb of paradise.

Barbourville was founded in the first year of the nineteenth century, named for James Barbour, whose donation of land convinced the state legislature to make Barbourville the county seat instead of Flat Lick. It was the hometown of two governors, a Supreme Court justice appointed by Abraham Lincoln, and Jimmy Carter's commerce secretary, Juanita Morris Kreps. In 1932 the town elected Kentucky's first woman sheriff, Jennie Mealer Walker, who one day felt compelled to arrest a stray mule for carrying a pint of moonshine strapped to its back.

The old center of Barbourville is orderly and flat, its streets radiating like spokes from the hub of the courthouse square. A banner hanging on a handrail of the courthouse steps announced "Prayer on the Square. First day of each month at 7 p.m. Praying for our region. Join us" . . . without identifying the "us." A life-size bronze statue of Daniel Boone, dedicated in 2012, stood beside the courthouse. He was portrayed, correctly, wearing a wide-brimmed hat rather than a coonskin cap. His face, a mite too handsome, flashed a wry grin. What may be Boone's

Daniel Boone statue at the Knox County courthouse,
Barbourville, Kentucky

only confirmed quotation was carved into the base: "I can't say as ever I
was lost, but I was bewildered once for three days."

As is the case with so many small towns, most travelers will never
see these sights. US Highway 25E once came through the town center
but was reincarnated decades ago as a four-lane bypass, tracing north
of the old downtown. It is cut from the side of a mountain on a shelf
of land lined with a predictable mixture of retail and fast food outlets:
Wal-Mart, McDonald's, and all the usual chain stores. If drivers thought
to look down from the bypass, they would catch glimpses of a spreading
cemetery, a grid of streets, a water park, and parts of the Union College

campus. The Cumberland River meanders somewhere down there, out of sight.

Barbourville is shrinking now. The town lost about 12 percent of its population in the previous decade, as the coal tapped out and local factory jobs moved away. But there is still the college, the county government, and five miles out of town, a tiny state park to mark the spot where Dr. Thomas Walker and his 1750 expedition built the first white settler's house in Kentucky. A reconstructed cabin stands at the park now, about the size of a modest modern bedroom. But the town has thrown in its lot with a more familiar pioneer: The Daniel Boone Festival each fall is the biggest party in town and, no doubt, a cash cow for the locals.

At precisely half past six the next morning, my iPhone rang, jolting me out of a deep sleep. My mental gyroscope took a few moments to calibrate as I staggered across the dark room and blinked at the number on the phone. The area code was mine, but I did not recognize the number. When I answered, a vaguely familiar voice barked, "Have you made it yet?"

"Robert?" I guessed it was Robert Bledsoe. *Wrong.*

"Have you *made it there* yet?" he asked again, more insistently—or at least more loudly.

"Who is this?" I mumbled.

"It's your old friend, John Boone."

"Uhhh . . ." My gyro was still spinning. *Who, and how in the world did he get. . . . Oh.* I had given a business card to John Wayne Boone back in Johnson City. That seemed like a long time ago.

"I just wanted to see how you're doing," he was saying. "Have you finished your walk?"

"Ummm . . ." I shook my head to clear it. "No, not yet."

"So, how's it going?"

Except for telling him that all was well and I was in Barbourville, the conversation was a blur. At the end he said, "Get in touch after you finish, okay?" I said that I would.

I put down the phone and fell back onto the brown patterned bedspread. I lay there gazing at the light brightening through the window blinds, glad that someone was thinking about me but annoyed about how early it was. But now that I was up—in fact a little later than usual for the last few weeks—I dressed and ate.

I considered getting back on the road, but thunderstorms were forecast for the afternoon and, more to the point, I needed a break and decided to take it while I had a literal roof over my head. This would be
a good day to read and write and talk to people. Grabbing my camera,
voice recorder, journal, and notebook, I made my way to the college
library.

Thanks to a quick phone call with Margaret, Dr. Hugo Freund,
professor of social and behavioral sciences, found me in the reference
section. He was a wiry man with curly dark hair, a goatee, and small,
round glasses. He spoke rapidly and urgently, sharing his passion for
Appalachia. In fact, Appalachian culture was his research specialty.
The Wilderness Road, Hugo said, may have been a conduit in the
early nineteenth century, but many immigrants—Scots-Irish, English,
German—decided to stay in the Cumberland Plateau instead of moving
through the mountains and then on to the Bluegrass. Below the Mason-
Dixon line, Appalachia is "not the South" as most people conceive it, but
a separate cultural region.

"That's one way to understand the residents of eastern Kentucky,"
Hugo said. People stayed, and so their ethnicity for the most part stayed
the same. By contrast, subsequent settlers in the South saw a lot of different groups come through. With its industrial growth, even relatively
isolated northeast Tennessee could claim a greater influx of people when
compared to southeast Kentucky. One of the paradoxes of the Wilderness Road, then, is that it evolved from being about movement to being
about settlement. What it did for wilderness, it did for migration: it ultimately brought both to an end.

After about a half-hour, Hugo gave me the names of several people
and books to consult, and we said goodbye. Feeling inspired, I pulled
a handful of local history books off the shelf. Hidden among the trivia
were markers of the area's rise and fall: Opening coal mines and factories. Overcoming great floods in 1946 and 1957. Building the bypass.
Closing coal mines and factories. And coping with the progression of
substance abuse, as relentless as kudzu.

I shut my eyes to think about the past two weeks, but the first thing
in my mind's eye was gray asphalt on my right and grass and rocks to
my left. I saw faces—Gary and Joan and Ron and Wes and Tammy and
Robert and Patty. I found myself thinking about economics, environment, and abstract concepts like "balance" and "harmony" and "dignity."

And then I found my mind drifting. No great revelations or earthshaking insights, although I was quickly learning how to read dogs.

I thought about the pain that occasionally fired down my right leg as I walked. I thought about the unceasing calculations of water. I thought about the urgency created by uncertainty—where to set up a tent, where to pee, where I might dive if that car came too close—and how that continual attentiveness brought me to life as few things did.

Next came not a thought but a vision or a dream (*surely, I was dozing off*): A golden eagle swooped down to grab a scampering chipmunk. I had seen eagles aloft several times along the way, but only one chipmunk, roadkilled in Virginia, its tiny white-domed chest glowing in the sun. I flinched as the eagle carried the chipmunk into the sky, and then my point of view switched so that I was rising with the animals. As we ascended, I saw the entire Wilderness Road stretched out below in one glance—like Jesus, looking down from a mountain, tempted with a view of all the kingdoms of the world.

I jolted awake in the library chair, my neck muscles snapping painfully. "All these I will give you, if you will fall down and worship me," the devil said to Jesus. So, what was *my* temptation? I had no idea.

I returned to the book on the table but felt distracted by a strange sense of unease. Step by literal step, I was learning about Appalachia, my adopted home, gaining insight and understanding. Or so I thought. Sitting in the quiet of a library, I realized how little I knew. The region seemed to defy being fully known. I recalled a warm evening more than three decades earlier, only weeks into my first year of college. Walking to the library, I turned a corner just in time to see the library's lights flicker on. Everything suddenly glowed pink and gold—the dusk sky, the library shelves—and I was changed in an instant, in the twinkling of an eye, from a cocksure academic achiever fresh out of high school into a boy who realized for the first time how much he did not know and how little he could ever truly know. It was the moment, I still tell my students, that I became a student.

So, here I was again, the student. After almost fourteen years of living in the region and more than a hundred miles of hiking, I did not know enough about Appalachia. At that moment it seemed like I never would. I was not lost, but I felt bewildered.

I needed to explore the town. I needed to talk to people.

Somewhere between the college and the town center, my phone rang again. It was my brother, Hank. Thanks to my GPS tracking gizmo and Google Maps, he had followed my route closely for a few days, right down to where I ate lunch in Pineville two days earlier. "I'm vicariously walking with you," he told me. He and his wife, Cindy, were planning to meet me when I arrived at Boonesborough, a thought that made me smile.

To say the streets, shops, and diners of Barbourville were bustling would be an exaggeration, but people were moving around and the town looked lively. At noon I found myself at Tammy's Café, near the courthouse square. The café took up most of the corner, but about one-third of the space was devoted to selling handcrafted goods to benefit a women's shelter. I sat at one of the half-dozen round tables set around the bare wooden floor and inspected the framed newspaper clippings and family photos dotting the pastel yellow walls.

The woman behind the checkout counter smiled sweetly and looked like everyone's favorite grandma. She wore a red-and-white striped apron and silver oval-framed glasses, and her strawberry-blonde hair glowed like a halo under the hanging light. Taking my order, she assured me that the sandwiches were excellent and advised me to save room for pie. Her name was Ethel Baker. Her daughter owned the restaurant, which was housed in the oldest building in town and came with the requisite legend of a resident haunt, Melba. (*Melba Ghost? Really?*) Two men and two women in their late twenties sat at the next table, and one of the women was telling the guy wearing a tie what a big deal the Daniel Boone Festival is. "You'll have to walk to work," she said. (*Was I watching a job interview?*) But the fall festival is worth the trouble, she added: Indeed, it is *awesome*. "Have you ever had deep-fried Oreos?" she asked. He had not. Her mock horror turned to delight at the chance to teach him about the delicacy.

The lunchtime traffic was busy enough to keep Ethel moving but light enough to let us grab snatches of conversation. After the rush was over, Ethel and a few other women sat to eat at a nearby table, close enough to let us chat. Ethel had once worked at the American Greeting Card Company in Corbin, about fifteen miles away, until it suffered the fate of most factories and all the coal mines in the area. A drug problem came to the county as jobs departed, like weeds in a vacant lot. The women agreed—mainly meth, mainly middle-aged users. They also agreed that the addicts need something to do, to get off "the cycle of welfare," which one woman said was a worse problem than drugs. "They say welfare breeds welfare," she said, without identifying the "they." That may be true, but this group resisted the idea of government spending to create jobs.

"So, how can the cycle be broken?" I asked. No one answered.

What I wanted to say but did not was that the world worked differently now, that the economic rules they—we—had absorbed as children and teens no longer jibed with a global marketplace, a widespread labor force, and high-tech and low-manpower coal production. I felt as if I had stumbled into a different conceptual time zone or a sort of permanent jet lag.

Margaret had arranged for dinner at the house of Dan Covington, the chair of the Union College biology department and, I was told, something of a chef. Tall and grizzled, he carried himself with a don't-give-a-damn swagger: two parts Texan blended with one part Bohemian. He smoked, drank, and laughed and cussed freely, and I immediately liked him. Two students, Sean and Wylie, were staying with him while they finished a final summer class before graduating in July. We all sat on his concrete patio while Dan's big black dog, Bourbon, roamed around sniffing and seeking strokes. Homemade barbecue simmered on the stove inside.

Sean hailed from New Jersey, but after graduation he planned to move to Louisville with his girlfriend, start a teaching career, and then begin a master's degree in history. His family members, Dan told me, were high achievers in the East Coast doctor–lawyer mold, and they were completely baffled by Sean's college and career choices.

Wylie was headed for the Army Reserves, hoping for eventual deployment. When he mentioned that he came from Middletown, Ohio, I told him I had met a girl from there only the day before, at the Wildcat Market. "Yeah," he said. "That's my sister." The small world of southeastern Kentucky immediately compressed even more.

Dan had come to teach at Union twenty-four years earlier. It was to be a stepping-stone, but after looking at other jobs in his early days, he found himself asking, "Why not stay?" and so he did. He focused solely on teaching, not research or writing. "I think I'm a good teacher," he said matter-of-factly. Wylie nodded in agreement.

When I told Dan about my trip, he chuckled and said that the US government defines wilderness as a place where you can graze cattle but not take vehicles.

"How do you call it wilderness if you can graze cattle on it?" he asked. It was a good question.

Dan's barbeque was tasty, and it paired well with early evening conversation.

After three hours we exchanged goodbyes, and I meandered around town in the fading, pink dusk. This town was pleasant, and I savored the hospitality. But by the time I returned to my room, I needed to pack and reorient to the road. After just one full day in a single place, my restlessness was rising.

15

CURSING AND BLESSING

Humans don't mind hardship, in fact they thrive on it;
what they mind is not feeling necessary. Modern society has
perfected the art of making people not feel necessary.

—SEBASTIAN JUNGER

ometime after eight in the morning, I stepped out of my room into heavy air under an overcast sky. I turned north onto a winding two-lane blacktop that skirted the western edge of the college campus and led to State Route 25E after a mile or so. Just before ascending to meet the highway, the road constricted to one lane at a sharp bend and passed under a narrow railroad bridge, forming a nasty blind spot with no warning signs or traffic lights. I scurried beneath the bridge, hoping nothing was coming from the other direction. The timing was good: A red Jeep Cherokee turned off the highway and passed me not far past the bend—but a few seconds later brakes squealed behind me as the Jeep came face to face with a blue sedan precisely at the one-lane underpass. They didn't crash, but the drivers froze in place for several beats until the Jeep yielded and reversed a few feet to let the car pass.

At US Highway 25E, I turned left, westbound. The road crossed Richland Creek, a clear stream about fifty feet wide that would join the Cumberland River in a mile or two. I felt a mental shift, thanks both to a day off the road and to the realization that, at my current pace, my trip would be finished in only a week. I felt like I had broken the back of this thing, but silently warned myself against complacency. There were still many miles to go and many unknowns—such as where I would sleep that night.

About an hour later, I wanted some coffee and needed a toilet, so I stopped at a convenience store: Spur Oil No. 2. Regular grade was selling for $3.29 per gallon—which would not be notable except that this price was fourteen cents less than it was directly across the four-lane, at Yeager's, a store that sells both gasoline and shoes. The man behind the Spur No. 2 counter explained that his store could sell cheaper because "we haul our own oil and cut out the middleman." Ken—early sixties, I guessed—wore aviator-style glasses and a trucker's cap. He was mild-mannered and eager to talk.

"It always gets busy around eleven," he volunteered. "Everyone comes to us for gas." He grew up nearby, in Stinking Creek. After graduating from high school in 1967, he, like so many others of his generation, moved to Michigan, where he built Cadillacs and drove trucks until returning to Kentucky in 1980, thanks to his wife's homesickness. He was glad for the chance to live elsewhere for a while but content now to be home. His favorite place was Holland, Michigan. ("They get two hundred inches of snow each year," he told me. It's actually closer to seventy, but it must have seemed like more.) His point in telling me his abbreviated life story was to emphasize how US Highway 25E had expanded from a two-lane to a four-lane road, and how the coal mines and factory jobs had almost disappeared, which was why he had left in the first place. He knew of a single remaining local factory, a dishwashing machine manufacturer in Barbourville.

I moved on, caffeinated and relieved, and soon passed Pleasant Ridge Baptist Church, a traditional white building with a steeple. The Ten Commandments were displayed out front. The roadside marquee sign read, "Choice Decides Destiny"—a view very much at odds with the pre-destination taught by classic Calvinism. *So much for old-time religion.*

By ten o'clock I was walking northwest on the old London-Barbourville Road, State Route 229—yet another winding, shoulderless two-lane, but relatively level and quiet after the highway. Trees crowding the edge of the road soon gave way to hayfields and grazing cattle. Suddenly, there was a scream of sirens. A Knox County Sheriff cruiser zipped past, headed toward US Highway 25E, followed closely by more than two dozen motorcycles, Harleys ridden by men and a few women, most of them with black leather and gray hair. Another sheriff's car trailed the convoy and then, a moment later, three straggling motorcycles.

A few minutes later, a bronze-colored 1990s-era Chevy sedan slowed down and stopped next to me. The passenger window lowered, and a white-haired woman in a bright purple blouse and a thick coating of makeup leaned across the front seat and spoke, *mezzoforte Appalachia:* "Could you tell me where (*suddenly pianissimo*) the goddam fucking main road is? (*forte*) Where the *hell* am I?"

I told her that US Highway 25 was about a mile ahead of her. "Thank you, sweetie," she purred. As she hit the gas and roared away, I glimpsed a Bible lying on the back seat of her car.

The terrain grew jagged over the next four miles, and the road felt desolate despite sprinklings of double-wides and small houses and the occasional passing car or pickup. I had seen only one person not in a car or on a motorcycle: a skinny man with long, black hair and beard, meandering down the road on a bicycle. We nodded to each other, but he kept going his serpentine way. I grew tired and impatient, wondering if I would see anyone else that day.

Perhaps I could make Levi Jackson State Park. It would be a long walk, about twenty miles, but it seemed possible—especially if there wasn't anyone to talk to.

Then suddenly there *was* someone to talk to. I spied a thin old man with slicked-back salt-and-pepper hair sitting in a folding chair by the road. He had a coppery, creased face with a nose that looked not so much broken as mashed down. A card table with a smattering of knickknacks that may or may not have been for sale was set up next to him. A shotgun leaned against the corner of the table, within easy reach. A holstered pistol and one shotgun shell rested in a spare folding chair on his other side.

Bobby Swofford, eighty-two, was a retired farmer. He had raised corn, hay, cattle, and tobacco—whatever would pay—on his hundred-acre farm. But he had long since sold all his stock and now simply worked in a garden that grew in front of a beaten-up trailer. His son Charles lived in a trailer next door, the only one of Bobby's nine children who had stayed in the area.

Bobby kept his seat as we talked, but a small black-and-white dog barked and sniffed around me and occasionally tried to nip my heels. Bobby yelled at him: "Cut that out, you damn dog!" The dog belonged to his son, Bobby explained, which might explain why whenever Bobby yelled at the dog, Charles poked his head out the door of his trailer— a hundred yards away—and also bellowed at the dog: "Shut the hell *up!*"

Bobby (left) and Charles Swofford

The dog would retreat each time, only to start up again after a minute or two, apparently intent on keeping Bobby from speaking his piece.

Bobby hated the way the world was turning out. He had grown up in Clay County—a rural, poor, isolated place—and he would go back if he could. Life on this two-lane back road moved too fast for his liking, a theme he strung together with a rope of thick profanity. (A sample: "Modern life has damn well fucked everything up. Damn fucking crazy people driving down this fucking road now. We got to live goddamn *modern* now.")

When I asked Bobby if I could take his photo, he almost jumped out of his chair: "Hell, *yes!* I've been wanting someone to take my picture."

We agreed his garden would provide a good backdrop, and he shouted across the road: "Charles! Get the hell out here. This guy's gonna take my picture, and I want you in it, too!"

Charles—thirty-something, dark-haired, skinny, and shirtless—emerged in jeans. "What?" he called back.

"This guy's going to take our picture," Bobby repeated. "I want you in it."

As Charles loped over, Bobby asked where I had walked from. When I told him I came from Barbourville that morning, he shook his head slowly, like a draft horse in harness.

"All the way? From Barbourville? You should get a ride." He shook his head again when I told him I had started in East Tennessee. "Damn," he said. *"Damn."* Then, after a slight pause, he said, "You know people have cars and trucks, don't you?" and we laughed. I believe we each thought the other one was a little crazy.

A few miles past the Swoffords' place, the road ascended beside one or two acres of bottomland dotted with rows of concrete rectangles. A couple of men seemed to be inspecting some of the pieces on the far side of the field but stopped when they spotted me. They waved, and one called out, "Where ya' walking?"

"Boonesborough!" I hollered back.

"That's a long way!"

Yup!

"Where'd you start?"

Tennessee!

"What? Really! Wow!" Then: "We're getting ready to stop for lunch, if you want to come in!"

Sure!

We rendezvoused at their office, a trailer crowded with desks and metal file cabinets, its walls sporting charts and calendars.

MJ and Jim Hensley—nephew and uncle—were my hosts. Their business, started by Jim's father some decades earlier, produces "specialty concrete structures," most of them designed to be buried, such as septic tanks, cisterns, and storm shelters. Jim, a mustached man with dark hair under a ball cap, was sixty-seven. MJ looked to be in his early forties, was bald, and had bright, friendly eyes.

As we sat and ate our bologna sandwiches on plain white bread, they told me that their family had migrated from North Carolina to Harlan County generations ago. They're related to the Hensleys whose settlement on a tall ridge near Cumberland Gap is now a living museum in the national park. When Jim and his wife had visited the place a few weeks earlier, they met a woman almost a hundred years old who had grown up in one of those cabins.

Jim (left) and MJ Hensley

Jim was a man acquainted with grief. His father had died just two weeks earlier, at age ninety-four. His younger brother had been killed four years before that, when he was riding his moped to work one morning. Two men stuck him with their car after being awake cooking meth all night. It happened on the road I was just traveling on. Jim told these short, sad stories as brief, informational anecdotes, without bitterness. When he learned my final destination, he told me about an excursion boat ride on the Kentucky River he and his wife took at Fort Boonesborough some years earlier. A small boat carrying a few couples buzzed around the cruise boat, and one of the men had mooned the crowd on the tour boat. "Some old woman got all upset," Jim said. "'Call the governor! Arrest them!'" Pause. "I just wanted to know how she thought she'd pick him out of a lineup."

We finished eating and stepped out into the sunny, humid day. Jim handed me some packaged crackers and granola bars to carry with me, and I felt a surge of gratitude. They posed for a photo next to five-foot-tall concrete storm shelters, and just then a woman drove in and started walking toward us.

"This guy here's a photographer for *GQ*," MJ told her. "We've been chosen as sexiest men alive, and we're doing a photo shoot."

I picked up his cue: "MJ, I told you, you're just on the short list. We haven't decided on the finalists yet." MJ and I laughed. Jim stood there quietly with a sly grin.

The steep banks and hollows eased themselves into rolling hills at the Laurel County line, and the road responded by becoming more level and straight. Three roadkilled turtles lay nearby, as if arranged for a still-life painting. All were large, one with a carapace at least ten inches across and claws almost two inches long. Its stomach, lined with green, yellow, and brown markings, faced the sky, split down the middle.

I was not sure how far I had already walked by the time I reached Benge's Store in midafternoon, but the day had turned to a slow boil, and I could feel my energy draining.

The store's name reminded me of Bob Benge, a notorious Cherokee fighter who joined the Chickamauga warriors, who were based in southeast Tennessee and led by none other than Dragging Canoe, the angry son who resisted his father's treaty at Sycamore Shoals. Depending on whose history we read, Benge was either a freedom fighter pushing back against the white incursion or an eighteenth-century terrorist. Starting in 1777, as the American Revolution spread, Benge led notorious raids on white settlements between Alabama and Ohio, mostly in East Tennessee and in the Virginia–Kentucky wilderness, including the area around Moccasin Gap and Kane Gap. The Virginia militia finally ambushed, killed, and scalped Benge in 1794 in what is now Wise County, making his famous red hair a gift for their governor. He, in turn, forwarded it to President George Washington.

The two women behind the counter of Benge's Grocery knew nothing of the Cherokee warrior. They did know that the state park was another five miles, however. I stifled a groan; I had miscalculated by at least two miles. Loitering in the shade of the storefront, I considered my options as I swigged chocolate milk and munched granola. I had no idea where I might camp if I stopped along the way. I was tired, but my legs did not hurt. A couple of additional unexpected miles would not make much difference, so I slung on my pack and started walking.

The road curled between a small gathering of modest houses before straightening out to offer clear views of cow pastures, scattered ranch-style homes, and the occasional minimansion. The houses gradually thinned out and finally gave way to tall pine trees and an outbreak of roadside historical markers. One commemorated the Campground Methodist Church, which had stood since 1811, thanks to the pioneering missionary Francis Asbury. Then came a marker for the Wilderness Road Inn, which was started by John Freeman in 1803 but burned down in 1962. A wooden fence about ten yards long shielded a collection of ten or so graves from the road, including the resting place of John Freeman himself and his family. Beyond that, a side road led up a hill to the cemetery of the Levi Jackson family, prompting the obvious question: Who was Levi Jackson, and why was he important enough for a state park to be named in his honor?

One could argue that the park should have been named for Freeman, who was more of the pioneer. Born in 1761 or 1764—road signs and genealogical records are inconsistent—Freeman fought in the Revolutionary War, moved to the new Commonwealth of Kentucky in 1802, and claimed as payment for his war service an extensive tract of land along the recently improved Wilderness Road. There he built a two-story tavern, which operated at least ten years before Jackson was even born. Still, at some point the two men became business partners, and Jackson married Freeman's youngest daughter, Rebecca. The two men ran the Wilderness Road Tavern and the Laurel River Post Office, and Jackson served as the first judge in Laurel County. After his father-in-law died in 1841, Jackson continued to run the inn until his own death in 1879, and the surrounding land became known as Jackson's Farm. On December 7, 1931, Colonel G. D. Jackson and Ella Jackson, the grandchildren of John Freeman, donated 307 acres of the family's land to the Kentucky State Parks System for a park that would honor the state's pioneers.

This gift of land was much more than the few acres the state had officially requested to commemorate an early pioneer debacle. Where a reconstructed mill now stands in the state park, a group of fourteen families moving from Virginia to central Kentucky made camp on the night of October 3, 1786. They had been vigilant against Native American attacks during their entire trip—but on this night, near the end of their journey and feeling confident and relaxed, they danced and drank until they fell into bed. For once they did not post a guard. A band of Shawnees attacked before dawn, killing at least two dozen people. The only survivors were a man, a woman, and an eight-year-old girl who was taken captive, married to a Shawnee chief, and then, seventeen years later, escaped back to the white world with her son. "McNitt's Defeat" was the worst single massacre in Kentucky pioneer history. The victims were buried at the site, which came to be known as Defeated Camp. At the time, the killings only inflamed the already-smoldering hatred of Indians and for a while served as a rallying cry for settlers: "Remember McNitt's Defeat!" was something akin to "Remember the Alamo!"

I arrived at the park around five o'clock, hot, tired, and sore and ready to stop. The swimming pool near the entrance beckoned, but I followed the signs to the campground, cutting through a vacant miniature golf course to reach the office and camp store. After paying for a spot, I rewarded myself with a Klondike bar.

The campground was arranged around a central loop road punctuated with diagonal slots for vehicles, like a pinnate leaf. It was full of machines and people, including sleek, gargantuan RVs, fifth-wheels, and many, many motorcycles. Kids scampered around while graying grown-ups sat passively in folding chairs or bustled about to get dinner on the picnic tables. I headed for one of the cul-de-sacs on the loop's perimeter that were reserved for tent campers. I could feel people watching me as I walked past the RVs and pop-ups. It was like walking through a parking lot, and I felt more self-conscious than at any other time on the trip—ironic because this was, after all, a campground. But this was not a campground to get away from it all. It was a place for those who liked to take it all with them.

Many of the RVs were almost the size of semitrucks, with modern aerodynamic curves and satellite dishes. A golf cart was parked beside one. Music filtered between the sites but not too loudly, and many of the radios were tuned to the same country music station. People sat in cozy semicircles next to their rigs while dinner sizzled on smoky grills. Children were out in force—younger ones running and shouting and tossing Frisbees while older ones stood around or blithely roamed the loop in small packs. I lost count of the "Friends of Coal" specialty license plates and stickers. One RV flew a black-and-white "coal miner" flag emblazoned with icons of picks and shovels. The place had the feel of an extended family reunion, a warm gathering with just enough movement, noise, and hidden alcohol to make the place vibrate, but not enough to disturb the peace.

I had never thought about the clientele for state park camping. There was a lot of money tied up in these big vehicles, but it was not Old Money. I concluded they were working people from the region who had saved their pennies, leveraged their land holdings, and mined, farmed, or retailed their way into the middle class.

A brown tent the size of a frontier cabin was already standing in the cul-de-sac, but there was no vehicle and no movement. In a few minutes, my tent was standing, tiny compared to the vehicles parked only a couple dozen yards away, like a bird perching near a herd of elephants. After putting my things in order, I walked to the communal bathhouse. As the warm shower soaked my head and back, I figured this must have been my longest day—more than eight hours and about twenty-two miles. That had not been the plan: I had just kept moving until I was close enough to the park to push on. It worked out all right, I decided. *But please*, I told myself, *never again.*

A red pickup truck with a topper was parked at the neighboring tent when I returned, and a young couple were moving around with their two children. The man and I silently waved to each other. I fired up my camp stove to boil water for freeze-dried beef stroganoff and peas. Three or four other cars pulled into our little primitive loop as I ate, and tents popped up like multihued mushrooms.

Night had come, and I was sitting at the table with my headlamp when the young man from almost-next-door—slim, dark-haired, mustached, and ball-capped—strolled over, introduced himself as Virgil Baker, and handed me an icy can of Pepsi. (A cold can of Pepsi—not Coca-Cola—must be the region's unofficial sign of welcome.)

"My wife noticed you didn't have a car, and I got curious," he explained, and so I told him a little about my trip. He and his wife, Nancy, were from Hazard, an old mining town in eastern Kentucky, and had a five-year-old daughter and a baby son. They had been promising the girl a camping trip, and so here they were for an overnighter. Virgil and I talked about nothing much—the weather, maybe—until he mentioned that he had worked in heating and air conditioning for the past year, since he got laid off from the coal mines. I was about to ask him about that when his baby's cry shot through the night. He glanced toward his tent, anxious and impatient even in the dim light. I thanked him for the Pepsi again, and we said good night. I hoped we could talk in the morning. This guy would have stories to tell.

I slept well except for the occasional need to dislodge myself from the side of tent and worm my sleeping bag back toward the center of the slick tent floor, which magnified the effect of any slight slope. I was out of the tent before seven and lit a fire to ease the welcome morning chill. The day began clear and pleasant and quiet. Grownups were just starting to stir and light fires and sip coffee. Kids were still sacked out. Virgil's truck was gone—not for long, I hoped. I wanted to talk more with him.

He returned while I was packing, carrying the family breakfast from McDonald's. His wife emerged from their tent, their little boy in her arms. I walked over to say hello a few minutes later. In the daylight, Virgil's blue eyes were striking, curious, and bright. Nancy, blonde and quiet, said hello but seemed guarded. Their boy, Blake, was eight months old. Their daughter, Brooke, was still asleep in the tent.

When I asked about his coal-mining job, his slight, constant smile did not waver. He had worked underground for six years, doing so well that he was promoted to supervise a fifteen-man crew. Unlike so many other eastern Kentucky men, he had not grown up in a mining family; his father worked in a shoe store. He married into mining, and Nancy's family helped get him get his first job. Maybe that was why his smile never dipped and his voice never betrayed bitterness or sadness as he described how his employer was bought by an Indian firm that planned to export Kentucky coal to fuel the booming economy of south Asia. But a lack of Indian infrastructure and an abundance of American tariffs left the owners with "a coal company they couldn't do anything with," Virgil said. He and about two hundred other men were among the economic casualties: they were let go on a Friday in April 2012—Friday the 13th, to be precise.

When he was laid off, Virgil decided not to follow the example of a friend who works in a West Virginia mine through the week and comes home only on weekends. Virgil instead changed professions, well on his way to earning an HVAC certificate from a community college. He

Nancy and Virgil Baker, with their son, Blake

had already landed a job, overseeing the heating and cooling systems in four medical facilities in Hazard. He was on call forty hours a week; beyond that, he was able to work on the side. Even so, his annual pay had dropped from $100,000 to $40,000. Nancy worked in the same health network, in the insurance billing department.

He said all this patiently, matter-of-factly. If he was angry, he disguised it well, even when he criticized the EPA. His complaints were not against regulations per se—he had seen water turn red after iron-packed slate was dumped into streams. He just thought the regulations were being applied too broadly, needlessly hurting the local economy. His example focused on regulations that called for streams to be restored after mining ceased. Until recently, he said, a "stream" was defined as a place where someone could launch a boat. But then the EPA expanded the definition to include gullies and, as Virgil pointed out, "you can't put boats there." Likewise, he believed that regulations about renewing mined lands were virtually impossible to fulfill without costing a company profits, and so several companies had simply stopped running mines, putting "a lot of people out of work." When I asked about the job potential of natural gas, he pointed out that even though gas was on the upsurge, the work opportunities were scarce. Once a well is tapped, it needs only one worker at a time "to turn it on and off," and so there were still big layoffs.

I liked Virgil and admired him and Nancy for the simple reason that they had read the writing on the wall and had adjusted, apparently without much resentment. He had learned a new trade, and together he and Nancy decided to stay close to their families—his family had lived in Hazard for four generations—rather than try to hang on to his old job or income. He was a rarity: a contented realist.

It was almost ten thirty when I left the campsite that morning. As I meandered through the park, I passed a four-foot-tall stone marker indicating the route of Boone's Trace and celebrating the sesquicentennial of Kentucky statehood ("Boone's Trace 1775–95/Kentucky—1792–1942"). This was an intersection of Boone's original route with the later, state-mandated Wilderness Road. From there, I walked by the world's largest collection of millstones, perched on a bank of the Little Laurel River. Then past the Defeated Camp Cemetery and finally to a road that led back to US Highway 25 and to London.

The road was busy on this fine Saturday morning in June. A convoy of forty-one motorcycles roared past, escorted by a sheriff. (*What was with the motorcycles?*) A string of car-related businesses lined the road on the way into town—car dealers and detailers, parts stores, and rental companies—bringing to mind the same sense of disconnect and irony I felt as I tramped into the campground the previous afternoon. Walking past RVs and trucks and campers, car washes, and a concentrated strip of auto retailing on a short stretch of road served as a reminder of how foreign the Wilderness Road had grown from what it had been.

Just past the fork where US Highway 25 merges with State Route 229—the road I traveled yesterday—an enormous cemetery spread out on a rolling hill. This was the A. R. Dyche Memorial Park, a gift from Russell Dyche to honor his father in 1935. I recalled that as editor of the local newspaper, Russell had exchanged numerous letters with historian Robert Kincaid in the 1940s, debating the likely route of the Wilderness Road. (The Dyche name showed up frequently in London, but when I asked a few locals about the family, the best guess anyone could muster was the self-evident fact that "they've been important in town." No one seemed to know why.) I was surprised to find a timeline drawn in blue and white chalk on the sidewalk in front of the cemetery. Almost a quarter-mile long, it outlined the earth's geologic history in what looked like proportional distances. I could easily guess the evolution-versus-creation sensibilities in a small Kentucky town, but at least one person here did not believe in a young earth.

Just before reaching the town center, a billboard solved the mystery of the motorcycles: "London–Laurel County Tourist Commission welcomes HOG Rally 2013." The Harley Owners Group had come to London.

Downtown looked attractive and active, with a mix of old and new buildings. The police department and city hall were housed in matching brown and green buildings, across the wide main street from a modern, four-story glass bank building. The Laurel County Courthouse was a handsomely refurbished colonial brick building, its clock tower topped by a weather vane. A row of squat, brick-faced storefronts lined the opposite side of the street.

The highlight of London for me, though, was Weaver's Hot Dogs (established 1940), which had drawn a lunchtime crowd. Booths lined each wall, and a row of tables ran through the middle of the dining room. Almost every seat was taken. Scores of framed photos—forty, sixty, a hundred years old—covered the dark paneled walls. Waiting for my cheeseburger, fries, and the splurge of an enormous chocolate-chip cookie, I studied the scenes of old London hanging around me: nearby East Bernstadt with the Rutledge Hotel, the Elk Hotel, the Laurel Grocery Building, and, in the foreground, the Warner Fertilizer Building. A stern couple named Gilbert and Maymie Porter looked down from a horse-drawn carriage in 1912. An avuncular man with thinning white hair, round spectacles, bowtie, suit and vest—Doc Crook—benignly gazed from his frame. A truck on a small ferryboat at Cumberland Falls, from the 1930s. Two photos of Bob and Ella Dyche. In one, they are a distinguished, trim couple standing in front of a 1930s era touring car, she in a plaid skirt and wool jacket, he in a blazer, tie, and flatcap, holding a walking stick. To the right of that photo, they are older, heavier, bespectacled versions of themselves, posed stiffly in front of a fireplace mantel decorated for Christmas sometime in the 1970s.

A chattering group of gray-haired grownups occupied the long table in the center of the room. They sounded like a family, and I considered interrupting them and starting a conversation. I wanted to ask how long their family had been in the area, if maybe an ancestor arrived in the days of Boone. But they looked so utterly absorbed in the moment and so happy that I sat quietly and pretended to study the photos while I eaves-dropped. After lunch I crossed the street to Mike's Hike and Bike Shop, the first outfitters store I had passed. Ben and Randall, friendly, hip, out-doorsy twenty-somethings, told me I might camp along the Sheltowee Trail, near Hazel Patch, about nine miles north. (The Sheltowee Trail, I later learned, is a 307-mile hiking trail connecting national forests and state parks in Tennessee and Kentucky. "Sheltowee" was Daniel Boone's name among the Shawnee: "Big Turtle.")

North of downtown, tidiness and quaintness gave way to rundown properties and then, where the road widened to four lanes, to a shadeless strip of small offices and retailers: a post office, a self-serve car wash, a lawyer's office, a fishing-and-muzzle-loading supplier, a dance studio. The Hissyfit Consignment Store. But one holdout stood among the ster-ile commerce. On an acre or so of elevated ground sat a white farm-house, almost invisible under its canopy of mature trees.

The post office identified the area as Pittsburg, Kentucky, which I rec-ognized as the place where Benjamin Logan parted ways with Daniel Boone during their 1775 migration. Boone had traveled north to Boones-borough; Logan had headed farther west, ultimately starting a settle-ment that bore his name, where the town of Stanford now sits on a wide spot on the road to Danville and Lexington.

Several more miles brought me to East Bernstadt, which appeared to be more of a collection of houses and farms than a town with a center. Traffic rumbling in the distance meant that Interstate 75 must be near. A sign pointed to St. John Swiss Reformed Church. *Of course! With a name like Bernstadt, this area must have started as a Swiss settlement.* The terrain then gave way to open farmland, long stretches of not much except for occasional Cape Cods and ranch-style houses—invariably white with black trim and roof—each separated from the road and from each other by enormous, flat lawns. Money was here.

Midafternoon, I found myself standing on an overpass looking down on the interstate, mesmerized by the stream of cars, trucks, and RVs. This trip would not be complete, I realized, without a nod to the interstate, the antithesis of wilderness. North of London, US Highway 25 never wanders far from Interstate 75, and as anyone who has seen *Cars* already knows, the coming of the superhighway permanently and profoundly changed the back roads and the communities they connect. Those communities, once the little links in a convoluted chain that pulled travelers across the country, usually shrivel to death, unless they retool themselves into rural refuges with quaint bed and breakfasts, cafés with distressed brick walls, vintage boutiques, and the occasional car mechanic. Not to rant against the interstate system: Walking to this spot had taken 18 days. Driving would have taken three hours. But there is, of course, a tradeoff. If you simply want to get from one place to another, take the interstate. But if you want to travel, there are other options.

On the opposite end of the overpass, a lumber mill filled the air with the scent of pine. At another flyover—the snaking two-lane crosses and re-crosses the straight highway at several places—I smelled a burst of honeysuckle. Then came ground that had been taken over by a dozen or more setups for yard sales, the latest in a string of tabletop vending since London. This weekend, it turned out, was the annual US Highway 25 Yard Sale, stretching across Kentucky between the Ohio River and the Tennessee border. I slowed down and waved at three old men wearing trucker's caps who stood near trestle tables piled with wares. They kept muttering to each other as they obviously watched me from behind their mirrored sunglasses. No one waved back.

Suddenly a deep, forested valley stretched to my right, bordered by a tall ridge on the horizon. This grand view took me by surprise after miles of gently rolling hills. By automobile, this scene would pass in a second and maybe go entirely unnoticed. But there and then, I caught myself almost weeping with delight. The dramatic view, I later realized, marked the change between the steep, mountainous eastern third of Kentucky and the rolling hills more typical of the central region, the geological border between Appalachia and Bluegrass.

Nearby, a roadside sign read Camp Wildcat. It was the site of one of the first Civil War battles in Kentucky and one of the earliest Union victories, in October 1861. A garrison of about seven thousand Union soldiers stopped a northbound Confederate campaign that had crossed the Cumberland Gap and followed the Wilderness Road—with skirmishes at Cumberland Ford (present-day Pineville) and Barbourville—as part of an effort, ultimately doomed, to win the commonwealth for the Confederacy. After demoralizing defeats earlier in the year, the Union was cheered by the news from Camp Wildcat, where about twelve thousand men fought but, amazingly, only sixteen were killed on both sides.

A Sheltowee Trail sign led me onto Hazel Patch Road, a winding and shaded blacktop that descended into a hollow shaped by a thin, meandering creek. I stopped at one of the few scattered houses where a graying, paunchy man stood talking to a tired-looking woman as a gaggle of yelling kids ran around them. A caged chicken hunkered in the back of a maroon minivan that had its tailgate open. The adults stopped talking to watch me approach on the gravel drive. I asked where I might camp nearby.

"I think there's a campground up around Livingston," the man said, "about five miles away." His voice was flat: the familiar mountain twang, but without expression. I shook my head—or maybe I felt my head shake—slowly. That's too far at this point, I told him. He threw a quick glance at the tired woman. I felt like I was already testing their patience. Then a light seemed to come on, and the man turned and pointed past the house to an open field spread out on the other side of the creek.

"The county owns thirty acres there," he said. "Go up in that corner, and no one can bother you." I started to thank him, but he had already turned back to his conversation. *Dismissed.*

A crowd was milling around a small church building that was barely visible through a thin screen of trees on the opposite side of the road. Bursts of laughter popped through the brush. *It must be a wedding!* Maybe I would worship there the next morning.

The road took a hairpin bend over the creek, and in a few minutes, I was walking alongside the big field, which was bordered by a split-rail fence and a handsome row of maple trees. Where the road turned to the right at a level railroad crossing, there stood a fence and a small monument consisting of three flagpoles, a Civil War-era cannon, and small plaque: Camp Wildcat. The gate was locked. A ragged brown barn stood a couple of hundred yards behind the fence. I climbed over and pitched my tent on a grassy shelf between the barn and the bottomland. This was about as close to wilderness I had come on the whole trip: no handy electrical outlets, no designated camping spots, no bathhouse. I used water purification tablets for the first time, not fully trusting what came from the solitary standpipe in the field.

As the sun dropped behind a ridge, the mosquitoes and gnats drove me into the tent, which was disappointing because the evening was clear and mild. The sky was almost dark, and I was settling into my sleeping bag when I heard a faint, distant buzz—electrical, not animal. Then a sterile, cool light suddenly flooded the tent. I was confused. Had a sheriff or park ranger come calling? I peeked outside: A security light mounted on the barn illuminated the night and snuffed any illusions of wilderness. I rolled over to keep the light out of my eyes and soon felt myself sinking into sleep to the distant sounds of bullfrogs, barking dogs, and coyotes. Occasional human voices drifted across the empty field. Then the trains came: one about every ninety minutes through the night, I reckoned—each one braking at a curve a hundred yards from my tent, squealing just below the frequency of a dog whistle.

16

RURAL RENEWAL

*We feel dislocated in nature in part because we have not
come to terms with our role, with engineering and with artifice,
nor with our utter dependence on the given world. We may long
for something pure, instinctive, organic, when we must instead
face the truth that everything we touch is thereby "artificial."
And not just face it but celebrate it, because to live out a
close relationship with nature may be to restore the
reverence that make us feel complete.*

—RICHARD TODD

By the time the sun crested a southeastern ridge to brighten and warm the hollow—properly pronounced "holler," of course—I was fed and packed and waiting for the tent to dry. This day, unlike most, I started with a specific destination in mind: Mt. Vernon, about fifteen miles away. There I would check into a motel and rendezvous with my younger daughter, Rachael, who was driving from her home in Lexington to meet me.

Feeling antsy, I packed the tent while its floor was still damp and started walking. It was Sunday, but the church building where the wedding had been the previous day was closed, its small parking lot empty. The church sign explained why: This was the Olive Branch, a messianic Jewish congregation that held its services on Saturdays. A Christian Jewish fellowship in Hazel Patch, Kentucky, of all places.

Back on US Highway 25, less than a mile away, the day already felt warmer, brighter, and more humid than in the hollow. The road is scenic at this point, two lanes with sweeping curves and trees hugging the shoulders, including magnolia trees with shiny dark leaves two feet

across and creamy blossoms a foot in diameter. But soon enough came
a section where a small hill had been topped to create a more level road,
exposing shale on both sides. The cut seemed gratuitous. "You could have
gone over it," I said aloud to no one in particular, surprised at my own
gut reaction. "Why not leave well enough alone?"

Yes. Why not? What explained this compulsion to alter the landscape,
to turn wilderness into something else? How do we choose when to let
it alone and when to literally blow it away? I thought of Jimmy Dean
Smith, a rumpled English professor I had met at Union College a few
days earlier. We'd sat in his office, the corner of a seminar room in the
college's oldest building. The walls were powder blue, like a child's bedroom. He wore a shaggy beard, a Hawaiian shirt, cargo shorts, and a wry
smile.

Southeast Kentucky, he told me, was "ground zero for thinking about
wilderness" because two competing points of view collided here. The
first could be represented by Dr. Thomas Walker, who built the first
white man's house in Kentucky back in 1750, less than ten miles from
where we had sat together. Walker's journal was as much inventory as
it was travelogue, itemizing the flora, fauna, and mineral resources that
could be extracted and used to good profit back east. Then there was
Daniel Boone who, according to his early biographer, John Filson, be-
moaned how quickly the wilderness was passing away within a few years
of his arrival.

Although Walker had the stronger historical connection to the town,
Barbourville "has decided that Boone is our guy," Jimmy Dean said. Exhibit A was the local fall festival named after the explorer. No doubt the
event capitalized on greater name recognition, but Jimmy Dean believed
that this choice also made a statement.

"We're marketing ourselves as 'the first frontier,'" he explained.
"There's an attempt to create a heritage trail in southeastern Kentucky."
He paused to weigh his words. "But there's only heritage and not much
else. What are the options? Maybe eco- and adventure tourism?"

It is hard to miss the irony of "marketing" wilderness to would-be
tourists—or, for that matter, would-be settlers in the eighteenth century.
Nor was the irony lost on either of us that it was Daniel Boone of all
people who lamented the retreat of wilderness, since he was largely responsible for the migration and development that destroyed it. By modern standards, Boone was no tree hugger.

But the idea of wilderness, Jimmy Dean said, is a "human construct." Until the time of John Muir, most Westerners assumed that "wilderness" or "nature" was either land wasted or land waiting to be used— "exploited," that is, to use a word that once carried more neutral and even positive connotations. (We still talk glowingly about the "exploits" of Boone and other adventurers, after all.) In this way of thinking, the land and all it contains exist primarily—if not solely—for human benefit, to be tamed and turned to "profitable" use. That was Dr. Walker's perspective, one echoed by coal-mining friends I had met along the way. Before the European Romantics of the nineteenth century, nature itself—whether "the natural world" or "human nature"—was to be harnessed, disciplined, tamped down, and, if necessary, scrubbed of its wildness. Such an agenda even carried theological overtones. Didn't God command the first humans to "subdue" and "have dominion" over creation? Didn't demons go to the wilderness when they were cast out? By contrast, when the Pilgrims came to the new world, they vowed to build "a city on a hill." In short, nature was a problem to be solved.

Sometimes it was indeed a problem. One of Jimmy Dean's students told him about a dead buffalo she saw on the road near Ewing, Virginia, where I had seen buffalo fenced in several days before. The roadkill seemed terrible, Jimmy Dean said, but only because buffalo now are few and far between and mostly confined. By contrast, other animals are not mourned when we see them dead on the road side. Indeed, they are considered pests.

"Deer are a problem now," Jimmy Dean explained, "and we can understand how early settlers viewed the big game: not as magnificent beasts that needed preservation and respect, even if they were 'harvested' in a reasonable way, but as vermin that needed to be controlled or even eliminated." To put it plainly: Losing a crop to grazing deer or stomping buffalo could spell the difference between survival and starvation. To frontier settlers, it was either them or the buffalo.

But now we want the wilderness back, or some approximation of it— a desire born from the legacies of nineteenth-century Romantics like Henry David Thoreau and John Muir, as well as our more complete understanding of the environmental problems that result from unfettered exploitation. People migrated west because they craved the freedom of open spaces, Jimmy Dean reminded me. The very space they craved, however, has almost vanished, largely by their own hands and the hands of their descendants. They—we—have felt the loss. So, Boone is our guy now, not Walker.

Almost as an aside, Jimmy Dean mentioned an Australian eco-philosopher named Glenn Albrecht. "He coined a word, 'solastalgia,'" Jimmy Dean said. "It describes the feeling you get when you're a stranger in your own place, especially when there's been some great environmental disruption." It is like nostalgia, literally "homesickness": a feeling of loss and longing. The difference is that solastalgia is not the result of leaving home, but of having home turned upside-down by catastrophe. It might be the aftermath of flood, fire, or stampede. It could also result from the wreckage wrought by the unrestrained work of humans—a mountain sheared off here, a river diverted there, a homeland rendered unrecognizable and exploited right out from under our feet.

Now, pausing to stare up at a mountain ripped apart, I thought about solastalgia. If Albrecht was right, people must wake up every day wondering why they feel homesick when they have never moved an inch.

Rockcastle River, yet another once-significant waterway reduced by the bump of a bridge, separates Laurel County from Rockcastle County. Maybe fifty yards wide and tinted drab olive, the river moved slowly. Floating yellow leaves took on a kaleidoscopic effect as they rotated in the leisurely current, flecks of pure gold on grimy green velvet.

About one and half miles into Rockcastle County, hungry and light-headed, I stopped to devour several handfuls of trail mix. I had hoped to come across a diner, but there was nothing.

Just south of the village of Livingston, US Highway 25 met Wildcat Mountain Road, where a big blue sign with white lettering advertised kayak rentals and "Daniel Boone's Historic Campground: Kentucky's oldest campground on the Wilderness Road, 1775." I silently cursed myself for missing that site by staying on the main road out of Hazel Patch instead of taking that back road, which probably followed the route of the original Wilderness Road more closely. I considered backtracking until a familiar jolt shot down my right leg, and I felt a surge of nausea. I walked on toward Livingston.

Bright, multicolored banners hung from light poles telling travelers that this was now a Trail Town. Sure enough, a prominent road sign pointed east to a trailhead. A little farther ahead, a sign memorialized

Private First Class David M. Smith, who was born in Livingston in 1926 and died in Korea in 1950, when he fell on a grenade in a foxhole. He was awarded a posthumous Congressional Medal of Honor and was returned home to be buried on a hilltop cemetery that overlooked the town.

With a burning leg and a woozy head, I dropped my pack in front of the Main Street Diner and eased into one of the mismatched chairs beside a plastic bistro table. A small black ashtray brimmed with cigarette butts. The morning was hot and humid, and nothing was open. I ate my last bagel, chomped more trail mix, and gulped water. Then a familiar hymn drifted through the air: "I surrender all. . . . All to Jesus, I surrender, I surrender all." I thought I was daydreaming before recalling that it was Sunday. A small, white-sided, black-roofed church building stood across the street. The sign in front of the church did not list its service times, which made me think that the people who were expected to attend already knew when to show up. Three doors down, a man and woman sat on their front porch, talking and squabbling. I thought about walking over to say hello. I thought about walking into the church. But I stayed put until my head stopped swimming.

At the sparse north end of town I saw a small shop called A Country Pedaler, a nifty wordplay for a bicycle rental business. The owner was a stout Midwesterner named Carl, who sat behind a desk just inside the open door. With cropped blonde hair and aviator-style glasses, he retained the military bearing he had learned in the Army. He and his wife, Bonita, had discovered Livingston during a vacation some years earlier and moved here from Ohio after he retired from the police force. Carl now also served as Livingston's part-time police chief.

A civic-minded man, he was eager to see his adopted home revive. Tourism might be the ticket, and he proudly said that the town was trying new things. (I thought of Jimmy Dean Smith's words.) The governor's wife was to visit in a couple of weeks to christen Livingston, population 226, as the state's first official "trail town"—hence all the signs and banners.

Carl had a renewal model in mind: Damascus, a small town in southwest Virginia where the Appalachian Trail and a popular rail-to-trail path, the Virginia Creeper, converged. That intersection had spawned an active tourist economy of bike shops, outfitters, and cozy cafés. But one difference, as Carl pointed out, was the lack of a fairly level and easy bike path in these Kentucky hills. The trails that did exist were difficult

Carl (Livingston, Kentucky)

and rough, more suited for hard-core mountain bikers than families on a Saturday outing. His own business illustrated the problem: He had rented only one bike in ten months. More visitors rented tubes for floating on the Rockcastle River than bicycles.

The town once thrived because of coal and because of its location on the so-called Dixie Highway, the major north–south corridor linking the industrial Midwest and the South. But when the interstate came in the 1960s, Livingston, like so many towns, was bypassed. The village had taken a more recent blow only a few months earlier, when CSX Railroad closed a maintenance yard.

But Carl saw signs of life—the schoolhouse was rebuilding!—and he was determined to make a go of it. A Country Pedaler—Livingston's "new business of the year"—had sponsored a festival that attracted a sizable crowd. The only problem involved the festival's minitriathlon of canoeing, running, and biking. The river was running too fast and high at the time, so the organizers canceled the canoeing portion.

The town needed more retailers, Carl told me. Even a store as basic as a Dollar General would attract shoppers and money and start reversing the economic slide. As he catalogued what it might take to revive the place, I thought it all sounded like a long shot, but maybe he knew something I did not.

He saw a connection between his entrepreneurial dreams and his role as police chief. No town can grow without a police department, he said, because people want to feel secure, which was almost impossible while the town and the surrounding county were suffering from a drug problem.

"When we arrived, the drug problem was as bad in Livingston as in Mount Vernon," he told me. "There were break-ins all the time, with some people even breaking into their own families' homes to get drugs or money for [drugs]." Since he took over as chief, there had been one break-in in Livingston. He credits the change to "being visible, being out in the community talking to people."

I sat in his office, listening and stretching my calves and drinking cup after cup of water. He offered me a granola bar as I left, which I gladly accepted. Only later did I realize that during the time I sat in the Country Pedaler, no one came in, no one passed by, and the phone never rang. Perhaps people were still in church. Maybe someone would come later.

Not far from the village a dead fox lay on the highway shoulder, having probably become roadkill within the last day. Its tail glowed a deep orange, almost red, and I instinctively sucked in a breath when I realized what I was looking at and how beautiful it was. Then another, unusual roadkill: a large turkey vulture sprawled at the base of a road-cut cliff. It was a big, black, ugly-faced bird, its neck locked into an unnatural crook. The bird must have lingered over the small, desiccated carcass next to it just a moment too long. *Greed kills.*

The scenery on this stretch was grand. Mile after mile of oaks and maples and pines, of rocks and hills and pastures and creeks, of brick-faced ranch-style houses interrupted by an occasional grand estate, quaint farmhouse, or desolate trailer. A grass trimmer whined in the distance. The sound of machinery was never far away: The drone of trimmers, the thudding of tractors, the hum of mowers. The roar, squeal, and rattle of trains. The hiss and buzz of cars and trucks.

Distant thunder and thickening humidity warned of coming rain, which arrived around one o'clock, alternating between tentative spits and confident showers. With an overpass of Interstate 75 in sight, I stepped into a bleak-looking convenience store for shelter and a snack. I dropped my pack near an empty table and scanned the meager shelves. I could feel the eyes of the scrawny clerk and a half-dozen customers watching me, as if I had interrupted something. I grabbed a bottle of orange juice and a candy bar. The clerk was cordial but all business. I did not linger.

Just before the interstate off-ramp, a narrow road ascended a short, steep hill to a broad apron of asphalt where I found an abandoned gas station and a motel called the Kastle Inn. The motel lobby door was propped open, but no one was around. The oversized parking lot was vacant except for four men huddled around three dark Eighties-era sedans parked on the opposite side. They must have detected movement because they all turned as one and looked at me. Their stares felt like a warning, and I retreated down the hill.

The center of Mount Vernon was another two miles distant—about a mile up to Chestnut Ridge and then down to the town, the seat of Rockcastle County. The rain had apparently waited to ambush me on the other side of the interstate, just as the road started to climb sharply. The drizzle turned steady and then hit hard. Harder. Harder yet, soaking me before I could fish my rain jacket out of my pack. Lightning and thunder crashed from the southeast and—just as I reached the top of the ridge—the sky fully opened, pelting the ground, the asphalt, the cars, and one lone, presumably half-crazed hiker. Within minutes the shallow culvert between the shoulder of the road and the base of a rocky cliff turned into a rushing stream.

Suddenly, in that moment, my point of view shifted. I was not the one walking in a thunderstorm. I was watching a character in a movie. It wasn't an out-of-body experience in the usual sense, but I felt strangely and pleasantly detached: This wasn't me but someone playing me, and I started laughing. I was having fun, not in spite of being caught out like this, but *because* I was caught out in the weather, caught out of my control, caught out in something like an adventure.

An old blue Honda Civic pulled alongside me and the driver, a dark-haired woman, rolled down her passenger-seat window and shouted over the rain: "Would you like a ride?" She had seen me walking and turned around to help.

"Thanks," I said, "but I'm on a trip that I need to walk the whole way." She nodded sagely. "I've had trips like that," she answered, giving me a thumbs-up. I stood still for a moment after she pulled away, feeling grateful and absurd and wondering what she had done in her past.

A few minutes later the rain stopped abruptly, almost precisely, as I pushed open the door of a tiny Valero convenience store. I started shivering in the warm, cramped shop, and a stocky clerk with horn-rimmed glasses let me draw a cup of old coffee on the house. What it lacked in flavor it made up in warmth. Before heading outside again, I put on my rain jacket over my dripping shirt, more to fend off the chill than the slackening rain.

Down to the town center, where the essential pieces of the county seat were lined up on Main Street: the storefront office of the local newspaper, a couple of low-slung banks with disproportionately wide drive-through lanes, a handful of small restaurants and cafés huddled at the base of old brick facades, as if propping up the redundant hotels and office buildings. Set apart from it all was the modernist, monolithic, almost windowless brown-brick county courthouse, like a big-city cousin visiting his down-at-the-heel kin.

I passed a road sign for Crab Orchard. I knew the place, a village about fifteen miles west, and had considered walking there. For some reason—perhaps because it was the home of William Whitley, an early militia leader and legislator—Crab Orchard was the original northern terminus of the official Wilderness Road. (It wouldn't be the only time a politician negotiated a public works project with his front door in mind.) Twenty years after Boone cut his trail, the Commonwealth of Kentucky, itself just a year old, decided to improve the old route, widening it to accommodate wagons and paving it all the way to the Cumberland Gap, first with logs and then with stone. But with increasing migration and trade on the Ohio and Kentucky rivers, the legislature departed from Boone's trace to take a more westerly track through Crab Orchard, Danville, Harrodsburg, and beyond, eventually reaching the Falls of the Ohio at Louisville. But here and now the sign indicating "Wilderness Road" followed US Highway 25 north, which would lead more directly to Boonesborough.

The deluge started again, and I took shelter under the awning of a storefront law office until the rain subsided. But any remaining dry spots on my body were soaked a half-mile later when a minivan plowed through a lane-wide puddle, drenching me with a rooster tail of murky water. "Of course!" I shouted to no one after my momentary stunitude passed. Then I started laughing again—loud and open-jawed and silly. I didn't know and didn't care if anyone could see or hear me. I felt entitled to a moment of sheer absurdity.

I was barely noticing the rain by the time I walked into the tidy and modest lobby of the Days Inn, where Rachael and I would meet. Water dripped from my hat brim. Mud was splattered on my pants. Two women clerks behind the counter—one in her twenties, the other somewhere north of fifty—looked up nonchalantly. They exchanged a quick glance (*What do we have here? Vagrant? Drunk? Old hippy?*) but otherwise seemed unfazed by the soaking sight standing there, asking about a room. Yes, rooms were available, the older woman said, friendly. As I filled out paperwork, she asked how I got so wet. I explained a little about my trip, and the three of us fell into conversation. The room was warm, and I didn't mind staying a little while. It had been only a few hours since leaving Livingston, but my last real human exchange felt like a long time ago.

The older woman, Jill Greenwell, had moved with her husband from Rockford, Illinois, to get "as far south as we could" while remaining in her husband's carpenters' union. They bought a piece of land on the edge of the national forest. "It's been a culture change, for sure," she told me, "but I'd rather have my land and the views."

Dalton Cummins—call her Dot—grew up just west of Mount Vernon. She, by contrast, was itching to move away as soon as possible—within the next few months, if she could, to study dental hygiene at a junior college in Lexington. "This is just a dead town," she explained flatly. "There's nothing, especially if you're young. People are like, 'You *live* in Mount Vernon?' It's just old people. Like at Denny's next door: nothing but old people. There just aren't any good jobs. Take Jill. She's got a degree, and here she is working at a hotel because there's nothing else for her."

As Jill handed me a key and told me about the breakfast bar, Rachael cruised into the parking lot behind the wheel of her little gray Mazda. A minute or two later, we were standing outside the lobby laughing because we had to keep ourselves from hugging because I would have soaked her.

Upstairs in my motel room—warm, plush, and confining—she and I chatted about the past two weeks while I unpacked, spread my damp tent and other gear to dry, and took inventory. Rachael had brought the box I mailed from Jonesville nine days earlier. As I restocked food—more trail mix and oatmeal—for a fleeting moment my gut knotted. I was calculating supplies for only a few days now, and the cool thrill of the approaching finish collided with the hot realization that the journey was almost over. In five or six days, I would unload my pack, take off my shoes, and simply be finished. It reminded me of an airplane landing: watching houses and trees fall upward—in the air, in the air, still in the air—until there comes a thump and a thud and a shimmy and a sudden splash of pleasure at being on the ground, immediately followed by the sinking knowledge that the trip is over. Boonesborough might be like that.

After I showered and changed, Rachael and I walked next door to Denny's. (*Dot would be amused.*) As we waited for her salad and my burger to arrive, I showed her photos and shared a few stories. Then she told me about her summer job at a big Lexington law firm and how a few days earlier she had accompanied an appraiser to a large horse farm that was up for auction. My mind turned to Daniel Boone, who is credited with launching the horse business in the commonwealth. At the first legislative meeting in Boonesborough in 1775, he introduced a bill to "improve the breeding of horses in the territory of Kentucky." He would surely be boggled by the modern Kentucky equine industry and its annual three-billion-dollar impact.

An hour later, as clouds and dusk came creeping in, Rachael and I hugged goodbye. Watching her car disappear around the corner, I felt a sudden shock of loneliness.

Rain started to fall again that night, and I considered my options as I crawled into what felt like a luxurious bed. The weather forecast predicted heavy rain the next day. And besides the soreness pestering my right hip and leg, my body seemed to register some other unfocused strain. Most compelling was an instinct that said I just needed to slow down, for its own sake. I had traveled about fifty-five miles in the last three days: too fast, I knew. With the end coming into view, I felt an urge, familiar from running, to keep pushing, to move faster. The racehorse within was straining at the reins and needed to be yanked back.

Finishing fast would miss the point. I was down to mere days, and I needed to savor them.

By the time I turned out the light and lay in the dark listening to pounding rain, I had decided to stay in Mount Vernon the next day. Back in Livingston, Carl had told me that Rockcastle County was plagued by drug abuse. I would use tomorrow to learn more about that.

17

JAPANESE BLUEGRASS AND OTHER MYSTERIES

*Life in America is viscerally uprooted. It's worth repeating that
most of the people who are here are the descendants of men and
women who came from other places, and so felt uprooted.*

—NORMAN MAILER

The rain that had pounded at one in the morning and at three and again at five thirty had stopped by the time I literally rolled out of bed with stiff thighs, sometime after seven. The morning sky, warm and humid, was lined with a low ceiling of stippled charcoal-gray clouds that induced claustrophobia. I lingered over the motel's complimentary breakfast, and by the time I started walking to the town center, the clouds were breaking up to expose small patches of pale blue. Maybe the forecast of all-day rain was wrong.

My first stop was the offices of *Mount Vernon Signal*, the county's first paper, launched in 1887. The *Signal* was "infamous," according to the town's official website, "for its continued use of typewriters into the 21st century." On this day, the handful of desks in the otherwise spartan room sprouted a few computer monitors.

A young bespectacled man came to the front counter. Doug Ponder was only twenty-four, but he had been the paper's editor for more than a year. After we traded some journalistic shop talk, I asked about the local drug scene.

Yes, he said, the paper had reported on that, noting its coverage of prayer meetings that had met at local churches every Thursday for seven weeks to pray for Rockcastle County. A regional organization, UNITE Coalition, focused on educating schoolchildren about the dangers of drugs, as does Chad's Hope, a grassroots effort in nearby Manchester. There were no rehabilitation centers in the county.

"People sweep the drug problem under the rug," Doug said in a soft accent. (The accents, I noticed, were growing more rounded.) Meth was the drug of choice, he said, mainly among middle-aged and older people. He believed—or hoped—that the problem had plateaued. "Why a sixty-year-old man would go on meth is a puzzle," he said.

The town, however, was ripe for revitalization, he said, mentioning Livingston's new "trail town" status as his only example. "We're trying," he concluded hopefully.

Mount Vernon's small center spread out from the courthouse. The first of three historical markers outside the entrance revealed that Rockcastle County, formed in 1810, was the fifty-second county in the common-wealth, carved from pieces of Knox, Lincoln, Pulaski, and Madison counties. It took its name from the Rockcastle River, so christened in 1767 by one Isaac Lindsey because of a nearby tall rock that, yes, resem-bled a castle. Dr. Thomas Walker had noticed the formation in 1750 but apparently had not named it, not even after the Duke of Cumberland.

The next marker remembered Colonel James Maret (1855–1936), who arrived in 1877—when he was even younger than Doug Ponder—and es-tablished the first telephone exchange and newspaper in the county, the selfsame *Mount Vernon Signal*. Maret was town clerk and the executive secretary of the Kentucky Good Roads Association.

The final marker described Boone Way, a ninety-six-mile stretch of road that ran between the Cumberland Gap and Crab Orchard—the basis of the Wilderness Road. Maret's name reappeared here because, in his capacity as the Louisville & Nashville Railroad agent and tele-graph operator at Mount Vernon, he advocated road improvement and was largely responsible for the cutting of the roadbed and its first paving. Boone Way was eventually incorporated into US Highway 25.

The main street of Mount Vernon, three blocks long, included several old buildings, a few retail shops, and some crumbling sidewalks. A li-brary. Vacant spaces including former stores, mechanics' garages, and a hotel. A homeless shelter stood next to an antique store, which stood next to a storefront church called the Bride of Christ in Jesus Name. And there was a recently opened café, a hint of resuscitation.

On a side street at the edge of town, I found Deb's Grab & Go, a tiny short-order place where I ate a second breakfast, a biscuit with gravy and a cup of coffee. A trim, professionally outfitted woman walked in to pick up an order for her office, and we chatted while waiting for our food. Danetta Allen was the county clerk. She seemed young for the job, but her family had roots four generations deep in the county. For ten years after college, she had worked as a real estate agent in her father's company before being elected clerk in 2010. Ms. Allen exuded a chamber-of-commerce optimism about the county's prospects, what with the mile-long stretch of country music heaven called Renfro Valley to the north and the new trail town status for Livingston to the south. (If Rockcastle County were a roulette wheel, everyone was putting markers on Livingston.) Our orders came, we said goodbye, and she left with her food. I stayed to eat mine at one of the tall counters.

The Rockcastle County sheriff's department was housed in a small one-story building next door, the bottom half covered with brick and the top clad with aluminum siding the color of brown mustard. It could have been mistaken for a mechanic's shop. Sheriff Mike Peters was sitting in his official SUV talking on a cell phone about some matter on the north end of the county. I introduced myself when he finished his call, and he said yes, he was willing to talk. His office was a no-frills, twelve-foot-square room dominated by a broad wooden desk. The plain, wall-mounted bookshelves were loaded with three-ring binders, a few award plaques, and hardbound books. Peters was a husky man with a small paunch, a full head of gray hair, and a thin mustache. He wore aviator-style glasses and smoked a cigarillo. A faint wheeze leaked through his soft baritone.

The problem with drugs, he said, was not particularly severe in southeast Kentucky or in Rockcastle County. It was "all over the state, all over the country." It just seemed more prevalent because of the small population; people here knew their neighbors or relatives, and they talked a lot.

He shared his impression that family, ironically, was one of the causes for the drug problems: "We're seeing the second and in some cases third generations of families with addictions," he explained. More critical still was the weak economy, which offered few jobs. "People are frustrated and disheartened," he said.

I mentioned meth, and the sheriff said meth was the big problem ten or fifteen years earlier, but there was "a lot of cracking down on that," and so getting the ingredients is harder. The current plague was prescription abuse—oxycontin and especially oxycodone.

Sheriff Peters patiently outlined the weird drug abuse economy of Appalachia, which is based on a symbiotic relationship between people with real pain, people with real medical degrees, and people with real money. Imagine a construction worker hurt on the job, the sheriff said. Maybe he's disabled for a year or for a lifetime, and his physician prescribes a powerful painkiller, say Percocet or oxycodone. With few if any prospects for a job, the man sits at home while his tolerance for the Perc or oxy builds, and before long he's craving constant and increasing doses. He's hooked, and even if there were any rehabilitation clinics in the county, he wouldn't have much incentive to go. Peters added that, while Kentucky law limits the number of refills, it is fairly easy to find an accommodating doctor to write larger or duplicate prescriptions that can be filled in out-of-state pharmacies, dodging state oversight. Florida was a favorite destination.

"It's just so darned easy to set up these pill mills," Peters said. "The feds cracked down, and Florida too, but there are still problems."

The way it works, he explained, is that a bankroller will rent office space close to a pharmacy, hire some version of an M.D., perhaps even install an x-ray or MRI machine—and they're open for business.

"It's all legal, so it's hard to fight the doctor shopping and pill mills," Peters said. "That's what bothers me the most. People are overprescribed. Why do you need to travel three states away if you're seriously ill, to get a prescription? I don't know."

Many addicts can't afford to make the trip, he said, so someone gives them money and loans them a vehicle in return for a portion of the pills they bring back. "Sixty percent of the pills usually go to these sponsors; 40 percent to the person who makes the trip," he said. He estimated the street value of black market prescriptions at about a dollar per milligram. Translation: A sponsor who gets 60 percent of a five-hundred-dose delivery stands to make $3,000 to $6,000.

Just then a thirtyish man knocked and walked in, holding the hand of his three-year-old son.

"My boy just wanted to meet a real policeman," the man explained. Peters was glad to oblige. He got up from behind his desk and shook the boy's hand and asked a few questions, patiently waiting for the boy to respond. This was the Andy Griffith in him coming out. After a few minutes, the man told his son to say thank you and then thanked the sheriff himself before leaving as quietly as they came. Sheriff Peters returned to his seat. He was patient with me, too, but clearly he was not enjoying our conversation as much. I asked about the number of drug-related arrests in the county.

"It's hard to say," he said. "If you count everything that's somehow related to the drug business—including public intoxication, theft—when someone is stealing to buy drugs—overdoses—my guess is 85 percent of all arrests are drug related." That seemed to me more than just another problem no worse than others, but I kept silent.

"My general observation is that we started this 'war on drugs' in the late seventies, but it hasn't worked," he continued. "The damn epidemic's gotten worse. How many billions of dollars have we spent, and it's not working." I asked why not.

"For one thing it's more socially acceptable. Plus, there's too much money to be made. We're talking about billions—*billions*—per year. We're dealing with national and international cartels. When you've got Mexican cartels dealing, it's too much. This is not like bootlegging. It's more prevalent."

He laughed—ironically or bitterly, I couldn't tell—when I asked about task forces. "There are three deputies and me. We have a total annual budget of $459,000—for gas and everything. The average size of a rural sheriff's department in Kentucky is ten officers or less. We had an officer for a while, through the HIDTA (High Intensity Drug Trafficking Area) program, paid by federal dollars, to bring FBI, DEA, ATF, and local forces together on task forces. We had the UNITE task force, but it was underfunded."

He wanted harsher penalties and wanted them enforced, but there would not be enough room in the prisons. So, given the alternatives, he leaned toward decriminalization.

"Speaking personally, I know a lot of European countries have decriminalized it, some even to the point of supplying addicts with a daily fix," he explained. "Some people won't like to hear this, especially in the Bible Belt, but it would probably be cheaper to do that. At least people wouldn't be on the streets stealing. Or we need major changes in education and start a rehab facility."

He did not sound hopeful. He knew he was outgunned—literally, in some cases—and certainly working with a much smaller budget than drug dealers. "It's like that old song," he said to me at one point: "'As Long as There's Money.' As long as there's a market, someone will supply a product."

Sheriff Peters and I talked almost an hour. I did not know what to make of our conversation. Some parts were not adding up. He had told me that the drug problem was no worse than elsewhere in Kentucky while also saying that the vast majority of arrests were drug related. If there were stricter enforcement, by his own admission his jail would not be big enough. But I soon found data that suggested the county's drug problem was in fact more severe than many other places, at least than other counties in the commonwealth. In 2012, for instance, Rockcastle County reported a drug-related arrest rate of 3,842 arrests for every 100,000 people—more than double the statewide rate of 1,201. The rate of drug-related deaths in Rockcastle County over the past five years, 43.6 per 100,000 people, was almost double that of Kentucky (23.06)— itself one of the states hardest hit by drug-related fatalities. Rockcastle County recorded an average of almost one drug-related death per week in 2012.

I wondered why the sheriff did not talk about these figures. Maybe his information was out of date. Maybe he felt overwhelmed by the scale. Maybe, given the limitations of a small department and a miniscule budget, he saw no reason to contemplate Rockcastle County's place in the big picture. I reminded myself that this was his home, his turf; he had grown up here and was elected sheriff in 2007. I was only a stranger passing through. Even so, I could not help but wonder if this conversation was indicative of what the newspaper editor meant by people sweeping the problem under the rug.

It was pushing two o'clock, and I felt hungry by the time I returned to my motel room to drop off my notebook and camera. I walked across the parking lot to Arby's, where a collection of Japanese tourists clustered in front of the counter. The twenty-one people in the group, mostly men, all crowded the counter, talking among themselves as they pointed at the backlit menu board. The tourists sported signed ball caps, cameras, tote bags, and daypacks. The three Arby's girls behind the counter sported slightly dazed expressions. The few other American customers were gathered on one end of the counter, eyeing the Japanese group with wary curiosity. I stood to the side, waiting for the crowd to thin.

A tall, thin Japanese man with straight, disheveled gray hair apologized to me. No need for that, I said. He kept motioning his fellow travelers ahead of him, determined to be the last person to order. This was a group of bluegrass fans on a ten-day tour, he told me. Most of them lived in Japan, but a few were immigrants to the United States. All were on their way to Indiana for the Bill Monroe Bluegrass Festival, by way of Kentucky and Ohio. He was the group's organizer and leader. His name was Saburo Inoue, and he was the editor of a small bluegrass magazine in Japan.

I asked if he knew about the Carter Family Fold near Hiltons, Virginia, and his face brightened. "Oh yes!" he said. In fact, he had been there several times, but regrettably this group would not make it there. His food came, and I placed a business card on his tray as I turned to order my cheeseburger. When it arrived, he waved me over to sit with him and a friend.

Saburo ("Everyone calls me Sab") introduced me to Akira Otsuka. They were not only friends but musical partners, members of a band called Bluegrass 45. Sab played banjo; Akira, mandolin. Having launched BG45 in 1967, in 2012 they organized an anniversary reunion tour around Japan: the forty-fifth anniversary for Bluegrass 45. I later found the group on YouTube. These guys were legendary in Japan and well respected in this country. The group had toured the United States twice in the early seventies, including a gig at the Grand Ol' Opry. They had recorded a few albums, and there was even a video from a concert during their 1971 US Tour. I recognized Sab, dark haired but still shaggy and even skinnier than he was now. The group was playing "Dueling Banjos"— a standard, except that each musician was holding his instrument behind his back or above his head, including the stand-up bass. And they played it well.

Akira stayed in the United States after their 1973 tour and had scored a brief solo career, playing with several big-name musicians. Now he was a programmer for a big banking company near Washington, DC. In the meantime, Sab's magazine, *Moonshiner*, kept 2,000 subscribers. It was available only in print.

As we ate, Sab said, "Many people ask, why bluegrass."

"I've been wondering that myself," I said, and he laughed.

"It's a universal kind of music," he answered. "And it might be hereditary."

I chuckled, but he smiled mysteriously and said, "Japanese people share DNA with the Melungeons," referring to a once-denigrated people with a murky ancestry who settled around these eastern mountains. Historians do not know exactly where Melungeons originated, but they are thought to be the mixed descendants of Cherokee, Scots-Irish, and other ethnicities. So why not Japanese as well? And it turns out that Japan boasts the second-largest bluegrass market in the world, according to the International Bluegrass Music Museum.

The tour group was headed to the Kentucky Country Music Hall of Fame and Museum in Renfro Valley after lunch, barely a mile from where we sat. Then they would resume their drive to the Bill Monroe festival. Sab and Akira talked fondly of Bill Monroe—and Doc Watson, too—as if they knew those musical legends personally. *Who knows? They may have.* Chatting with a couple of Japanese bluegrass legends at a fast-food restaurant in Mount Vernon, Kentucky, anything seemed possible.

18

RICHES AND POVERTY

A road . . . even the most primitive road, embodies
a resistance against the landscape. Its reason is not simply
the necessity for movement, but haste. Its wish is to avoid
contact with the landscape; it seeks so far as possible to
go over the country, rather than through it.

—WENDELL BERRY

An old Irishman was keeping Dot occupied in the motel lobby when I lugged in my pack to check out.

"What's missing in the world is *truth*," he was saying. "I'm not talking about specifics. It's *truth*." He punched out the last word as if that would explain everything. He claimed to know twenty languages, including Hebrew and Arabic so he could study the Bible and the Koran for himself, and to have traveled the globe. Dot, bless her, listened patiently as he dispensed his worldly and world-weary wisdom. She and I caught each other's eye just long enough for her to raise one skeptical eyebrow. Some minutes later, as I walked into a cool, bright morning, I contemplated whether this exit on Interstate 75 was a crossroads for the world. Between Japanese bluegrass fans and Irish philosophers, Mount Vernon might be as diverse, per capita, as Times Square.

Crossing under the interstate, I entered Renfro Valley, which comprised one straight, nostalgic mile of packaged rurality and country music. The cabins, even the authentic ones, seemed like backdrops in a theme park. The Historic Lodge Restaurant was housed in an elongated cabin, its logs painted robin's-egg blue and chinked in white. A white-lettered sign painted on the side of The Big Red Barn advertised "Home of Renfro Valley Barn Dance: Home of Real Country Music Shows." Those shows date back to 1939, the brainchild of John Lair, a homesick

Kentuckian living in Chicago who decided that the world needed a weekly dose of country music entertainment via WLS-AM radio. Thus was born the Barn Dance. By the time he died in 1985, Lair had turned Renfro Valley into a magnet for rising or falling country acts.

Two RV parks huddled together on the other side of the road, but no music fans were stirring at nine in the morning. Nothing was open, not even the limestone-clad Kentucky Country Music Hall of Fame. Through the small window in the front door, I could see guitars hanging from rough wooden posts and folding chairs lined up, waiting for a concert. Soft yellow light fell between exposed rafters to illuminate a wall crowded with plaques and other displays.

Renfro Valley was too small to have any outskirts. It simply came to an end, and then the blacktop ribbon of US Highway 25 curled between stands of trees. Less than a mile from the Hall of Fame stood a long, low-slung building that housed a food bank and a used-clothing store named, respectively, Grateful Bread and Grateful Threadz. These were conjoined twin ministries of the Christian Appalachian Project (CAP), one of the largest private nonprofit organizations in the region. Renfro Valley might have been closed, but the two Gratefuls, the only clothing store and food pantry in the CAP network, were already humming. A half-dozen cars and trucks were parked in the gravel lot.

The clothing store was spacious and clean, with plenty of room to walk the carpeted floor between well-organized clothes racks. A short passageway connected the Threadz with the Bread. There stood three long rows of floor-to-ceiling stainless steel wire shelves, all stocked with orderly rows of canned vegetables and soups and boxed meals. A cardboard box big enough to hold a kitchen range was loaded with bananas. Two commercial-sized refrigerators and freezers lined one wall.

I was browsing the Threadz store when a tall, fortyish woman with brown hair and a welcoming smile asked if she could help me.

"I'm passing through and just was curious about this place," I said, and we introduced ourselves.

Sherry Barnett was a volunteer, as were all but one of the people who worked at this site. She quickly sketched information about the store and pantry, which had been located in Mount Vernon until the previous year. The new building was larger and more accessible for people with handicaps, but it was less convenient for townspeople, many of whom did not drive. Even so, about nine hundred people had come for food in the previous month alone—all from Rockcastle County, all living below the poverty line. The food bank was serving more than thirty-eight hundred different people per year in a county that reported just over 17,000 people in the 2010 census. Individuals, grocery stores, restaurants, and even other food ministries donate the food, and a volunteer had arrived a few minutes earlier with a sizable contribution from a local Kroger.

"Families can pick up free food only once a month," Sherry said, "but a lot of them come more often. They come in for friendship, for a hug."

Sherry grew up in Renfro Valley. The place had not changed much, she said, except that sometimes the weekends were more crowded, depending on who was playing. "Loretta Lynn performed a few weeks ago," she said, "and so you can imagine how that was."

Another volunteer, a bright-eyed twenty-something from Ohio named Allison White, had signed on for a year because she was "at loose ends." Her year was almost over, but she "just loved" the area and wanted to stay and teach school and lead Bible studies.

Was it ironic, I wondered aloud, that a food pantry stood within sight of a big-money entertainment complex? Neither Sherry nor Allison took the bait. Sherry said she hoped to see more connection between the community and their ministry, but those prospects seemed remote when I asked about the four child-drawn posters tacked on the food pantry wall—almost the entire output of an awareness-raising program at the elementary school a few weeks earlier. The event was intended to attract people from the community, but total attendance could be counted on two hands.

As we said goodbye, Allison handed me a cold bottle of water and a banana she had grabbed from the big box and wished me well. I was grateful indeed. The day was already heating up.

The CAP is one of the dozens of organizations—faith-based, secular, or governmental—that blossomed in the region during the War on Poverty in the 1960s. A Roman Catholic priest named Ralph Beiting launched CAP as an interdenominational ministry that has since expanded into scores of camps, schools, and centers that offer housing assistance, counseling, and other kinds of help. The entire organization operates in sixteen counties in southeastern Kentucky with an $80 million annual budget, most of it coming from donations of cash and materials.

The history of the War on Poverty can be spelled out with an alphabet of initiatives: CAP, VISTA (Volunteers in Service to America), AV

(Appalachian Volunteers), CAAs (community action agencies), ARC (Appalachian Regional Commission), the EOA (Equal Opportunity Act of 1964), and the short-lived granddaddy of federal action in Appalachia, the OEO (Office of Economic Opportunity). They were united by an overall goal of addressing and alleviating the chronic poverty in America's inner cities and Appalachia. As Appalachian scholar Ronald Eller stated in *Uneven Ground: Appalachia Since 1945*, the efforts "brought hope and empowerment to millions in Appalachia, fueling a nascent regional identity."

But while the organizations were united in what they wanted to accomplish, they were frequently divided over how to achieve that goal. There was a "great divide between self-help efforts promoted by government and private programs and [contrasting] calls for structural reform, alternative development, and social justice being made by a growing number of activists and community leaders," according to Eller. "Proponents of this more radical perspective, however, remained in the minority during the height of the War on Poverty. Most antipoverty programs sought to extend social services to the poor and accepted the idea that if the poor could be trained to think and act like middle class Americans, they would be successfully absorbed into the larger society."

Even so, for all these tensions, the War on Poverty—along with the Civil Rights Movement and the Vietnam War—shone a bright light on profound social divisions in America and in Appalachia. As Eller noted, the antipoverty campaign "revealed just how deeply Americans differed in their visions of democracy and the good life." Appalachia had always been flyover country—regarded as strange and backward, but in fact barely regarded at all. That seemed ironic to me, considering how much of American history and identity grew out of the region.

At the top of a long ascent on a stretch of empty road, the hills rolled rather than soared and pastures opened up. The topography was changing, and I guessed this marked the subtle geologic border between Appalachia and the Bluegrass region.

I felt glad to be paying closer attention to the land now, even gauging the shifts in topography that might seem as subtle as a mood change. I wanted to appreciate the importance of land as keenly as the importance of breath. City-raised humans like me, those who do not make their living from the soil, tend to overlook the land and take it for granted, with the exception of those occasional moments of awe at a spectacular view or horror at an environmental calamity. But the land, I started to realize, is vital almost beyond words, and not just for its economics. This simple declarative sentence sounded trite but true when I spoke it aloud: *The land is a source of identity.* I recalled Tom in Himyar, who returned to a place where he had not lived for decades and still regarded it as home, although everything had changed. I thought of Wes back in Gate City, who felt displaced even though he lived only ten miles from where he grew up. *The land is a source of identity.* I remembered Robert and Patty and the few acres they had acquired in Clinch Valley. Ron Short, who had Powell Mountain and all its nooks as his backyard, believed that, were Daniel Boone plopped down here today, he'd still recognize the place. *The land is a source of identity.* It is a truth, but one frequently washed out of sight like stars above streetlights.

Farms, forests, rivers. Junkyards. Eroded timber roads. Litter-clogged streams. Below ground, mazes of coal mines where thousands of men earned their living and hundreds met their deaths. All around, wild animals thrive, some protected within national forests. To the east, mountains are stripped and flattened and scalped. After two hundred forty years, we still cannot reach a consensus on how best to balance conservation, preservation, reclamation, and development. The land yields life as much as livelihood, growing people and societies as much as it grows corn and hay and tobacco.

I recalled a few days earlier, when my morning reading included verses from the biblical book of Deuteronomy. As the people of Israel paused on the threshold of the Promised Land, their old leader, Moses, approaching death, pleaded with them to stay true to their covenant with God. Time and again, Moses spoke about the land. It was entwined with the people, with their existence as a nation, with their very connection to God. Their identity, their survival, and their prosperity would depend on how well they attended not only to their relationship with God, but also to their relationship with the land. The land was not a mere stockpile of natural resources to be garnered, but a gift to be appreciated and nurtured. That struck me as a surprisingly relevant lesson that should have resonated in the old Bible Belt.

My thoughts were interrupted when I noticed a skinny young man, dressed all in gray and carrying a full pack, walking toward me on the same side of the road. "Where you headed?" I asked as we got close. He vaguely gestured ahead of him—southward—without breaking his stride or looking at me. "Wherever," was all he said.

The New Hope Holiness Church is housed in a plain white building and has a front lawn the size of a football field. The property line was obvious: it was where the church's neatly mown grass met the slightly shaggier neighboring property—and where a Romney–Ryan yard sign stood, seven months after the election. It was planted as close as possible to the church property without being on it, an inch beyond the scrutiny of the Internal Revenue Service.

The land opened up, flat and green, revealing Interstate 75 to the left, parallel to my road. The blur and hum of the highway drove thoughts of wilderness from my mind. Railroad tracks ran parallel on my right, and the smattering of houses and small businesses hinted that a train stop once stood here in Conway. Something still happened here at least once a week: A big black barn on the far side of the train tracks advertised "Live Music, Saturdays, 7 p.m."

I stepped into a cavernous produce store that was joined to a store that sold carpet, rugs, and floor tile. No one was in sight, but I was glad to see a restroom in the short corridor connecting the fruit with the flooring. When I emerged a few minutes later, a man with a goatee and wearing a ball cap was leaning on a broom near the passageway in the produce side, and a blonde woman in a striped polo shirt stood behind the counter. They spoke politely, but the man eyed me warily. I bought an apple and a small bottle of Ale-8-One, a famous Kentucky species of soft drink something like ginger ale. They offered only perfunctory answers to my small-talk questions, obviously uninterested in conversation. I stepped onto the porch to snack and to pull a tick off my arm.

Less than an hour later, the flat, straight road—which felt foreign after so many miles of curves—started rising into hills again, reminiscent of Appalachia but without the towering heights. I was approaching Boone Gap, the last high point on the route before Boonesborough and the boundary between the watersheds of the Cumberland and Kentucky rivers. There were signs at the crest, including a "No Parking" sign in front of a wide spot that offered a fine view through a line of trees down to a valley. On the opposite side loomed a sheer wall with the familiar vertical grooves in exposed yellow-and-gray rock, the scars of yet another blasted and graded hill.

Descending, the road crossed into Madison County at its southernmost point. Fort Boonesborough perched on the county's extreme northern edge, about thirty miles away, where Otter Creek flowed into the Kentucky River. I had entered my last county.

----- **19** -----

THE CENTER OF THE UNIVERSE

We are all of us seeking a homeland, dear, even though
we have only seen and embraced it from afar. We are
all of us strangers and pilgrims on the earth.

—FREDERICK BUECHNER

The two and a half miles between Boone Gap and Berea were populated by jumbles of houses and oddly juxtaposed businesses. In front
of a small white office building and a block of self-storage units, a
sign hand-lettered in red marked "THE HaRVEST FAMILY MIN-
IStRY NON-PROfit HELP StORE." Signs painted by the same hand,
hanging on a chain-link fence, said clothes were available—as were furniture, beds, tools, books, shoes, TVs, household items, movies, "AND
MOre!" Later a single-story chain of pale yellow buildings with bright
green metal roofs served as home to Fitness, Friends and Fun *("Join
Today!")*. The center offered zumba daily, cardio, personal boot camps,
a smoothie bar, child care, and Brazil butt lifts.

About a mile from the center of Berea, a colorful sign pointed to
the artist's district, which I followed to Weaver's Bottom Craft Studio.
A guest room waited for me there, assuming that Sam Rosolina, the
twenty-something son of friends back in Tennessee, had come through
with his offer to find a place for me to stay in the town where he had
attended college. Hot and sweaty, I entered the long, narrow shop. The
place glowed, thanks to large windows that let the sun reflect on worn
wooden floors. Colorful cotton, linen, and wool lay on tables and were
draped over wooden racks—doilies, napkins, hand towels, coasters.
Room-size rugs hung from the high walls. A central aisle, laid with a
steel-blue runner, was flanked by wooden looms. A sturdy, compact man
wearing a craft apron over a plain white T-shirt and blue jeans looked

up from a loom that was about the size of a Mini Cooper. His graying ponytail reached the middle of his back.

"You must be the walker," he said. Sam, bless him, had indeed come through. Neil Colmer was counting varicolored threads stretched halfway down the central aisle. This shop belonged to him and his wife, Mary. At one time, they had also rented a couple of upstairs rooms as a bed and breakfast, but that part of the business did not pay, and so they just made the rooms available to friends and to friends of friends. Thanks to Sam, I came as the friend of a friend of a friend.

Neil and I chatted a few minutes, but he did not seem to know much about me other than that I was "the walker." Eager to return to work, he directed me to a narrow, steep staircase adjacent to the shop, which climbed to a hall running the length of the building. A roomy, sparse kitchen and a small, common bathroom anchored one end of the floor. At the other end, luggage and clothes lay strewn on the floor of the larger of two bedrooms—evidence that Sam and a couple of his friends had arrived as expected. (A few weeks earlier Sam and I realized we might rendezvous in Berea, when he would be in town as part of an alumni panel talking to students about graduate school.) My room was painted robin's-egg blue, trimmed in white, and decorated with the Colmers' handiwork. A handmade white cotton cover draped over the bed, and two small rugs lay on the wood floor. A compact writing desk stood next to a window that looked over the street toward the old train station. I showered, changed into my clean-ish shirt and pants, and draped my sweaty hiking clothes on a quilt rack. Within an hour, after easing down the steep stairs with stiff thighs, I headed to the town center. I was to rendezvous with Sam and his friends at a coffee shop that, I was told, I could not miss.

Berea is composed of three communities. There is, of course, the rural southern town of stores and banks and schools and chain restaurants and homes of various sizes and conditions. This is the part of town familiar to residents and passed by visitors on their way to the town's other sections. The artists' district, comprising about ten blocks, is home to shops like Neil and Mary's: weavers, crafters of furniture and musical instruments, painters, and sculptors. Then there is Berea College, which spreads leafy green and brick-red through the central part of town.

Town and college intersect at College Square, the vibrant heart of Berea. Here are clustered small specialty shops, bistros, and professional offices, such as the suite of Berea Healing Arts that housed the kinds of businesses not usually found in small southern towns: an acupuncturist, a massage therapist, a holistic nurse, a "center for mindful living practices," and an "intuitive consultant." On the northeast side of the square is a row of white facades, dominated by Boone Tavern, a two-story, colonnaded high-end restaurant and hotel that the college owns and operates, as it does several of the businesses in the town center. One of them, five doors down from the Tavern, is the obvious hangout of choice, Berea Coffee and Tea, which the locals affectionately call BC&T

The interior of BC&T—dark, wooden, and softly lit—features overstuffed couches and broad coffee tables around the edges of the room and another half-dozen scattered mismatched tables. Baristas, mostly Berea students or recent graduates, were shuffling behind the long wooden counter that was worthy of a Western saloon, beneath an enormous blackboard which listed the menu of drinks, scones, sandwiches, and salads. Customers could wend through the building to a back patio, which is where I found Sam and more than a dozen other people seated around umbrella-topped patio tables shoved together. Among them were the college's new president, Lyle Roelofs, and his wife, Lauren, who had arranged this informal "meet and greet" between students and several visiting alumni, including Sam.

When I walked onto the patio, Sam jumped up to greet me with a smile and hug, which is typical for him. Slight of build but large of personality, Sam can fill a room with warmth and energy without a trace of smarminess. With his straight, shaggy, light brown hair and kind, wide, blue eyes, he could have stepped out of central casting as an easygoing and earnest singer–songwriter—which is not far from the exact truth. Currently, he was a doctoral student in chemistry at the University of Tennessee.

Several alumni from his era were there too, but Sam was so much the wheel within the wheel that I started thinking of the group, inevitably, as Sam's club. His welcome punched my ticket to immediate credibility, if not total coolness. When he stopped the conversation around the table to introduce me and my walk (*"He's already walked fifteen miles today!"*), I heard a few sincere oohs and aahs.

Every liberal arts college is distinctive: special places, one and all, as their websites will tell you. Berea College fits the bill. Founded in 1855 by an abolitionist minister named John G. Fee, Berea was a nineteenth-century rarity, intended from the start to provide a good education for men *and* women, whites *and* blacks, particularly those who came from the hills of Appalachia with much promise but little money. Berea's intentionally multiracial student body made it not just unique but controversial. Besides that, the college has never charged tuition. Instead, every student works for the college to pay for his or her education. Among other jobs, the sixteen hundred students staff enterprises like BC&T and the Boone Tavern, tend the college-owned organic farm that sends produce to the college's food services, or work in other college-owned nonprofit businesses. The college seems to have its own economy.

The gathering on the patio started to break up—it was pushing six o'clock—and Sam and several friends invited me to join them for dinner at an Italian restaurant around the corner. I chatted with Ryan, a husky, dark-haired guy who said he "worked for the man" without offering specifics. Monica was a thirty-something grad student in ecotechnology who worked at a fitness center to pay her bills. Joshua taught high school chemistry in rural Tennessee. Matt was not a Berea alumnus but was a certified friend of Sam in the same graduate chemistry program. He was planning to hike the Appalachian Trail. Seth was the youngster, newly graduated from Berea and getting ready to travel to eleven countries in eleven months with a Christian mission organization. Donia was working on a doctorate in drug development at the University of Kentucky, commuting seventy miles every day between Berea and Lexington so she could take care of her grandparents. By her own reckoning, she was also a crackerjack plumber, a fact that her otherwise lovable grandfather had trouble recognizing. "The kitchen sink sprang a leak, and he insisted on fixing it, which he couldn't do after six hours and six trips to Lowe's," she told me, before adding with a smirk, "I finished the job in fifteen minutes."

After dinner we returned to BC&T, where I was introduced to Lilly Belanger and her mother, Sarah. Lilly was—no surprise—great friends with Sam and his fiancée. She had moved to New York City to work with a nonprofit organization whose mission was to get people to live with smaller carbon footprints. Her current project was a campaign to have plastic shopping bags banned in America's biggest city. For her part, Sarah worked as a mentor in the local middle and high schools. But John,

Lilly's father and Sarah's husband, was a "local hero," according to Sam. Once a successful physician in Berea, he now devoted his time and efforts to a health clinic in Paint Lick, a small community about ten miles northwest of town. If local residents did not have insurance—which was common—they paid only twenty dollars or whatever they could afford. His casualness about money apparently went way back. John grew up in a well-to-do family, Sarah said, but when she brought him home from college to meet her family, his shoes were held together with duct tape.

Just then a boisterous man the size of a linebacker and the fashion sense of a dairy farmer walked in and boomed a greeting to the Belangers. This was Craig Williams, leader of the Kentucky Environmental Foundation, a cofounder of the Nobel-winning Vietnam Veterans of American Foundation and winner of the 2006 Goldman Environmental Prize—"the Green Nobel"—an award received, Sam whispered to me, from the hand of Robert Redford. Williams and the Belanger women chatted about family and started reminiscing about some happy event they attended years ago, before Lilly was even in school. Maybe a picnic, I assumed, or an outdoor concert. It turned out they were recalling a 1991 antiwar protest at the Kentucky state capital.

After an hour, our little group, minus a few who had already said goodnight, walked a mile through the slant light and thick humidity to the old train station, converted into a visitor center, across the street from Weaver's Bottom. Sam and Ryan grabbed their guitars and soon were sitting in the middle of the center's small garden area, strumming and singing while the rest of us stood around them in a half-circle, occasionally joining in but mostly watching and listening, now and then calling out a request. Another couple arrived, Meghan and Jacob, and Meghan and Sam sang a few duets. But in a little while—I lost track of time—the songs drained away with the light, and the friends started trading stories and catching up on who had moved where, who had gained and lost jobs, who had married whom, and who had broken up. I withdrew to one side and watched, tired and full and mellow as the sky turned dusky blue and a thin crescent moon rose over the station's roof.

Someone had brought a board game called, fittingly, Ticket to Ride, produced by a company called Days of Wonder. But no one was playing. I found myself transfixed by the abandoned box, its names working a strange effect on me. These were "days of wonder" for a group of twenty-somethings a few years out of college, at the start of their adult lives.

Half of them were launching on trajectories through graduate schools and on to fulfilling careers and good paychecks. A few had already stumbled and were groping toward the future, their early hopes tempered by fear. No one can know what waits around the bend.

Just like Melissa and me, I thought. She and I were already living in England at that stage of our lives. We were only kids then, I realized. Nostalgia washed over me, warm at first but then turning hot as memories of the three intervening decades unspooled in my mind—terrific and terrible, amazing and agonizing. How could we have known then what would be coming our way? For the first time on the trip, I felt close to tears.

Somber thoughts and tears did not seem suitable for a fine summer evening with a group of newfound, young, and hopeful friends. I said goodnight and walked through the small plaza, across the street, and up to my room. The sky was not quite dark, but I was ready for bed and ready to let Sam and his friends enjoy the rest of their time together— and ready to not think about my first years out of college. As sleep overtook me, random guitar chords and snatches of conversation drifted across the street and into the open window.

The beep-beep-beep of pedestrian crossing signals around Berea's College Square in the morning was almost nonstop and annoying. True, this was a complicated intersection, laid out like a river delta as the main road branches and then branches again, with an island in the middle. But this was not New York City, for goodness' sake, and the beeps seemed to overpower a town whose entire population could fit on a single block in Brooklyn.

The home of the Loyal Jones Appalachian Studies Center stands on one corner, a tall, brick-faced modern building where the college campus abuts the town center. The center is named in honor of its founder and first director, an alumnus and retired professor at Berea. By all accounts Loyal Jones—such a wonderful, noble name—is regarded as an Appalachian Renaissance man: farmer, musician, scholar, author, 1960s activist for the region, storyteller. He still lived in town and was a regular customer at BC&T. I had arranged to meet him there this morning, another contact via Sam.

The center, the first of its kind, is part academic institute, part museum, part archive, and part launching pad for Appalachian awareness and activism. A prominently displayed quotation from author Wendell Berry declared its sensibilities: "To know about strip mining or mountaintop removal is like knowing about the nuclear bomb. It is to know beyond doubt that some human beings have, and are willing to use, the power of absolute destruction. This work is done in violation of all the best things that humans have learned in their long dwelling on the earth: reverence, neighborliness, stewardship, thrift, love."

There must have been a mix-up or a problem because Loyal Jones did not arrive. He and his wife were well past eighty. After almost two hours of waiting and several cups of coffee, I decided to explore the town and left a note for Loyal Jones with the bushy-haired guy behind the counter. Loyal Jones received my note from the coffee shop and emailed me that night. There had indeed been a mix-up; he did not think our meeting was confirmed, and, regretfully, he could not meet today. (We agreed to try again sometime when I was traveling through the area. We eventually met briefly the following September.) I walked out into a bright, sweltering morning.

Across a side street from Boone Tavern is Union Church (officially named Church of Christ, Union), one of two congregations launched by the Rev. John Fee before he founded the college. Fee was lured to the area by the prominent Kentucky politician and abolitionist Cassius Clay, who gave ten acres of unexceptional land to his antislavery ally. "Open in full equality to all races and non-sectarian, the church had a leading part in establishment of Berea College in 1855 and in the cause of racial equality in this area," according to a nearby historical marker.

Strolling through a residential area a half-mile down the road, I met a short, stocky man walking his small, blond mutt. The man did not tell me his name, but the dog's name was Bailey. After thirty-two years of farming in Garrett County, he—the man, not the dog—had moved to Berea three years ago after a quarrel with his landlord. But he did not like "the city." A friendly, garrulous man who smiled easily, revealing two missing teeth, he wore his slick, emphatically parted black hair over black horn-rim glasses. He had no discernible chin. When I asked what he thought about the college, he replied in a gravelly twang, "Did you see the new dorm they're building? A friend of mine works there, and he told me that the insulation caught on fire, and that set 'em back. It was supposed to open in July, but now it'll be August." He seemed to take some pleasure in the college's misfortune.

Kim and Joseph Claytor

After wandering around the town center, I wanted to talk with someone who knew the town but was not connected with the college, so I
walked into a real estate office at random. Joseph and Kim Claytor
shared the office—he was an accountant, she was the estate agent—and
they shared a love of Berea, where they had lived for fifteen years. They
agreed that, by and large, the town's three main communities peacefully
coexisted.

"The people and the college are incredibly tolerant of each other," Kim
said. "If locals pass by some protest rally at the college, they'll just say,
'Well. . . .' That's a favorite word, 'Well.' As in, 'Well, there they go again.'"
She and her husband laughed in recognition.

"I think of Berea as the Berkeley of Kentucky," she said. "It's more
open-minded here, and the town generally welcomes new ideas coming out of the college. Even if people aren't exactly sure what to make of
something, they believe people have a right to their opinion."

The town's culture, according to the Claytors, was set by the Reverend
Fee. Not yet forty years old when he established the town in the 1850s,

he christened it in honor of the biblical city where the apostle Paul found people "more noble than those in Thessalonica, in that they received the word with all readiness of mind, and searched the scriptures daily." A fervent abolitionist, Fee aimed to create a multiracial, egalitarian, and well-educated island in the middle of a slave state.

Fee's social experiment attracted like-minded people, but its first decade—which would include the Civil War—was full of troubles. Fee's slave-holding family disowned him. He was repeatedly beaten up, almost lynched, and eventually run out of town in 1859, in effect exiled until after the war.

Fee and the other reformers returned in 1866, restarted the college, and began a long-term program of integration on all fronts. But strong resistance remained, and Fee was its regular target. A pacifist, the minister never retaliated or defended himself. "But then everyone who tried to hurt him would die within a month of their attempts on his life," Kim told me. "Eventually people started leaving him alone, either because of the guilt of hurting someone who didn't fight back or because they worried about the strange deaths."

Not only did his church and his college welcome people of all races, but Fee also instituted policies of selling property in the town to blacks as well as whites, a truly unique initiative. By 1876, landownership among blacks almost matched that of whites. One scholar concluded that "perhaps no other community in the South resembled Berea in its pattern of interspersed land ownership."

In 1904 the Kentucky legislature put a stop to the college's forty-year interracial "experiment"—three years after Fee's death and eight years after the *Plessy v. Ferguson* US Supreme Court decision enabled Jim Crow laws for another half-century. The Day Law, "an Act to Prohibit White and Colored Persons from Attending the Same School," was aimed directly at Berea College, then the only integrated school in the state. Upheld by the Supreme Court in 1908, the law stood until it was amended in 1950 to allow individual schools to decide whether to integrate. At that point—four years before the *Brown v. Board of Education* decision overturned Plessy and ultimately killed the Day Law—Berea became the first school to readmit black students. Among them was the roommate of Kim Claytor's father.

Today, about 25 percent of the college's enrollment is composed of minority students. The town itself, however, is far less diverse, especially

Mary and Neil Colmer

considering its progressive history. Over 90 percent of Berea's 13,561 residents in 2010 were white and only 4.6 percent were African American, according to the Census Bureau. Which is to say, Berea looks much the same as other small towns in the region.

Back at Weaver's Bottom, Neil Colmer was working on a custom-ordered tartan blanket, adjusting the tension on the dozens of strands of yarn stretched perhaps three or four yards from a wooden loom to another piece of equipment. He worked efficiently, quick but unhurried, almost silent except for his soft humming. Neil had started weaving when he was a student at Berea in the late sixties, as part of his work program. "I hadn't done anything like that before, and now here I am," he said.

And now here was Mary, returned from running errands. She was nearly as tall as Neil, with an aquiline nose and a toothy smile that creased her eyes into slits. Her gray hair was pulled back in a bun.

They first met at a country dance in the summer of 1969, when Neil worked at a camp in Massachusetts after his sophomore year. Mary was a camper. "One night we danced together," Neil explained, "and that was all for seven years." They met again at a folk-dance school in Berea—*dancing again!*—but did not remember each other. They fell in love and were married the following year ("We got our marriage papers on April 1, 1977, and had a party on 7/7/77, at 7 p.m.," Neil said with a wide grin.) They were married eleven years before they realized they had first met at that camp years before.

Neil and Mary opened a studio in 1983 and bought their current shop six years later; the seller accepted a one-dollar down payment. The "Bottom" in the shop's name, Mary said, referred to the "courage and persistence" that it took to make the business go. There were the inevitable lean times, but now they owned the building free and clear. Their business is cyclical, and it had been slow that season. Most of their trade came from townspeople and tourists, with occasional commissions—such as the tartan Neil was working on—and sales were increasing from their Facebook page. "We reach 137,000 people in twenty countries," Mary reported. "We have 2,000 followers per week, in fifteen languages."

The three of us chatted as Neil continued working—adjusting the spread of the yarn across the loom, threading the strands through what looked like a four-foot-long comb, anchoring them to provide tension, just so, before he started weaving. They started explaining the weaving process, and my mind swam with the details.

Creating sixty inches of fabric takes just over fourteen hundred threads, Neil said. "The process starts with warping . . ." Mary interrupted him.

"*Planning,*" she said. "Planning is first, and absolutely necessary. How many yards, how many pounds."

Depending on the size and intricacy of a design, weaving a piece could take just a few hours—dish towels, say, or scarves—or it could take days that stretch into weeks. I pointed to an intricate couch throw, woven in red and white. Just setting up the loom for that piece would take twenty hours, Neil said.

Our conversation drifted from the particulars of what they did to the minutiae of where they lived. A spring runs under the parking lot at the old railroad depot across the street. A tornado blew through town in 1996 and ripped off the roof and back wall of their shop.

"If you hang in one place long enough, you hear a lot of stories," Mary said. "I remember a man who played Santa Claus for twenty-eight years,

Neil Colmer at work in Weaver's Bottom

until he suffered a stroke. I used to ask him for world peace. 'I'm working on it,' he'd say." Mary paused, somber for a moment. The peace-loving Santa had long since died.

Then brightly and randomly Mary announced, "Jesus' robe must have been woven in a tube." I didn't understand.

"It was seamless," she explained. "That would have been rare." Small wonder, she added, that the soldiers gambled for it.

Neil had finished for the day as we talked; the tartan would require a few more days. He and Mary packed up to go home. We said our good-byes, and they wished me well for the rest of my trip. I said I had enjoyed my stay in the town.

Mary replied, "We've had people come in who told us that Berea is the center of the universe."

---- 20 ----

BATTLEGROUND STATE

To be an American is to move on, as if we could
outrun change. To attach oneself to a place is
to surrender to it, and suffer with it.

—KATHLEEN NORRIS

Just before eight the next morning, I pulled the cornflower-blue door shut, said good-bye to Weaver's Bottom, and turned north. A slight, humid breeze puffed at my back, and clouds were stacking up to the west. Richmond, the seat of Madison County, was the day's goal, about thirteen miles away. Tomorrow was Fort Boonesborough and the end, a realization that stirred a familiar ambivalence. The walking now felt normal. It was the stopping for more than one night, even in a place as pleasant as Berea, that seemed odd and extravagant. I caught myself squinting, as if peering through an imaginary mist made up of thrill and sadness in equal parts.

The town's northern edge was perhaps a mile from the genteel town center, but its atmosphere was light years away—a typical small town with a four-lane strip of retailers and fast-food joints. One shopping center was predictably named Boone Square. At the very end of this ribbon of commerce stood a three-unit plaza, painted pale yellow and consisting of The Rock of Ages Wedding Chapel, Jobee's Discount Wedding Shop, and Joyce's Alterations. It was a one-stop wedding arcade: Get a dress, get it altered, and get married, all within a few steps.

The road then narrowed to two lanes, lined by fields, fences, and trees. The traffic was busy this morning. A big church loomed to my left. "Enlarging our territory, to God be the glory," its sign proclaimed, which sounded high-handed even to my Christian ears. Perhaps the territory in mind was just across the road, where dozens of new brick, upper-middle-class homes spread across the rolling hills and out of sight, like a fleet of reddish brown boats drifting on a bright green sea.

By late morning the western sky bulged with a wall of gray and black clouds. When the storm came, it came fast and fierce. The blue sky switched to gunmetal gray, and within a few minutes the breeze turned into a moderate wind and then got stronger. The sky cracked with lightning and unleashed a barrage of rain just as I reached a line of small trees. I pulled on my rain jacket and hunched in the lee of the trees, perching on the bank of a shallow culvert less than ten feet from the shoulder of the road. It was almost dark as dusk now. Wind and rain, punctuated every few seconds with lightning and thunder, thrashed the little trees behind me and seemed determined to wash away the road. Traffic slowed and then thinned and then almost disappeared. For distraction, I focused on the water rising in the culvert, wondering if it would reach my shoes.

And then, almost as suddenly, the storm ended, leaving behind only a gentle drizzle as the great wall of weather moved east. (I later learned that this storm had caused flooding and damaged buildings in Lexington, thirty or forty miles away.) The culvert was now a fast-running stream, topping out a quarter-inch from my toes. I stood, stretched, slung on my pack, and laughed at my good fortune and folly.

- - - - - - - - - - - - - -

Battlefield: An unexpected name for a place as peaceful as a golf course and as domesticated as a middle-class subdivision. But there it is, a few miles south of Richmond, named after a Civil War battle fought on this spot of rolling ground. The two-day engagement in August 1862, which involved about fourteen thousand soldiers, was the single Confederate victory in an ultimately doomed campaign to wrest Kentucky from the Union. A commemorative park occupies the site, including an impressive, two-story brick Federalist house that stood during the war and now serves as a visitor center. A few miles away, another home from the era is the golf course's clubhouse.

Earlier battles were fought nearby, including one that almost stopped Daniel Boone and his companions in their tracks. The site of "Twitty's Fort," named in honor of William Twitty, one of Boone's trailblazing

crew, is a few miles east. There, only fifteen miles from their final destination, the group was ambushed by a Shawnee party. Twitty was shot in
his knees. His slave, Sam, was killed instantly. Another crew member,
Felix Walker, was also wounded. With Twitty and Walker incapacitated,
the group hunkered down and built a small defensive shelter. Boone dispatched a messenger back to Richard Henderson, urging him to hurry
with supplies and reinforcements. Twitty died from his wounds a few
days after the attack and was buried there, next to Sam. After a week,
Walker had recovered enough to be borne on a litter between two horses,
and the expedition struck out for their destination.

Fort Estill, four miles southeast of Richmond, was one of several
small, early settlements. This one was erected by James Estill, a militia
captain best known for being killed by a Wyandot war party in the gruesome 1782 Battle of Little Mountain, about twenty-five miles away.

*McNitt, back near London. Twitty. Estill. Kentucky seemed to revel in
its pioneers' defeats.*

The Blue Grass Army Depot is a more modern and observable reminder of battlefields, enclosing more than fourteen thousand acres of
rolling hills, woodlands, and facilities that store conventional and chemical weapons. Its tall chain-link fence runs parallel to the road for several
miles. The facility was built in the 1940s, displacing about two hundred
family farms. As one of several military depots around the country, this
site was chosen presumably because it was close to good transportation
systems—roads and railroads—and far away from vulnerable coastlines.
One of its tasks now was to monitor and destroy chemical weapons, as
required by a series of treaties brokered by the North Atlantic Treaty
Organization.

An entrance to the depot on US Highway 25 is large enough to accommodate semi-trucks. An apron of asphalt the length of a football field
separates a metal-and-glass guardpost from the road, and four concrete
barriers, each the size of a compact car, stand like sentries across the
apron. As I approached the guardpost, a compact, muscular man in a
blue uniform emerged. "Can I help you, sir?" he asked in a practiced
monotone. I introduced myself and started to tell him about my interest
in the depot. He listened patiently for almost ten seconds before interrupting. "You cannot be here, sir. You'll need to go to the main gate.
You cannot be here." I asked where the main gate was located. Pointing
south, he said it was located on US Highway 421, almost two miles back.

I thanked him and mentally calculated my options as I retreated from the guardpost. I turned north.

Heavy construction clogged the road just south of Richmond. The scene was reminiscent of the route out of Johnson City weeks earlier, including the memorable roadkill. Here was the carcass of a skunk. There, a leathery corpse the size of a large cat or small fox, looking like prehistoric remains from a peat bog.

Approaching the center of town, I had no idea where I would spend the night. It would be ironic, I thought, if my last night on the road were the only one when I didn't find shelter. Stores and businesses started to crowd closer. A sign at Uncle Charlie's Tender and Juicy Meats advised passersby, "Don't stress. Dreaming about bacon is normal." Across the street, a banner at the Honda Power Equipment dealer announced that firearms were available.

This was Big Hill Avenue, named for the place where Captain Estill was killed, and it looked like a half-mile of seediness sprinkled with a few mainstream businesses. Several small liquor stores. An old, low-slung motel with peeling paint and a weedy parking lot, where a few people listlessly sat in front of rooms. A dance joint. A tire store. An insurance agency. A liquor warehouse. In quick succession I passed three men and a woman walking on the sidewalk, all skinny and all sharing a similar vacant look in their eyes. A fourth man said "Hi" and grinned as we passed, revealing tobacco-stained teeth. But the scene abruptly changed, literally on the other side of the railroad tracks. Grass was mowed; stores were modern and clean. A tidy brick sidewalk ran alongside a cemetery. One more bend in the road and downtown Richmond came into view.

The Madison County Courthouse dominates Main Street, of course: a soaring, white, colonnaded building, churchlike except for the clock tower in place of a steeple. Monuments and markers punctuated the building's front face. On the southeast corner, a stone pillar topped by the bust of a man wearing a floppy hat honored the early pioneers. A nearby interpretive marker noted that Madison County was formed in 1786, only eleven years after Boone blazed his trail. Kentucky was still part of Virginia then, and the new county was named to honor Virginia son James Madison, at that time a thirty-five-year-old lawyer and rising politician. Madison had yet to draft the Constitution or swear to preserve, protect, and defend it when he took his place as the nation's fourth president in 1809. Richmond, settled in 1785 by one John Miller and named after the Virginia capital, became the county seat in 1798.

Another marker informed readers that the courthouse was built in 1862 and Union prisoners of war were kept here after the Battle of Richmond. Eight bronze plaques embedded in the sidewalk in front of the courthouse formed the county's "Heritage Walk of Fame." The first plaque was for Daniel Boone. Then came suffragist Laura Clay; James Estill; Monk Estill, the first slave freed in Kentucky, 1700s–1835; the Rev. John Fee, "founder of Berea College, abolitionist"; Kit Carson; Cassius Marcellus Clay (the early politician, not the boxer who became Muhammad Ali); and Hall of Fame baseball player Earl Bryan Combs, who played for the New York Yankees in the 1920s and 30s.

Rain was spitting again, and I took shelter under a store awning to consider where I might pitch my tent. A slightly balding middle-aged man stopped to ask if I was walking across America. A short woman with glasses and dishwater blonde hair stood next to him. No, I told them, I'm just on the Wilderness Road. "We saw you earlier, coming up on US 25," she said, "and we wondered what you were doing."

Lewis and Lois—they did not give their last names—had just driven through nineteen states in sixty days, "in that van right there," he said, pointing across the street to a copper-colored minivan.

"It was *supposed* to be to celebrate our thirtieth anniversary," Lois said.

"Supposed to?" I asked.

"We came to Richmond to file divorce papers," she explained. Lewis held up an envelope.

"Then we're going back on the road," he added.

"Pardon?" I asked, thinking I misheard him.

"Yeah, we want to finish the trip," he said, clearly more enthusiastic about that notion than she was. As he talked with excitement about where they had been and where they would go, she would shrug and mutter. "I just can't take his other . . . *friend* anymore," she said at last.

"She doesn't understand my needs," he said without missing a beat and then finished outlining their itinerary. When their travels were done, he would return to their home in Virginia, and she would move in with their daughter who lived in Berea, which explained why they came to the Madison County seat.

Then he said, "If you want to see some great crystals, let me tell you where," and she joined in, equally thrilled about what they had found in upstate New York.

"It was just magical," she said.

"I was blown away," he said.

We chatted a few more minutes, and then Lewis said, "Well, I guess we better go do this," waving the envelope. "Then back on the road."

Lois shook her head and mouthed "No way," and then followed him across the street to the courthouse.

Watching them go, I noticed a small hike-and-bike shop: maybe they would know where I might camp. I walked in and had barely started to tell the guy at the register what I needed when he said, "Oh yeah oh yeah oh yeah. Go to the fire station. There's one downtown here and one at EKU. They let people do that *a lot*." He told me directions, and I headed for the downtown station, a couple of blocks away. At Fire Station No. 1, the woman behind a lobby window looked confused when, after explaining my trip, I asked if I could camp there.

"The guy at the bike shop said people do that sometimes," I added, wondering if I looked as stupid and desperate as I felt.

"We've *never* done that," she answered. Her voice was friendly, but she was not smiling.

I stood there dumbly, frustrated and tired and ticked off at the guy in the bike shop and wondering how I might persuade the woman to let me stay. I do not know how she interpreted my silence, but she suddenly said, "The chief's here. Let me see what he says." She disappeared into another part of the station. A moment later, a robust, mustached fireman wearing a white uniform shirt emerged and introduced himself as Chief Buzzy Campbell. He was built like a rugby player.

"Well, we've never let anyone camp here before," he said, "but I don't see why we can't." He paused before adding, "But we don't have much green space. Let me show you what we've got."

He led me through a large common room, out the back door, past the enormous garage doors and across the broad driveway. He pointed to a small patch of grass wedged into the very corner of the property, nestled between the driveway, a short retaining wall topped by a chain-link fence, and a five-foot-tall white metal cube that was the station's emergency generator. My tent would easily fit on the grass patch, I told him.

"Well, make yourself at home," he said. "Let us know if you need anything." I thanked him, we shook hands, and he walked back into the station.

What a strange symmetry, I thought as I unpacked my tent: Sheltered at a fire station on my first day and again on my last night. I decided I was a fan of firefighters everywhere.

My tent up, I was organizing my gear when a high-pitched drawl called through the tent wall: "Hey, Jim. Are you in there?"

I poked my head out and saw a trim man with a close-shaved head walking toward me. Captain Janson Hurt—thirty-something, I guessed—was that night's shift captain, and he was a fine host. "Need a shower or want to do some laundry? Just let me know. . . . Want to use the kitchen? No problem. . . . Need to use the bathroom? We'll leave that door unlocked, and you can go in through there."

I was hesitant at first—it seemed too easy to take advantage of their hospitality—but I stank and I was wet, so I accepted all his offers. Suddenly the sun broke through a cloud in the clearing sky. *It must be a sign.*

After a quick shower, I joined Janson on the overstuffed sectional sofa in the large common room, which included a kitchen on one end and a large-screen TV on the other. A conference table in the middle was stacked with three-ring binders and papers. When other men entered, their faces registered surprise or a flash of suspicion until Janson introduced me.

I asked how he got into firefighting.

"Firefighting found me," Janson replied, explaining that he had enrolled in a co-op program when he was a student at Eastern Kentucky University, there in Richmond. The work suited him. He not only liked the physical aspects, but the work also let him "think outside the box" (his words), which was essential when needing to respond quickly in unexpected situations. Like many firefighters, he held a second job on the side—in his case, installing flooring—which was possible with the fire department's schedule of twenty-four hours on, forty-eight hours off.

Neither he nor the other guys who came and went—Dave, Richard, Joey, and others—could name the worst fire they had ever worked, but all had seen gruesome scenes. Some of the worst, they agreed, were road crashes, like a semi not long ago that was hauling water and crashed on the interstate. The army depot could also be challenging. It housed the last supply of chemical and neurological weapons, which by treaty would

Capt. Janson Hurt (front) and Chief Buzzy Campbell of the
Richmond, Kentucky, Department of Fire and Emergency Services

be destroyed in a few years. I recalled reading about occasional toxic gas
leaks in the last several years—nothing that escaped into the air or put
the public at risk, but the accounts reminded me of the potential dangers
these guys faced.

"You don't really get scared," Janson said. "You put on your helmet and
then just rely on your training." Richmond provided posttrauma support
for the firefighters in the form of debriefing teams and chaplains. But the
best help, the men agreed, was just talking about it back at the station.

One and all, they liked Richmond. The town still maintained the familiar small-town feel Janson remembered from his childhood, but they
appreciated the recent growth, too, thanks in large part to the com-
muters who worked in Lexington, twenty-five miles away. (Janson noted
that there were three golf courses around town when he was a kid; now
there were seven.) EKU was booming too, attracting big-name acts like
Blue Man Group and Jerry Seinfeld to its new performing arts center.
"*Seinfeld!*" Janson exclaimed with a laugh. "In *Richmond!*"

But not all was well. Beside the university, Richmond was home to a Sherwin Williams paint warehouse and a Yuasa-Exide battery plant. That is to say, the town is home to a lot of chemicals. That translates into greater potential hazards that firefighters must contend with.

"Exide used to be a bad place for us, and I didn't like going there, not even for inspections," Janson said. "I was in there one time, and acid dripped on my boot and burned a hole through the toe."

Yet the city had recently closed a fire station near one of the big manufacturers that used a lot of chemicals—the crew preferred not to identify the company—thus increasing the fire department's response time from two minutes to at least ten minutes. The consensus was that it was only a matter of time before the city paid for that bit of efficiency.

Fire departments seem to attract military veterans, including two of guys in the room, Joey and Dave. Both had been twice deployed to Iraq. Others, like Janson, came through the fire protection administration degree program at EKU. A student in the co-op program was working with them now, a rising senior who had just come into the room—dark hair, glasses, a little doughy around the edges. The regulars played pranks on him and assigned him the kind of grunt work they knew well. But the young man told me that he loved the work and the atmosphere.

"He's a good guy," Janson told me after the student left, "but he's never done much outdoor work, and it shows." *For example?* "Well, every day we test all the equipment, including the chain saws. He didn't know how to work one." Janson was diplomatic, but he seemed to doubt whether this student would make the cut.

The place was in constant motion around me, with firefighters coming and going to finish chores or pick up food or grab a nap or do any number of other things I did not see. In the kitchen I prepared my last dinner on the road, one of my freeze-dried pouches. Afterward I walked into the early evening to explore the town, mentally convincing my feet and legs that they could still take a few more steps. The sky now was cloudless and dry and glowing with slanting sunlight.

I meandered to EKU, a prettier and greener campus than I expected, and came upon a statue of Daniel Boone, the toe of his bronze boot rubbed shiny by students wishing for good luck on exams. Unlike the statue in Barbourville, this Boone wore a dubious coonskin cap. Circling back toward downtown, I passed Irvinton, once a luxurious private home with a Wedgwood blue exterior, but now a visitor center and

Daniel Boone statue at Eastern Kentucky University, Richmond, Kentucky

museum surrounded by a city park. A small geometric marble monument to "Christmas Angels" stood in the park, in memory of "children who passed too soon." Twenty names were carved into the base, and the city held an annual ceremony each December to remember the latest child-hood deaths. Then I wandered through the town center, returning to the fire station just as dusk turned to dark.

I changed into a T-shirt and shorts and hunkered down to write notes from the day, but within a few minutes Janson came over and invited me to watch the NBA finals with the crew. "Thanks," I said, "but I need to do some writing." He shrugged.

"Well, I've got something for you," he said, holding out a neatly folded navy-blue T-shirt emblazoned with the crest of the Richmond fire and rescue squad. "It's just one of my old shirts, but I'd like you to have it."

I stammered a heartfelt thanks. He said good night and walked back inside. About two minutes later, I realized that I was being an idiot: I could write later. Hanging out with these guys was a one-time deal. I changed into Janson's shirt and crawled outside to find him and three other guys sitting at the picnic table on the small patio, ignoring the basketball blaring on the TV inside. They welcomed me, joking about my joining the department.

One of the guys, I found out in conversation, was having girlfriend problems. She wanted him to spend his day off with her. He wanted to go fishing with his pals. The barbs flew fast: "She's got you, man." "You'll be fitting for a ring soon." "Yeah, a ring in your nose." Laughs all around. He had been married three times before. Janson leaned over to whisper to me that several of the guys had "women troubles." An occupational hazard, perhaps, but Janson told me he was happily married.

When I told them about Lewis and Lois—the traveling, divorcing couple I met that afternoon—the men shook their heads. One whistled softly in disbelief. "Now *that's* messed up."

21

WHITE LIGHTS, RED HOUSE, BROWN DOG

*All places are stories, stories we tell to ourselves. We have
no choice, because all inhabited places, no matter how pure,
are in fact polluted with meaning. No place is one-dimensional.
We share our environment with too many disparate
people who are telling their own stories.*

—RICHARD TODD

Shouting men and a thumping engine roused me. The light in the
tent glowed gray-green. I needed a few moments to remember
that I was at a fire station in ... *where?* ... Richmond. It was one-
thirty in the morning. Poking my head outside, I saw two men—no,
three—silhouetted in a pure white light blazing through the tall garage
doors. They were blasting water at something I could not see and at the
moment did not care about, but it explained the light and noise. Simply a
routine equipment test and cleaning, I was later told. Toppling back into
my sleeping bag, my head thumped the hard ground through my leaky
air pillow. Soon enough I heard men's voices again, but now morning sun
flooded the tent. Seven o'clock—time for the shift change.

I quickly pulled on shorts and my official Richmond Fire and Rescue T-shirt and climbed out into the morning. I did not want to miss
Janson before he left. A couple of pickup trucks were parked in the driveway, and a dozen men or so—some in uniform, others in jeans, T-shirts,
and ball caps—were bustling around. A few of the guys going off duty
shouted their plans to go fishing. And there was Janson, in jeans and a
T-shirt, who introduced me to the day-shift captain, Brent. I told Janson
I would be in touch: I owed him a shirt, after all. We laughed and said
goodbye.

On the road before nine, I felt drawn to the end of my trip like an animal to water. Fort Boonesborough State Park lay only thirteen miles to the north, and I reminded myself to resist the temptation to hurry or to pass up people or places. "I'm not done yet," I said aloud to myself.

State Route 388, which started on Third Street, would lead directly to the park. The road passed Madison Central High School, a handsome brick building with art deco flourishes. It passed the predictably named Daniel Boone Elementary School. It rolled beyond the sprawling Shawnee Run Apartment complex, where anything resembling the road's shoulder gave way to a steep grassy bank that made walking difficult and downright dangerous when cars approached. The road crossed Otter Creek on the outskirts of town, and road and stream would more or less follow each other the rest of the way. This creek was much on Daniel Boone's mind in March 1775: His destination was the confluence of Otter Creek and the Kentucky River. There the land was level and fertile and surrounded by protective hills, with plenty of game and fresh and navigable waters. The location also happened to sit at the most distant point of Henderson's Transylvania Purchase, a fact that may or may not have been a coincidence.

After passing under a highway, the road, now dubbed Red House Road, ran parallel not only to the creek but also to a railroad track for several miles. There was the old, familiar pattern: Roads followed the rivers, and railroads followed the roads. For some distance the road and the railroad tracks aligned in almost military alignment, with the creek always flowing nearby.

A mile or so outside of Richmond, the land opened up to my right in a picturesque view under the vibrant blue sky, featuring waves of green hills, a large hayfield, a pond, a black horse fence, and a white colonial-style home. A house nestled into a hillside on the far side of a field, and a tree-covered ridge rose behind it. To the left stood a substantial dairy farm flanked by smaller homes. The whole scene was punctuated with tall, leafy trees. A word sprang to mind: *harmonious*. When white settlers came, they found forests and canebrakes. From that wilderness, this place emerged over the course of generations. In stark contrast to the ruin and imbalance evident in so many other places, this stretch of road provided a welcome reminder that, with forethought and patience, people could cooperate with nature as they carved out a home for themselves and tried to make it pay.

Tommy Rice (left) and Butch Barber

A few miles farther, at the crest of a hill, an iron-and-brick gateway caught my eye — or maybe it was the "For Sale" sign in front. A modern and expansive ranch-style house was barely visible through the gate, at the end of a quarter-mile-long tree-lined driveway. The place seemed quiet, and rolling meadows spread behind the estate. A couple of hundred yards later, a man was sitting in a wheelchair on the opposite side of the road, under the shade of a tree. His hair was gray, his nose slightly bulbous, and his eyes friendly but sad. When I stopped to say hello he looked at me inquisitively and kindly but did not answer. A tall, wiry man mowing the small lawn stopped the machine and walked over. His name was Tommy Rice, and he was mowing for his neighbor, Butch Barber, the man in the wheelchair. Butch had suffered a stroke sixteen years earlier, leaving him paralyzed on one side and unable to talk. Tommy — sixty-five, soft-spoken, and polite — lived across the road, next door to the gated estate. When I told him what I was doing, he said I would have been welcome to camp in his yard last night. He said he liked to travel too; he and his wife had recently returned from a road trip to Nova Scotia. He sorely wanted to visit Alaska — but not on a cruise because "all you see is a lot of coastline." Instead he would rent a car and "drive around to see what we can see. I'd *love* to do that."

I asked about the estate for sale. The property—which Tommy said included not one but two houses, a thousand acres, several barns, and a helipad—belonged to Garry and Penny Marshall, the TV and movie producers. Their mother had lived here for years, according to Tommy, until she grew too frail in her old age and was moved to a nursing home in Cincinnati. "The locals hope it's not bought and turned into any kind of housing development," he added. "That would be their right, of course, but we sure hope that doesn't happen. All those houses would ruin the view." (The property was eventually sold, apparently to a group of Chinese businessmen.) Regardless of whether his information was accurate about the property or its owners, Tommy was certainly correct about the view, which overlooked a broad, green dale that seemed to stretch for miles.

Up ahead was the actual Red House, he told me, for which the road was named. "A good old farmer" named Harold Bucher owned the place now. "If you see him in his yard, go up and meet him," Tommy advised. Tommy needed to finish the mowing, and I needed to finish walking, so the three of us—Tommy, Butch, and I—shook hands and said goodbye. As I hoisted my pack, Tommy said, "Generally, I find that if you're nice to people, people are nice to you."

After a few more miles—past farms, occasional clusters of small houses, and a wide concrete bridge spanning Otter Creek—the Red House stood at the top of a long, curved driveway. The maroon brick house featured a wraparound porch and white trim, shaded by several lofty trees and surrounded by acres of rolling fields. Black horse fences and a row of red rose bushes formed a border between the road and the upsweeping front yard. A sign mounted on the fence said, "Harold Bucher, Master Conservationist: soil, water, wildlife, forests."

Two young men and a gangly, slightly stooped older man were walking from the house to a white pickup truck parked at the top of the driveway. By the time I reached the truck, the older man was behind the wheel, and the two young guys were sitting next to him. The man spotted me in his rearview mirror and waited for me to come to his window. "Can I help you?" he asked, sounding wary.

I said I was looking for Howard Bucher.

"Well, I'm *Harold* Bucher," he replied tartly.

How stupid of me. I apologized. I could understand his suspicion of a stranger from the road. Who knew how many drifters must stop here? Then I said the magic words: "Well, Tommy Rice said I should introduce myself."

He brightened. "Are you a friend of Tommy's?"

As of about a half-hour ago.

Harold extended his hand to shake. I introduced myself and gave him a brief rundown of my hike. I wanted to know about the house and its history. The main part was built in 1810, he told me—originally the home of Colby Quisenberry and his wife, Lucy, who was the sister of Billy Bush, one of Boone's crewmen in 1775. The Quisenberrys lived at the home for twenty years ("and had thirteen children," Harold noted). Situated on the road from Richmond to Boonesborough and Winchester, Mrs. Quisenberry started cooking meals for travelers who would stop for the night, including farmers driving their hogs to the Cincinnati market. "She would feed the Indians for free," Harold added. "She was afraid of them." The house was sold to the Cobb family in 1837 for $900, who turned it back into a private home. The property remained in that family for a full century.

Harold, who worked for IBM before retiring, bought the house and the surrounding thirty acres in the 1970s. He had done well by his farming: he now owned four hundred acres, raised hay, and bred cattle. The "master conservationist" sign on his fence indicated an honor from the state for good land management practices, and I asked what he thought about how the land was being used around the region, especially in eastern Kentucky. Harold paused, weighing his words. His answer began with the past.

"Everyone raised corn and burley tobacco, and they raised their own food with gardens and needed to grow feed for their livestock," he said. "In most cases, the land has been taken good care of." He went on to describe the improvements he had made to his property, but I was lost in mulling over his answer, which surprised me some. I had seen plenty of places where the land was so obviously neglected or abused. Perhaps he was thinking specifically about this pleasant corner of Madison County, or maybe he understood how people closely connected to the land gave it better attention. People whose lives and livelihoods depended on the health of the land would indeed did take good care of it, if only out of necessity. It was an obvious point—or it should have been.

He and his two young companions needed to leave, and we said our goodbyes. Back on the blacktop, however, I felt myself slowing down, not from tiredness but from a sudden reluctance to finish. My earlier eagerness to reach the end had given way to a desire to savor the last few miles. Most of the early travelers on this route, I realized, would probably laugh at such a luxurious notion.

But what about Daniel Boone? I was not so sure. Boone seemed to appreciate the journey as much as the destination, if not more. He always found a reason to start moving again, and so it was with his most famous settlement.

Boone did not stay long in Boonesborough nor, for that matter, in Kentucky. The Boonesborough fort construction began in late spring 1775, but that autumn Boone returned east to retrieve his wife, Rebecca, and their ten children, making the Boone women the first white female settlers in Kentucky.

Over the next several years, Fort Boonesborough and the other two Kentucky settlements—Harrodsburg and Logan's Station, later known as St. Asaph and now as Stamford—were regularly harassed by Native American warriors who were encouraged and often armed by the British army during the American Revolution. In July 1776, for example, a Shawnee hunting party kidnapped Boone's fourteen-year-old daughter, Jemima, and two friends. Boone led the dramatic and successful rescue mission that became one of the most famous episodes of the frontiersman's life.

The year 1777, "the Year of the Bloody Sevens," was particularly terrible, with scores of fatalities on all sides and harsh sieges at Boonesborough and Harrodsburg. The casualty numbers look small by modern standards, but with fewer than two hundred white settlers in Kentucky at the time, the year was proportionally devastating. The regular raids, battles, and sieges frustrated the settlers' efforts to build fortifications, cultivate crops, and distill the salt essential for preserving meat and other needs, a problem made worse by the lack of any good salt springs near Boonesborough.

Near desperation, in late January 1778 Boone led a party about forty miles north to Blue Licks, to collect salt for the settlements. There they were discovered and surrounded by a Shawnee raiding party. Rather than face almost certain extermination, Boone negotiated a surrender, a decision that saved the group but would later haunt him. The whites were taken north across the Ohio River to a Shawnee town, Chillicothe, on the Little Miami River, near present-day Dayton. Boone spent four months in captivity.

It might be more accurate to say that it was a sort of captivity. The Native Americans sometimes adopted white prisoners to fill in families who had lost members to war or pestilence. The Shawnee knew and respected Boone, and Boone generally respected and liked the Native Americans he knew. He was adopted by Chief Blackfish, who gave him the name of Sheltowee, or Big Turtle. (Boone's adopted name is memorialized by the modern-day Sheltowee Trace National Recreation Trail, which runs between central Tennessee and Kentucky. The trail crosses the Wilderness Road near where I camped at Hazel Patch.) Boone bided his time but then made a truly daring escape in June after learning that the Shawnee were planning a major attack on Boonesborough.

Sneaking away one night, he trekked one hundred sixty miles in four days to alert the settlers and direct preparations for the assault. Blackfish and his warriors arrived in September. Boone guided the negotiations, which grew increasingly strained over three days. Running out of patience, Blackfish issued an ultimatum: surrender or starve. Shots were fired, and the Shawnees blockaded the small, wood-picket fort. Prolonged days of tense quiet periodically erupted into brief, intense, and sometimes deadly exchanges as bullets, arrows, and torches flew between the picket walls and the surrounding forest. The siege lasted three weeks and was lifted only after a brave white settler evaded detection, rode two hundred fifty miles back to the Watauga-area settlements, and returned with reinforcements—all within ten days.

In the aftermath, however, Boone's apparent friendliness with the Shawnees at Chillicothe aroused the suspicions of other settlers. Thus, for his troubles, Boone, a captain in the Virginia militia, was court-martialed and accused of treachery by two other settlers, including his daughter Jemima's father-in-law. Richard Callaway claimed that Boone had given up too easily at Blue Licks and had secretly collaborated with the Indians and thus, by extension, with the British. Boone was swiftly exonerated— largely due to the testimonies of other men taken with him—and promoted to major. Still, he felt personally wounded by the suspicion and ingratitude.

While Boone was a captive, Rebecca had given up her husband for dead and returned to North Carolina with her children. In the fall of

1778, he went east to join them. The family returned to Kentucky the following year with about one hundred more settlers, including one Abraham Lincoln, whose grandson, his namesake, would become president. But the Boones would not stay in Boonesborough: Disgusted by hints of old suspicions and frustrated by the lack of progress in establishing the settlement, the Boones and some twenty other families moved ten miles north and started anew with Boone's Station, near present-day Athens. They made the move on Christmas Day.

Tragedy struck the Boones in August 1782, in one of the last battles of the American Revolution, coincidentally at Blue Licks. Lord Cornwallis had surrendered at Yorktown the previous October, ending the conflict in the east, but fighting continued on the western frontier. A party of nearly two hundred Kentucky militiamen—Lieutenant Colonel Daniel Boone among the leaders—had pursued a British-backed raiding party. Against the advice of Boone and other officers, the commander ordered an attack, leading his men straight into an ambush. Almost half of the detachment was killed by a group of fifty Loyalists and three hundred Native Americans. Boone's twenty-three-year-old son, Israel, was shot through the neck as his father stood only a few feet away, helpless as he watched his son die. The old frontiersman later described the day as the worst of his life.

The next twenty years passed more peaceably for Boone as he took up a more conventional life: tavern keeper, Virginia state representative, shopkeeper, and surveyor. When the three-year-old state of Kentucky announced plans in 1795 to upgrade the Wilderness Road, he petitioned the first governor, his old friend Isaac Shelby, to appoint him as the project's overseer. The job, however, went to two other men, and Boone felt slighted. Shelby apparently believed, with some justification, that Boone's strengths did not rest in government-level detail and administration. Furthermore, Boone was already gaining an exaggerated but not entirely inaccurate reputation as a debtor who ignored court summons. By that time, however, he was also an international sensation, thanks to the publication in 1784 of *The Discovery and Settlement of Kentucke*, written by a traveler from the east named John Filson.

By all accounts Filson was a mild-mannered, scrawny schoolteacher—a sort of Ichabod Crane type—but he had braved the Kentucky backwoods to write a history about this new land that was capturing the American imagination. When he heard stories about a hunter named

Daniel Boone, Filson sought Boone out and pried grand stories out of him. The resulting book—part history, part biography, part yarn spinning and public relations puffery—launched Boone's reputation as a frontiersman extraordinaire to the eastern cities and beyond, even across the Atlantic. In his lifetime, Boone was elevated from long hunter to legend, the idealized natural man whose status was burnished in a wave of dubious "biographies"—most of them fabrications—that depicted a proto-Tarzan swinging through the forest to escape Indians when he wasn't gleefully slaughtering them by the dozens. The first American action hero, Natty Bumppo of James Fenimore Cooper's *Leatherstocking Tales,* was modeled on the real and exaggerated exploits of Boone. Thanks to Americans' embrace of frontier legends—as well as Boone's own tendency to sometimes embrace and sometimes debunk the stories—sorting fact from fiction has taken generations.

But Boone, despite his reputation and efforts at domestication, did not seem able to settle down. He and Rebecca and various combinations of their surviving children would move several more times in Kentucky and beyond: Marble Creek. Limestone (now Maysville), where he ran a tavern and general store. Point Pleasant, Virginia, a strategic junction of the Ohio and Kanawha rivers in present-day West Virginia. A secluded cabin near present-day Charleston, West Virginia, around the time Kentucky gained statehood. Back to Brushy Fork, Kentucky, in 1795. But eventually he grew tired of Kentucky. Compensation promised from the new state government went unpaid. Many of his land claims were refused, confused, or stolen in the land-grabbing free-for-all of Kentucky's first years of statehood, and he was forced to sell most of what remained to pay debts. His last full year in the commonwealth was emblematic of his mixed fortunes: In 1798 the Kentucky legislature named a county in his honor, and the Kentucky judiciary issued an arrest warrant for his failure to honor a court summons. The following year, he and Rebecca left Kentucky for good and moved to Missouri, near present-day St. Charles, where their son Nathan lived. There they settled once and for all to farm and hunt and watch their family grow.

Rebecca died in 1813 and was buried on their son's land. Boone followed her seven years later, at the remarkable age of 85. But if Boone had had enough of Kentucky, in 1845 Kentucky officially decided it had not had enough of Boone. The legislature voted to bring him back and promptly sent a party to fetch him. The delegation exhumed the bodies of Daniel and Rebecca, carted them back to the state capital of Frankfort, where the Boones were reinterred, their graves marked with a grandiose stone monument. Even in death, it seemed, Daniel had trouble finding a home.

For its part, Boonesborough would never thrive, despite the ambitions of its proprietor, Richard Henderson. Henderson envisioned a tidy town with lively commerce, the capital of the new state of Transylvania. But that dream died in less than two years, in large part because Henderson the entrepreneur overplayed his hand. He hoped to convince the other, older Kentucky settlements at Harrodsburg and Logan's Station to join his Transylvanian colony. But they balked when he pressed his dubious claims of land and tried to impose land fees on other settlements. Support for Henderson outside Boonesborough evaporated.

Although the settlement was growing, its destiny as a backwater town was sealed in December 1776, when Henderson's formal petition to create a new state of Transylvania—with Boonesborough as its capital—was firmly rejected by the nascent American Congress, leaving the territory as part of Virginia. That result should have come as no surprise, given the era's political and financial realities. Politically, with the Americans barely surviving their desperate fight for independence, Congress was in no mood and in no position to enable a potential breakaway, particularly from its largest and most powerful colony. If the politics were not enough, then the failure of Henderson's scheme was guaranteed by the financial interests of Virginia and its leaders who held stakes west of the Alleghenies—George Washington, James Madison, and Thomas Jefferson among them. Even so, Henderson was granted two hundred thousand acres farther west as a kind of consolation prize, and today Hendersonville, Kentucky, bears his name. Boonesborough, however, would wither in just a few decades.

That any of the early Kentucky settlements survived is something of a wonder. The pioneers faced myriad threats, many of their own making through some combination of ignorance, stubbornness, selfishness, and sloth. Boonesborough's troubles began mounting from the start. Boone immediately saw that the settlers' unrestrained hunting would yield terrible consequences. In May 1775—only six weeks after he and his crew arrived—at the first and only convention of the proposed Transylvania colony, Boone proposed limits on taking game. His motion passed, but before the year was out, the great buffalo herds had retreated, and the people of Fort Boonesborough faced starvation.

The settlers took three years to complete the fort stockade wall and did so only in the face of an imminent attack by a Shawnee force. By the time a physician named William Fleming took stock of the Kentucky settlements in late 1779, they were enduring terrible conditions. At Harrodsburg, for example, Fleming observed, "The Spring at this place is below the fort and fed by ponds above the Fort so that the whole dirt and filth . . . putrified [sic] flesh, dead dogs, horse, cow, hog excrements and human odour all wash into the spring which with the Ashes and sweepings of filthy Cabins, the dirtiness of the people, steeping skins to dress and washing every sort of dirty rags and cloths in the spring perfectly poisons the water and makes the most filthy nauseous potation of the water imaginable." Boonesborough, with thirty houses, was almost as bad.

Fleming grew increasingly concerned about the welfare of the people as the most brutal winter in living memory set in, its harshness only magnified by Kentucky's primitive conditions. By Christmas 1779, the ice was two feet thick on the Kentucky River at Boonesborough. Cattle froze to death in the fields, and more than five hundred head perished while traveling the Wilderness Road. Settlers were forced to eat their horses. As the historian Robert Kincaid noted, "All sections of Kentucky were paralyzed from the middle of November to the latter part of February. Most of the smaller streams froze solid in their beds. Snow and ice continued through the winter, and not a drop of rain fell. . . . In the forests maple trees cracked liked pistols and burst open as the sap froze. Through the nights the sleep of the settlers was broken by the frantic struggles of buffalo and other animals. All wild life was almost exterminated."

As if in a biblical famine, life on the Kentucky frontier ranged from difficult to harsh to deadly for about seven years—but fortunes began to turn in the early 1780s. The Revolutionary War ended and, with it, the British incitement of Indian attacks. The respite allowed settlements to rebuild, see their crops through to harvest, and enjoy longer spells of normalcy. The attacks on travelers also decreased, both on the old road and, significantly to the north, on the Ohio River. The river route—faster, cheaper, and now as safe as overland travel—funneled settlers into the

Northwest Territory north of the river as well as to the south, bringing with them more goods, more people, and more security. While some would-be Kentuckians returned to the east, often doing their best to discourage any westbound settlers they met on the Wilderness Road, the west had opened forever.

Even though the travels by road and river were still arduous and life on the frontier harsh, people came by the thousands, determined to create new homes in the wilderness. The growth was exponential: In 1780, around 45,000 settlers and their slaves were living in Kentucky, then a county of Virginia. Ten years later, the numbers had grown to 74,000. Kentucky was admitted as the fifteenth state in the Union in 1792, and by the turn of the nineteenth century, its population had ballooned to 152,000. In another decade, the census counted almost 407,000 people.

Boonesborough, however, was left behind. As Kentucky marched toward statehood, a push to locate the state capital at the old settlement was rejected in favor of Frankfort. The inevitable growth of river trade on the Ohio and then the Mississippi tilted the traffic toward Lexington, Louisville, and points west, which doomed any big ambitions for Boonesborough. The settlement was even abandoned by the road that created it. When Kentucky commissioned the improvement of the Wilderness Road, the route did not follow Boone's Trace but took the more westerly fork to link the Cumberland Gap with Louisville.

After its initial growth, Boonesborough gradually shriveled to way-station status. For some years the place boasted a post office, a general store, and other amenities common to villages, but its population was already declining by 1800. The 1810 Census counted sixty-eight people in eight households, including twenty-three white men, thirty white women, and fifteen slaves. A proposed town plan filed with the county office that year never came to pass. The 1820 census did not even record Boonesborough as a separate township, and by the middle of the nineteenth century, it had "almost disappeared as a village," according to one state history. Except for the occasional historical commemoration, Boonesborough was essentially forgotten until 1963, when the state park was created.

- - - - - - - - - - - - - -

My next few miles toward Boonesborough were quiet and unremarkable. Gentle rolls gave way to steeper hills, like a blanket crumpled and wedged between steep knobs on one side and Otter Creek on the other. The road narrowed and lost its shoulders as it followed the curves of the creek. Here I saw the first and only live snake of my trip. It lay curled by the road until I came within a few feet, when it slithered under some leaves. The snake was the diameter of my thumb and not even a foot long, greenish-brown with two yellow stripes running the length of the body: a harmless garter snake. I added it to my tally of animal sightings over twenty-three days. Snakes: This one alive, the other eleven dead. Turtles: ten, one alive. One fox: dead. Deer: two dead, two alive. Turkey vulture: dead. Other birds: countless, most alive. One skunk, dead. One cat, dead. Dogs: many alive, maybe three or four dead. Three raccoons, all dead. Possums: twelve to fifteen dead, including one today—flattened and decomposing, its ribs and leg bones spread white in the sun, its tiny teeth grinning up at me. The remains of other numerous and unidentifiable animals.

The early afternoon was warm but pleasant in the shade, and my mind was wandering as I approached a small house separated from the road by a narrow yard and a stunted, scraggly hedge. I had just passed the first clump of bushes when a low growl rumbled behind me. I turned around to see a handsome pit bull the color of creamed coffee emerge from beneath the hedge. His shoulders were about knee high. His steel-gray eyes locked on mine. *Oh damn,* I thought. His growl deepened and then he started to bark. Adrenaline surging, I kept facing him, walking backwards and clambering to switch my trekking poles to my right hand so I could fish for the can of dog Mace in my zipped left pants pocket. Then other growls and barks started behind me: three mutts stood shoulder to shoulder, blocking my path. They were smaller than the pit bull and seemed to take their cues from him. I instinctively veered into the middle of the road to keep them all in my sight. I swung the trek poles back and forth to keep all four at bay, but when I concentrated on the pit bull to my left, the others stepped closer. When I wheeled to face them, the pit bull closed in. I had invaded their territory, and they were not letting me pass.

Movement in front of the small house caught my eye. A skinny, shirtless man with blond hair was walking along the front of the house, only a few yards away and apparently oblivious. Finally, I reached the Mace and followed my rule: If a dog got close enough to bite the end of my trek pole and did not back off, I would shoot. The coffee-colored pit bull came and I sprayed the stuff, the color of stale piss, into his snout. He hesitated, shook his head with a bemused *"What the . . . ?"* expression, licked around his muzzle, and then started approaching again. I emptied the can into the dog's face in three more streams, with the same lack of results. All four dogs were getting closer as we circled each other in this weird dance. They must have sensed my fear.

The little drama could not last much longer, if only because of a blind bend in the road just ahead. If the dogs didn't get me first, then a car or truck would barrel around that curve and take us all out, man and beasts together.

Enough was enough. Pushing my frustration and anger to the surface, I stopped walking and started yelling at the dogs as loud as I could, waving my arms and trek poles: "Go on! Get away! Get the hell out of here!" I took a deliberate step toward them and then, feeling inspired, started barking back. The three smaller partners froze, crouched, and backed away. The pit bull stopped, cocked his head in confusion, and re-treated just far enough to let me step sideways up the road—still staring down the dogs, still pointing my trek poles like mutated swords—past the house, past the short driveway, and past the small black pickup truck parked there. When I was about fifteen feet past the drive, with the dogs now hunkered under the rear of the truck, the skinny man came out to the road. His hair hung in a ponytail down to his shoulders and was shaved on the sides. "Shut up! Get back here!" he shouted at the dogs. The pit bull stooped low and the other dogs scattered into the yard. The man did not acknowledge me at all: I might have been a leaf blown down the road. I turned and walked away fast with a racing heart and rubbery legs, cursing under my breath.

The next couple of miles passed quickly before I reached a place where steep banks and trees crowded the shoulders, leaving little room to walk. At a tight curve to the left, where the road ascended slightly, I estimated about another mile to the park. Instead of a shoulder, there was a steep weedy hillside separated from the road by a three-foot-deep drainage ditch. I heard the grumble of a diesel engine ahead. I halted about ten feet from the curve and perched on the edge of the road, using my trek poles for balance, trying not to slide into the ditch. I waited. An immense white pickup came hurtling around the bend. The scene felt familiar. It was almost identical to that recurring vision from several nights before I started the trip: I was walking on a narrow, wooded road when a truck would come tearing around a curve. In my dream, I braced for impact. But in the reality of a sunny June afternoon, the driver and I caught each other's eyes, and he easily adjusted. No problem.

After another short sequence of woods and fields, the trees cleared, the road rose slightly, and suddenly Fort Boonesborough State Park was spread below me. The first thing I saw was a swimming pool with a corkscrew slide besieged by kids in bright bathing suits. Beyond the parking lot, a grassy field sloped down toward a distant line of trees that screened the Kentucky River from view. If my bearings were right, I stood on Hackberry Ridge, where Boone and his men arrived on April 6, 1775, and gazed down upon a herd of about three hundred buffalo. Where bison once roamed, cars and campers now parked.

I knew that my brother, Hank, and his wife, Cindy, were waiting to meet me at the site of the original fort, as arranged. But rather than walk on, I shed my pack and eased down onto the road's grassy shoulder, opposite the park entrance. There I sat, not quite ready to be finished. Not quite ready for reentry.

My first feeling was relief. I had made it through the near-misses, the stormy nights, and the exhausted days. I had survived my inflamed hip and even those crazy dogs only a few miles before. I said thanks to God and raised my canteen in salute and then waited for an epiphany, in vain. I reckoned that I simply needed to catch my breath and drink in the scene. Revelation would come later, or so I hoped.

After five or ten minutes, feeling a familiar restlessness, I hoisted my pack and walked into the park.

----- **22** -----

HEADING HOME

Every traveller has a home of his own, and he learns
to appreciate it the more from his wandering.

—CHARLES DICKENS

A fifty-foot-by-fifty-foot square of gray stone wall, just over four feet tall, was the finish line: the 1930s-era memorial on the site of the original Fort Boonesborough. A weathered, rectangular concrete block the size of a small sarcophagus stood in the center of the square, inscribed with the names of about fifty of Fort Boonesborough's original settlers, including Daniel and Rebecca Boone and their children.

I felt a hopeful jolt of ego as I walked across an open field, thinking that maybe, just maybe, a few people would notice something odd was happening and a small crowd would gather and applaud and snap pictures and post them online, where I would go viral—all ludicrous, of course. As far as I knew, only my brother and his wife would meet me.

But as the memorial came into view, I was surprised—thrilled—to see not only Hank and Cindy but also Melissa's sister, Barb, and brother-in-law, Gary, who had come down from Illinois. Then I heard the tinny plinking of a distant banjo. After a moment of bewilderment, I recognized the tune: the theme song from the old Daniel Boone TV show. *"Daniel Boone was a man, yes a biggg man..."* With a sly smirk, my brother was walking toward me, holding aloft an iPad, like a waiter with a tray serving up the hokey music. Mild disorientation (*What the...?*) was followed by mild annoyance (*He has got to be kidding...*) and then mild amusement (*I should have known...*). I smiled (I think) as my family surrounded me, all chattering at once.

"I need to finish," I said to no one in particular. "I need to get inside the fort." I held out my camera, and someone took it and captured an image of my pack and backside as I climbed the steps up and over the monument wall. A white paper banner, six feet long, was draped atop the memorial, emblazoned with block letters:

S. J. (JIM) "GRIZZLY" DAHLMAN
DANIEL BOONE WILDERNESS TRAIL &
THE WILDERNESS ROAD

Sycamore Shoals, TN—Cumberland Gap, VA—
Fort Boonesborough, KY
May 22–June 14, 2013

A toy flintlock rifle, a powder horn, and—*really?*—a fake coonskin cap rested on top. My brother's doing, no doubt. In all my planning, I had given little thought to what the finish might look like. This was as good as anything and better than a lot of other possibilities. It was silly and comical and completely what I needed. *Bless his heart.*

My family wanted to know everything at once, and we stood next to the banner talking while I swigged water.

Did you camp every night? *About half the time.*

Were people friendly? *Almost without exception . . . almost.*

What was the best day? *Hard to say.*

The worst? *Hard to say.*

Any run-ins with animals? *Yes—very recently, in fact.*

"You're not as skinny as I expected," Barb said. No, probably not, I told her, thanks to generous people along the way and roadside diners serving soup beans and cornbread.

I planned to camp in the park that night—the only fitting finish—but only after we rendezvoused with my daughter Rachael for dinner in Lexington. The first order of business, however, was to secure a campsite.

Hank and I climbed into his silver Saturn Vue and drove in search of a park office. The speed, about thirty miles per hour, startled me after not riding in a vehicle for more than two weeks. At a small kiosk at the entrance of the main campsite, which was already clogged with RVs, a short, thin woman with short, thin hair the color of ash took my money and reached for a parking pass. Seeing an opening, I jumped.

"I don't need a parking pass," I said, pausing for effect. "I *hiked* here. In fact, I walked the route of the Wilderness Road, all the way from Tennessee. I just got here."

"Uh-huh," the woman said flatly, unsmiling, as she held out a pass. "Here you go. Have a nice day."

Hank and I met the others back at the monument, and we all ambled over to the aptly named primitive campground area. The sites were scattered across a low, wooded area between the fort site and the RVs. Surely this was Sycamore Hollow, where Boone intended to build the fort until his boss, Richard Henderson, arrived. Henderson chose the higher spot closer to the river, where the stone monument now stood, a football field's distance away. Sunlight filtered through the trees of the hollow, but the campground still felt inexplicably dank and disordered. A faint boggy smell rose from what might have been a creek bed meandering between the sites. The only amenities were a few shared standpipes and rusted fire rings at each site, several containing half-consumed logs, bits of singed paper, smashed soda cans, crushed Styrofoam cups, and scraps of food. Only a few sites were occupied.

After searching for a few minutes, I was ready to settle for a level, grassy, cleaner-than-most site under a tall sycamore. Then Hank called down: He had found a spot on a small rise. At first, I resisted his suggestion, more from pride than good sense, but once I walked up the knoll, I saw that it was obviously the better location. As I pitched my tent, Hank and Gary kibitzed about its placement while Cindy and Barb stood to the side, loudly observing that I had managed just fine on my own for almost a month. After I stowed my gear, Hank, Cindy, and I climbed into their vehicle, and Barb and Gary followed in theirs. We made our way to the replica fort, which was situated on a hill about a mile away.

The fort wall was built of broad, wooden horizontal logs. A sign near the gate listed the admission price at $8 and the closing time at five o'clock. It was already past four. Several pale tourists were wandering around the open space inside. An overgrown garden occupied the center of the compound, and farm tools that evoked pioneer days—a wheelbarrow, a plow, wooden buckets—lay nearby. When I asked the woman at the ticket booth if I could speak to someone who knew about the fort's history, she cocked an eyebrow.

"Anyone in particular?" she asked stiffly.

Ready for my cue, I said, "No. You see, I just finished walking the Wilderness Road, all the way from East Tennessee. I just got here this afternoon. I'm writing a book and was hoping . . ."

"Well, we're not supposed to do that," she said.

I paused, expecting her to add, *"But in this case..."*

She didn't. Instead she silently stared at me, apparently waiting for me to either hand over $8 or leave. More than picket walls were defending this fort. I shrugged, walked back to my family, and told them what happened, which gave us all a good laugh. Gary pulled out a camera and asked me to pose next to the sign. "You've just walked three hundred miles," he said as he snapped a photo, "and here's what it will take to get in: eight bucks." We climbed into the cars and drove away.

A four-lane highway led us to Interstate 75, now choked with Friday afternoon traffic—an abrupt reintroduction to a once-familiar world. When Daniel Boone and his fellow pioneers walked this ground two hundred forty years ago, it was a different creation. Could they have imagined that these hills would one day be streaked with swaths of concrete as wide as the rivers they had forded? Could they have known the land would be overrun, not by bison but by rumbling vehicles that could travel as far in an hour as they could in a week?

Those pioneers, of course, had initiated this transformation by the mere act of coming and building: Plant a crop. Raise a house. Establish a fort. Drive back the buffalo. Pave the road. Lay out a town. Divvy up the land. These individual acts of surviving and civilizing, small in themselves, accumulated into a cascade of development—the first pebbles of an avalanche that they could scarcely have predicted or stopped, even if they had wanted to. The push toward development, once unleashed, would never stop. Were Boone plopped down in the same place today, would he indeed recognize it, as Ron Short believed? Seeing how much had been torn down, shorn off, built up, and shoved around, I was not so sure. Old Daniel might find himself bewildered once more.

We arrived at my daughter's snug townhouse in about an hour, and soon I was basking in a warm shower with good water pressure. Another hour and we were sitting on the sun-drenched patio of a trendy barbecue joint, our family conversation swinging between my hike and their various pieces of news. They raised a toast with beer, and I felt warm with appreciation for their coming and for our being together. Then as if by a secret signal—perhaps a shift in sunlight at the end of a long day—we started to move. Hank and Cindy said goodbye and left for their home in Ohio. The rest of us returned to Rachael's house. Excitement, adrenaline, and daylight were all fading, and I asked Rachael to take me back to the park. Instead of the interstate, we drove a rolling back road, past Hootentown and Lisletown and Athens (with a long a, as in "hay"), until we crossed a wide and barren bridge high over the Kentucky River and descended to the state park.

The campground was now crowded with cars and tents and trailers and pickups, all parked helter-skelter, some separated by only a few feet. Kids and a few grownups chased each other around. Two or three gas-powered generators chugged in the middle distance, and slightly sweet smells of grilling pork and beef drifted through the air. It was dark when Rachael and I said good night at my little gray-and-yellow tent. She would return for me in the morning.

The night grew warm and muggy. For a few minutes I silently griped about the chaos and the noise until I recalled that this pandemonium was nearer to the experience of early settlers than the orderly and quiet corrals of other parks. I lay on top of my sleeping bag, sweating lightly and half-listening to shouts and conversations drift through the night. *No, you can't walk down to the river; it's too dark.* Motorcycles roared and screeched in the distance. *Amy, would you care to get me another Pepsi while you're up?* Hurried footsteps crunched on grass and twigs close to my tent. *Tommy, slow down and wait for your sister!* Lights flickered and flared through the tent walls.

I felt mildly intoxicated by a brew of feelings: relief, satisfaction, success, completion, and others that I couldn't quite name. I had walked those miles of asphalt without getting myself killed. I had met many good people and was befriended by some. I believed that, as I had hoped, I gained a fresh and deep appreciation for Boone and the other pioneers, despite their complicated legacy—or maybe because of it. I had indeed come to know this swath of Appalachia better—slowly, closely, deliberately. The journey was often exhilarating, often exhausting, frequently boring, occasionally frightening, and constantly eye-opening. *I loved it.*

Now it was all but finished. Tonight was the last night this tent would serve as home. Tomorrow I would sleep in Lexington, and the day after I would be back at my brick-and-mortar house in Tennessee. The rate of reentry was almost unimaginable. After taking almost four weeks to get here, it would take about four hours to get back.

For a moment I felt suspended between a desire to return to my ordinary life and an urge to keep moving. The journey suddenly felt too

short. But as the campground fell quiet and drowsiness crept into me, I
knew it was time to go home.

Home. That old moving target.

A chilly fog hung over the predawn campground, but it would burn off
in the morning sun. Only a few other people were stirring as I tramped
over to a picnic shelter and parked myself at an aluminum table to eat
my usual breakfast. By the time Rachael arrived, around nine thirty, the
sky was clear, the air was warm, and my gear was packed. We loaded
her little gray Mazda and returned to the replica fort, where the same
woman was sitting in the ticket booth. I felt for my wallet.

I told her I had only a few questions about the fort, and now she was
more welcoming: I could go talk to a woman in the gift shop. "It won't
cost you anything to go in there," she said, pointing toward one of the
log cabins hugging the fort's wall. There, a friendly babushka-type in
frontier garb—simple linen bonnet, a white bib apron over a floor-length
gray dress, moccasins—directed me to a cabin on the opposite side of the
fort, where I would find an older man with a bald head. "Talk to him,"
she said. "His name's Bob. He knows everything about this place."

Bob Caudill, age seventy-three, sat on a rough wooden bench in the
shade of the cabin, polishing a flintlock rifle. He wore a white frock shirt
tied loosely at the throat, leather breeches, and moccasins. The only
modern thing on him was a pair of square, silver-rimmed bifocals. And
indeed, he seemed to know everything about the original Fort Boonesborough and this replica, built in the 1970s. He nodded toward individual features as he described them.

The dimensions and shape of the replica wall were the same as the
original's, he said, but the cabins were built larger to accommodate visitors and displays. Bob tilted his head toward the door behind him. "You
want to take a look inside?"

Rachael and I stepped into a one-room treasure house of frontier
craftsmanship, chockablock with powder horns, flintlocks, pistols,
eighteenth-century-style tools, leather pouches, wooden and tin cooking
utensils, and ornaments made of bone and antler—all laid out on a great
rough-hewn table or hung from wall pegs. The room, redolent of leather
and oil, glowed golden with all the handiwork. Bob had made everything
on display.

Bob Caudill

He crafted his first powder horn as a teenager in late 1950s and his first flintlock in 1962. He was especially proud of one particular powder horn, dark brown and cream, cradled in a wooden rack, displayed front and center on the table. It was an exact copy, he said, of an original powder horn on display in a Louisville museum. Scholars said it probably originated in North Carolina's Yadkin Valley, where Daniel Boone once lived. "It's entirely possible," Bob said, "that Daniel Boone himself might have carried that original horn."

Bob knew the land surrounding the fort, and not only because he had hunted on it before the park was established. His ancestors arrived in 1779, stopping at Boonesborough for a few days before pushing north another ten miles, to settle at Strode's Station, near present-day Winchester. Bob lived on the thirty-three acres remaining from the family's property there, and he aimed to stay as close as possible both to where they lived and how they lived. His home was a three-room cabin that he built by hand, with no running water, no telephone, and certainly no internet. His main accommodation to the modern era was that he was forced to drive between his home and his interpreter's job at the fort,

A sample of Bob Caudill's craftsmanship

where he had worked for seven years. "I wish I could just take my canoe," he said. "It's only six miles by the river, but it's not practical with all the changes and diversions."

We chatted until other visitors approached, and he excused himself to greet them. Rachael and I wandered around the fort, accidentally cheating the park out of a couple of $8 admission charges. We started with the three "timeline cabins," laid out to show in succession how settlers improved their lives through the early decades. Beds, for instance, went from being little more than piles of straw stuffed into big linen sacks on a dirt floor, to ticks resting on raised platforms, to pole beds, recognizable ancestors of four-poster beds. As roads and river routes improved in the early 1800s, trade with the east increased, bringing more ironwork, more fabrics, and more attention to decor.

My thoughts kept circling back to Bob Caudill as we wandered. He was the closest thing to a reincarnation of Daniel Boone I had met on my trip, and here he was, serendipitously, at the very end of the journey. One difference, however, was that Boone always seemed ready to move on, while Bob was always determined to stay.

I envied him a little for that. I had once said that I wanted to point to a place on a map and call it home—but Bob had been born directly into that gift, a legacy of generations. I had no idea what it meant to be so intimately connected to a place and obviously never would.

But that's all right, I thought. *His way of life can't be for everyone.* The idea surprised me. *When did I figure this out?* The realization must have crept up on me, like those moments in the morning when we see the night mysteriously turn to day but can't pinpoint the exact moment of change.

Or perhaps I had been thinking about the meaning of home all wrong. Rather than existing in some generational or even transcendent connection—the geographical equivalent of a soul mate—home presented itself in the most practical, mundane terms possible. Home is where we do the bulk of our living. It is where we literally spend—or invest—our lives, whether or not we can point to a spot on a map. Home felt less about *where*, and more about *what* and *who*: What are we doing there, and who is with us to make it home?

"Home lies in the things you carry with you everywhere," wrote Pico Iyer, "and not the ones that tie you down." Even the travelers on the Wilderness Road—including Bob Caudill's ancestors and a long hunter named Daniel Boone—seemed to understand that. And after all those miles on foot, I understood, too.

Rachael and I explored the fort for a few more minutes until there was nothing more to see, nowhere else to walk. We climbed into her car for the drive back to Lexington, where we would meet up again with family and wait for Sarah to arrive from Johnson City to retrieve me.

The morning had turned bright and breezy. Cumulus clouds cruised overhead. As we pulled onto the highway and gained speed, I rolled down my window and let my hand surf the warm air, like some dreamy kid on his way home.

THE END.

Acknowledgments

I am deeply grateful to the many people I met during the journey on which this book is based, who shared their food, their homes, their land, their wisdom, and their stories with exceeding generosity. I hope that I have presented them well.

Thanks to students, colleagues, and administrators at Milligan College, many of whom offered enthusiastic support, provided assistance in research, and generally showed great tolerance as I worked on this book. Thanks also to the Appalachian College Association, which provided generous financial assistance through a faculty research grant. I am grateful to the University of Tennessee Press for its partnership in publishing this book, particularly to Thomas Wells, Linsey Sims Perry, Jon Boggs, and Laurie Webb Varma.

A number of individuals provided valuable research assistance, including Michelle Ganz of the Lincoln Library and Museum at Lincoln Memorial University, Harrogate, Tennessee; Jeffrey Harbin, then of the P. H. Welshimer Library at Milligan College; Tammy Kirk of the US Army Corps of Engineers (Nashville District); Martha Wiley, then a ranger at the Cumberland Gap National Historical Park; and staff members of the Filson Historical Society in Louisville, Kentucky, and of the Archives of Appalachia at East Tennessee State University in Johnson City, Tennessee. Thanks also to Loyal Jones of Berea, Kentucky, a leading light of Appalachian scholarship and activism, who kindly shared his time and his rich experience.

Joan Boyd Short and the Daniel Boone Wilderness Trail Association were always hospitable and generous as they shared their knowledge and insights. Thanks to Dave Ramsey and the staff at Mahoney's Outfitters in Johnson City, Tennessee, for their advice and assistance. Thanks to my new friends at Union College in Barbourville, Kentucky, for their hospitality, particularly then-Chief of Staff Margaret Senter.

The Master of Fine Arts in Creative Nonfiction program at Goucher College in Baltimore was crucial in lighting the spark and providing direction for this book. I felt privileged to work with an exceptional group of teachers and writers, many of whom I count as colleagues and friends. Thanks to my faculty mentors for their instruction, insight, encouragement, and tough editing love: Tom French, Diana Hume George, Suzannah Lessard, Joanne Wyckoff, and Webster Younce. I was also fortunate to work with not just one but two fine program directors, Leslie Rubinkowski and Patsy Sims. Many of my fellow students—

too many to list here—provided helpful advice, incisive critiques, and steady encouragement. I especially want to thank several fellow alumni in an ongoing writers group who provided excellent suggestions and constabt support: Jennifer Adler, Heather Bobula, Theo Emery, Erica Johnson, Tom Kapsidelis, Pam Kelley, Carol Marsh, and Kim Pittaway.

This book has also benefited from friends who read drafts at various stages, invariably offering good feedback and welcome encouragement: Babs Boter, the late Dale Brown, Andrew Hicks, Jennifer Holberg, LeRoy Lawson, and Natalia Suit, as well as a group of fellow writers in the remarkable church my family attends, Hopwood Memorial Christian Church, including Gayle Brown, Laura Hardy, Ben Lee, Miriam Perkins, Eric Perry, Melodie Perry, and Grete Scott.

This book would not exist without my family, who were always supportive and patient (even if occasionally bewildered by this endeavor). Their encouragement and love mean more than my words can adequately express. Thanks to Hank and Cindy Dahlman and to Gary and Barbara Vance for meeting me at the end of the road. Thanks to Seth and Abby Tramel, not only for being part of a wonderful new blended family but for sharing their enthusiasm for this project. Thanks to Matthew Smith for creating the map—and even more for choosing to join the family. My daughters, Sarah Dahlman Smith and Rachael Dahlman, have been a source of joy throughout this project—not to mention throughout their lives—and their practical assistance and constant encouragement helped make the journey and the book possible. Finally, I have been blessed with a most cherished reader, copy editor, and friend who, a few years after my trip along the Wilderness Road ended, began another kind of journey with me when she became my wife, Stacy Dahlman.

Appendix

ORGANIZATIONS AND PARKS

Numerous nonprofit organizations from Pennsylvania to Missouri are dedicated to conducting research, providing education, raising awareness, and generally celebrating the legacies of Daniel Boone and other early travelers. Several in the southern Appalachian region have particular interest in the Wilderness Road, including:

Daniel Boone Wilderness Trail Association: http://danielboonetrail.com/
Friends of Boone Trace: http://www.boonetrace1775.com/
The Boone Society: https://www.boonesociety.com/pages/

At least six state parks and one national historical park are located along the routes:

Sycamore Shoals State Historic Park, Elizabethton, Tennessee
(http://tnstateparks.com/parks/about/sycamore-shoals)
Warriors' Path State Park, Kingsport, Tennessee
(http://tnstateparks.com/parks/about/warriors-path)
Natural Tunnel State Park, Duffield, Virginia
(http://www.dcr.virginia.gov/state-parks/natural-tunnel#general
_information)
Wilderness Road State Park, Ewing, Virginia
(http://www.dcr.virginia.gov/state-parks/wilderness-road#general
_information)
Cumberland Gap National Historical Park, Middlesboro, Kentucky
(https://www.nps.gov/cuga/index.htm)
Levi Jackson State Park, London, Kentucky
(http://parks.ky.gov/parks/recreationparks/levi-jackson/)
Fort Boonesborough State Park, Richmond, Kentucky
(http://parks.ky.gov/parks/recreationparks/fort-boonesborough/)

Notes

Prologue

1 "John Filson" John Filson, *The Discovery and Settlement of Kentucke and an Essay towards the Topography, and Natural History of that Important Country*. 1784. Reprint, Ann Arbor, MI: University Microfilms, Inc. 1966, 49.

Chapter 1

9 "From pioneer trails" Ann Brigham, *American Road Narratives: Reimagining Mobility in Literature and Film* (Charlottesville: University of Virginia Press, 2015), 4.

14 "Teddy Roosevelt later called the fight" Theodore Roosevelt, *The Winning of the West*, vol. 2, "From the Alleghanies to the Mississippi, 1777–1783," chap. 9, under the section "After the Victory," http://www.gutenberg.org/cache/epub/11942/pg11942.html.

14 "according to an interpreter" Chad Bogart, interview by S. J. Dahlman, October 11, 2012.

14 "But the British Crown was far away" Robert Kincaid, *The Wilderness Road* (Middlesboro, KY: Lincoln Memorial University, 2005), 94.

16 "They brought the payment in a wagon train" Scholars dispute the figure of ten thousand pounds, placing the value at closer to "a pittance" of £2,700. See, for example, Claudio Saunt, *West of the Revolution: An Uncommon History of 1776* (New York: W.W. Norton, 2014), 23, 217.

16 "Whole nations have melted away" Jeff Corntassel, "Dragging Canoe," http://www.corntassel.net/archive_draggingcanoe.htm. See also Robert J. Conley, *Cherokee Thoughts: Honest and Uncensored* (Norman: University of Oklahoma Press, 2008), 89.

17 "But even before the treaties were signed" John Mack Faragher, *Daniel Boone: The Life and Legend of an American Pioneer* (New York: Henry Holt, 1993), 112–113.

Chapter 2

26   "It doesn't take long before your conscience gets sticky" Maurice Manning, "Notes on 'The Natural Man,'" in *A Companion for Owls: Being the Commonplace Book of D. Boone, Long Hunter, Back Woodsman, &c.* (Orlando, FL: Harcourt, 2004), 82.

28   "Appalachian men made good soldiers" "Appalachia" gained common currency as a regional label in the first half of the twentieth century. For statistical purposes, the term "Appalachia" refers to the region as defined by the Appalachian Regional Commission: "a 205,000-square-mile region that follows the spine of the Appalachian Mountains from southern New York to northern Mississippi. It includes all of West Virginia and parts of twelve other states: Alabama, Georgia, Kentucky, Maryland, Mississippi, New York, North Carolina, Ohio, Pennsylvania, South Carolina, Tennessee, and Virginia" (http://www.arc.gov/appala chian_region/TheAppalachianRegion.asp).

28   "What is certain" Alice Cornett, "The Sgt. York Syndrome," *Baltimore Sun*, November 11, 1991, http://articles.baltimoresun.com/1991-11-11 /news/1991315046_1_appalachian-counties-vietnam-war.

29   "The tales surrounding Daniel's childhood" 11. Faragher, *Daniel Boone*, 9.

Chapter 3

37   "All conservation of wildness" Aldo Leopold, *A Sand County Almanac and Sketches Here and There* (New York: Oxford University Press, 1989), 101.

39   "While the main plant covers nearly eight hundred sixty acres" Eastman Chemical Company, *Kingsport Facts and Figures Through 2012*, brochure.

39   "The company consistently appeared" Eastman Chemical Company. "Eastman Ranks among Top Five U.S. Materials Companies in Newsweek's 2012 Green Rankings," November 1, 2012, http://www.eastman .com/Company/News_Center/2012/Pages/Eastman_Ranksamong _Top_Five_US_Materials_Companies_in%20Newsweek.aspx.

39   "The last major study, in 2010" Roger L. Thomas and Richard J. Horwitz, "South Fork Holston River Monitoring," The Academy of Natural Sciences of Drexel Univ., n.d., http://www.ansp.org/research /environmental-research/projects/holston.

46   "Built about 1777 by Captain John Anderson" The plaque was placed in the early twentieth century. Later research determined the blockhouse was built earlier, probably by 1775.

Chapter 4

49 "Being in so alien an environment" Pico Iyer, *The Global Soul: Jet Lag, Shopping Malls, and the Search for Home* (New York: Vintage, 2000), 288.

49 "[F]or nearly its whole length the Wilderness Road followed the streams" William Allen Pusey, *The Wilderness Road to Kentucky* (New York: George H. Doran, 1921), 65.

50 "By the time they slogged through the knee-deep mud" Kincaid, *The Wilderness Road*, 165.

53 "Estill, whose lone surviving image" Southwest Virginia Museum Historical State Park, "Benjamin Estille" [*sic*] n.d., http://www.swva museum.org/benjaminestill.html.

60 "Trinity Sunday is always difficult" Trinity Sunday, one week after Pentecost, is observed in honor of the Trinity, the Christian teaching that the Godhead exists in three persons—Father, Son, and the Holy Spirit. This is a core teaching of most Christian churches, but it is a complex doctrine and has often been controversial (to put it mildly), which explains why it can be "difficult" for preachers and teachers.

Chapter 5

63 "What is straight?" Tennessee Williams, *A Streetcar Named Desire*, scene 9 (New York: New Directions, 1980), 145.

65 "his cocktail of prescription drugs, including Ambien" Ambien is the brand name for zolpidem, a sedative prescribed primarily to treat insomnia. It is generally prescribed for short-term use, usually two weeks or less. It can be habit forming. "Zolpidem," Medline Plus, n.d., U.S. National Library of Medicine, https://medlineplus.gov/druginfo/meds /a693025.html.

68 "It was not uncommon on Friday nights" Ronald E. Eller, *Uneven Ground: Appalachia Since 1945* (Lexington: University Press of Kentucky, 2008), 22.

69 "Within two minutes I knew that J. E." J. E. is a pseudonym, to protect his privacy.

Chapter 6

80 "Memories need to be shared" Lois Lowry, *The Giver* (New York: Houghton Mifflin, 1993), Nook edition, 114.

80 "to identify, preserve and promote historically significant sites" Daniel Boone Trail Historical Society, n.d., http://www.danielboonetrail.com.

87 "It was in part the effect" Frederick Jackson Turner, "The Frontier in American History," *Report of the American Historical Association,* 1893; quoted in John Campbell, *Southern Highlander,* 41, note 1.

87 "[T]he discovery of salt springs" Campbell, *Southern Highlander,* 41.

87 "In his 2003 book on the environmental history of the Appalachians" Donald Edward Davis, *Where There Are Mountains: An Environmental History of the Southern Appalachians* (Athens: University of Georgia Press, 2003), 155.

88 "Duffield reported a population of 91" US Bureau of the Census, 2010 Census Interactive Population Search, n.d., http://www.census.gov /2010census/popmap/ipmtext.php?fl=51.

Chapter 7

92 "If you don't know history" Michael Crichton (attributed).

94 "Joan said it was reminiscent of Foxfire" Foxfire began in a high school English class in 1966, when the students created a magazine, "honing their writing skills on stories gathered from their families and neighbors, and producing articles about the pioneer era of southern Appalachia as well as living traditions still thriving in the region." Today, Foxfire includes not only the ongoing student-produced magazine, but also twelve volumes of *The Foxfire Book* and a museum and heritage center in Mountain City, Georgia. https://www.foxfire.org/about-foxfire/#history.

94 "The high school eventually merged with another regional school" Powell High School consolidated with Appalachia High School in 2011 to form Union High School.

96 "Depending on the level of authenticity" Tony Horwitz, *Confederates in the Attic: Dispatches from the Unfinished Civil War* (New York: Vintage, 1998), 10–11.

Chapter 8

100 "The journey I'm taking is inside me" Haruki Murakami, *Kafka on the Shore,* Trans. by Philip Gabriel (New York: Vintage, 2006), 397.

104 "They had, however . . . invested heavily in lobbying" Figures from the FEC. Reported by the Center for Responsive Politics, http://www .opensecrets.org/lobby/induscode.php?id=E1210&year=2010.

104 "In a sweep of inspections" Ken Ward Jr., "MSHA Finds Hundreds of Violations in Inspection Sweep," *Charleston (WV) Gazette,* May 6, 2010, http://www.wvgazette.com/ News/montcoal/201005060852.

105 "He claimed the mines were required by law to restore" I heard several former coal miners make similar claims. That is a misunderstanding.

Regulations require permittees to restore the approximate original contour of the location mined, according to Kentucky's Division of Mine Reclamation and Enforcement (DMRE), which is part of the commonwealth's Energy and Environment Cabinet. The location also needs to be returned to its approximate original contour.

105 Mountaintop removal is specifically defined as mining that removes a coal seam "from outcrop to outcrop." (Compared to other types of mining, few mountaintop operations—technically speaking—are in production.) When mountaintop operations cease, the permit holders are required to restore the land to "conditions capable of supporting land uses which the areas being mined supported prior to mining or higher or better alternative uses," according to DMRE Director Courtney Skaggs. "Mining operations have to restore the productivity of the land. Mountaintop removal operations have specific post-mining land uses that can be approved: industrial, commercial, residential, agricultural, or public facility. Forestland is not an approved postmining land use that can be utilized on a mountaintop removal operation, pursuant to the regulations." Skaggs referred me to the Kentucky Administrative Regulations—specifically 405 KAR 20:050. (Courtney Skaggs, interview by S. J. Dahlman, February 1, 2018.)

111 "I was later surprised to learn" US Bureau of the Census, *Consolidated Federal Funds Report for Fiscal Year 2010* (Washington, DC: US Government Printing Office, September 2011), 1–2.

Chapter 9

115 "People are always moving, even those standing still" "Road Trip," © 2012 by Kurt Brown. Used by permission. Revised and published as "Road Trip with Stars Around My Ankles," in *I've Come This Far to Say Hello: Poems Selected and New,* by Kurt Brown (Rochester, NY: Tiger Bark, 2014).

118 "Big Jim, however, escaped north" Faragher, *Daniel Boone,* 252.

118 "The murder of the Boone and Russell boys" Robert Morgan, *Boone: A Biography* (Chapel Hill, NC: Algonquin, 2008), 136–138.

119 "According to Nathan Boone" Neal O. Hammon, ed. *My Father, Daniel Boone: The Draper Interviews with Nathan Boone* (Lexington: University Press of Kentucky, 2012), 41–42.

Chapter 10

131 "You see how little nature requires to be satisfied" Faragher, *Daniel Boone,* 84.

135 "Silver Leaf was the only place" Daniel Boone Wilderness Trail Association Trail Map, http://danielboonetrail.com/trail-map.

142 "Rose Hill was doing good" A spokesman for DeRoyal later confirmed that jobs had been moved overseas from Rose Hill. "We understand when it's personal," Michael Smith told me in a phone interview. "We held off for a long time, until the early 2000s. If we'd kept things as they were, we wouldn't have a company." Mr. White also emphasized the company's many large donations and philanthropic works in the region. "There's a familial and geographical loyalty to the area that's still there," he said. As of January 2018, DeRoyal employed fifty-six people at its Rose Hill facility. The corporate headquarters are in Powell, Tennessee. (Michael Smith, phone interview by S. J. Dahlman, January 12, 2018).

Chapter 11

144 "[We] are by no means divided, or readily divisible" Wendell Berry, *The Unsettling of America: Culture and Agriculture* (San Francisco: Sierra Club Books, 1996), 18.

147 "The school and the road were named" Kincaid, *The Wilderness Road*, 47–48.

147 "Walker also named another major waterway" Thomas Speed, *The Wilderness Road: A Description of the Routes of Travel by Which the Pioneers and Early Settlers First Came to Kentucky, 1886* (New York: Lenox Hill, 1971), 14.

157 "But great herds once roamed farther east" Davis, *Where There Are Mountains*, 111.

157 "A long hunter named Isaac Bledsoe reported" Stephen Aron, *How the West Was Lost: The Transformation of Kentucky from Daniel Boone to Henry Clay* (Baltimore: Johns Hopkins University Press, 1999), 25.

158 "But something changed by the late 1600s" Davis, *Where There Are Mountains*, 39.

159 "Cherokees and then long hunters brought their harvests" Davis, *Where There Are Mountains*, 206.

159 "Deerskins were more profitable than buffalo hides" Aron, *How the West Was Lost*, 55.

159 "As historian Stephen Aron succinctly states" Aron, *How the West Was Lost*, 25.

160 "The last wild buffalo in central Kentucky was killed in 1793" Brent Altsheler, "The Long Hunters and James Knox Their Leader," *The Filson Club History Quarterly* 5, no. 4 (October 1931), 173.

Chapter 12

161 "Stand at Cumberland Gap and watch the procession of civilization"
Turner, quoted by Mary S. Sheridan, ed., *America: Readings in Themes
and Eras* (Lanham, MD: University Press of America, 1992), 185.

164 "When this is done the great Gap" Lucien Beckner, letter to Robert L.
Kincaid, August 2, 1946, Kincaid Papers, Lincoln Memorial University
Library, Harrogate, TN, 1–2.

165 "Five years later, work began" Mark Woods, "An Appalachian Tale:
Restoring Boone's Wilderness Road," *Cultural Resource Management* 5
(2002): 22.

165 "The first white man known to have crossed it" Kincaid, *The Wilderness
Road*, 27.

166 "legend has it that in 1863 President Abraham Lincoln" "About LMU,"
Lincoln Memorial University, last modified July 2012, http://www
.lmunet.edu/about/mission.shtml.

166 "'This rock,' according to the 1835 diary" Lindsay Patterson, "Observations of an Early American Capitalist," *The Journal of American History* 1, no. 4 (1907): 664–665.

167 "I saw no cleft, but part of the rock had been blasted away" Kincaid,
The Wilderness Road, 351.

Chapter 13

169 "The very least you can do in your life" Barbara Kingsolver, *Animal
Dreams* (New York: HarperCollins, 1990).

170 "The crater was only one of 'four geologic elements'" Steve Kortenkamp,
"Impact at Cumberland Gap: Where Natural and National History Collide," *PSI Newsletter* 5, no. 2: 2, http://www.psi.edu/sites/default/files
/imported/news/newsletter/summer04/Summer04.pdf.

180 "A nineteenth-century historian, Thomas Speed" Speed, *The Wilderness
Road*, 68–69.

180 "The company was named for Wallsend, England" Tim Cornett, *Bell
County, Kentucky: A Brief History* (Charleston, SC: The History Press,
2009), 20.

182 "Tracy, who worked at The Flocoe" Her name is changed to protect her
privacy.

Chapter 14

188 "First, he said, the coal companies are required to restore 90 percent"
This interpretation repeated some misunderstandings about the regulations, as noted in chapter 8.

188   Milligan College in Tennessee, where I teach, is another example. That
       school began in 1866, a secondary academy for children in the impover-
       ished, isolated mountains. Originally named for the small creek running
       along its property, the Buffalo Male and Female Institute was elevated
       to college status twenty-two years later and renamed—with thanks
       from generations of alumni—to honor the president's favorite profes-
       sor, Robert Milligan, a classics professor at what is now Transylvania
       University in Kentucky.

190   "Based on census data from the ten counties" Those ten counties (Carter,
       Washington, and Sullivan, Tennessee; Scott and Lee, Virginia; Bell,
       Knox, Laurel, Rockcastle, and Madison, Kentucky) had a total popula-
       tion of 605,385 in the 2010 census. Boston Combined Statistical Area
       (CSA) has a total population of 7,559,060 and 60 colleges and univer-
       sities, including associate-level and special-focus schools (Carnegie
       classifications).

197   "Two students, Sean and Wylie" Their names are changed to protect
       their privacy.

Chapter 15

199   "Humans don't mind hardship, in fact they thrive on it" Sebastian
       Junger, *Tribe: On Homecoming and Belonging* (New York: Twelve,
       2016).

200   "The roadside marquee sign read, 'Choice Decides Destiny'" Classic
       Calvinism teaches that God has predestined each person for salvation
       or damnation. According to the Westminster Confession of Faith (1643):
       "God from all eternity did by the most wise and holy counsel of his own
       will, freely and unchangeably ordain whatsoever comes to pass. . . . By
       the decree of God, for the manifestation of his glory, some men and
       angels are predestinated unto everlasting life, and others foreordained
       to everlasting death."

206   "On December 7, 1931, Colonel G. D. Jackson and Ella Jackson" Ken-
       tucky State Parks, "Levi Jackson History," http://parks.ky.gov/parks
       /recreationparks/levi-jackson/history.aspx.

207   "The only survivors were a man, a woman, and an eight-year-old girl"
       Jessamine County Family Database, http://jesshistorical.com/Jessamine
       %20County%20Kentucky%20Families/b145.htm.

Chapter 16

217   "We feel dislocated in nature in part because we have not come to terms"
       Richard Todd, *The Thing Itself: On the Search for Authenticity* (New
       York: Riverhead, 2008), 120.

220 "He coined a word, 'solastalgia'" See, for example, Glenn Albrecht, et al., "Solastalgia: The Distress Caused by Environmental Change," *Australasian Psychiatry* 4, issue 1 Supplement (February 1, 2007): S95–S98. doi: 10.1080/10398560701701288.

221 "The owner was a stout Midwesterner named Carl" For personal reasons, Carl requested that only his first name be used.

222 "The village had taken a more recent blow" *Journal of the CSXT Historical Society* 2, no. 1: 17, http://www.csxthsociety.org/journal/2013v02 /v02n1/csxthsjournal2013v2n1-2013conventionhfs.pdf.

227 "He would surely be boggled by the modern Kentucky equine industry" Holly Wiemers, "Study Shows State's Equine Industry Has $3 billion Economic Impact," *UK AgNews*, September 6, 2013, http://news.ca.uky .edu/article/study-shows-state%E2%80%99s-equine-industry-has-3 -billion-economic-impact.

Chapter 17

229 "Life in America is viscerally uprooted" Norman Mailer, interview with J. Michael Lennon, 1998, qtd. in Becky Bradway and Doug Hesse, *Creating Nonfiction: A Guide and Anthology* (New York: Bedford/St. Martin's, 2009), 558.

234 "In 2012, for instance, Rockcastle County reported a drug-related arrest rate" The Foundation for a Healthy Kentucky, "Drug Arrests (per 100,000 population), 2012," http://www.kentuckyhealthfacts.org. The data was calculated by the Kentucky State Data Center, using data from the Kentucky State Police *Crime in Kentucky Annual Report* and FBI Uniform Crime Reports. Population estimates come from the US Census Bureau.

234 "The rate of drug-related deaths in Rockcastle County" Svetla Slavova, Terry L. Bunn, and Wei Gao, *Drug Overdose Deaths in Kentucky, 2000–2013* (Lexington: Kentucky Injury Prevention and Research Center, 2015), 2–3, 12.

234 "Rockcastle County recorded an average of almost one drug-related death per week" Stephanie Smith and Nadia Kounang, "Prescription Drugs 'Orphan' Children in Eastern Kentucky," December 14, 2012, updated December 3, 2013, https://www.cnn.com/2012/12/14/health /kentucky-overdoses/index.html.

236 "And it turns out that Japan boasts the second-largest bluegrass market" Naomi Gingold, "Meet the Musicians Behind Japan's Vibrant Bluegrass Scene," *Morning Edition*, NPR, October 30, 2016, https://www.npr.org /2016/10/30/498827939/meet-the-musicians-behind-japans-vibrant -bluegrass-scene.

Chapter 18

237 "A road . . . even the most primitive road" Wendell Berry, "A Native Hill," *The Hudson Review* 21, no. 4 (Winter 1968–1969): 601–634, http://www.jstor.org/stable/3849275.

238 "By the time he died in 1985, Lair had turned Renfro Valley" Pete Stamper, "The History of Renfro Valley," Renfro Valley Entertainment Center, http://www.renfrovalley.com/info/renfrovalley-history.php.

239 "The entire organization operates in sixteen counties" Christian Appalachian Project, *50 Years of Faith, Service and Compassion: Annual Report 2014*, 8–9 http://www.christianapp.org/pdfs/AR+FY14+For+Web.pdf.

240 "As Appalachian scholar Ronald Eller stated" Eller, *Uneven Ground*, 93.

240 "There was a 'great divide'" Eller, *Uneven Ground*, 127–128.

240 "As Eller noted, the antipoverty campaign" Eller, *Uneven Ground*, 129.

240 "That seemed ironic to me, considering how much" See, for example, Jeff Biggers, *The United States of Appalachia: How Southern Mountaineers Brought Independence, Culture, and Enlightenment to America* (Berkeley, CA: Counterpoint, 2006).

Chapter 19

244 "We are all of us seeking a homeland, dear" Frederick Buechner, *Open Heart* (London: Chatto and Windus, 1992), 198.

251 "Not yet forty years old . . . in honor of the biblical city" Acts 17:10–11, King James Version.

252 "By 1876, landownership among blacks" Richard D. Sears, *A Utopian Experiment in Kentucky: Integration and Social Equality at Berea, 1866–1904* (Westport, CT: Greenwood Publishing Group, 1996), 82.

252 "The Day Law, 'an Act to Prohibit White and Colored Persons'" Richard Allen Heckman and Betty Jean Hall, "Berea College and the Day Law," *The Register of the Kentucky Historical Society* 66, no. 1 (January 1968), 35–52.

252 "Upheld by the Supreme Court in 1908" *Berea College* v. *Kentucky*, 211 U. S. 45 (1908).

253 "Over 90 percent of Berea's 13,561 residents" US Bureau of the Census, *Quick Facts*, Berea city, Kentucky, https://www.census.gov/quickfacts/fact/table/bereacitykentucky/PST045216.

Chapter 20

256 "To be an American is to move on" Kathleen Norris, *The Cloister Walk* (New York: Riverhead, 1996), 243.

258 "There, only fifteen miles from their final destination" Kincaid, *The Wilderness Road*, 103–104.

258 "One of its tasks now was to monitor and destroy chemical weapons" Phone interview with Mark Henry, public affairs officer, Blue Grass Army Depot, by S. J. Dahlman, May 29, 2015.

Chapter 21

267 "All places are stories, stories we tell to ourselves" Todd, *The Thing Itself,* 79.

272 "In July 1776, for example, Boone's fourteen-year-old daughter" Faragher, *Daniel Boone*, 131–137.

273 "Boone's adopted name is memorialized" US Department of Agriculture Forest Service, "Sheltowee Trace National Recreational Trail," n.d., https://www.fs.usda.gov/recarea/dbnf/recarea/?recid=70839.

275 "Thanks to Americans' embrace of frontier legends" Several modern biographies have done admirable work in describing the real Boone, in truth a remarkable man even without the fanciful tales. Among them are John Mack Faragher's *Daniel Boone: The Life and Legend of an American Pioneer,* and *Boone: A Biography,* by Robert Morgan.

277 "At Harrodsburg, for example, Fleming observed" Kincaid, *The Wilderness Road*, 152–153.

277 "As the historian Robert Kincaid noted" Kincaid, *The Wilderness Road*, 151–152.

278 "The growth was exponential" Mark Spencer, *The Bloomsbury Encyclopedia of the American Enlightenment,* vol. 2. (New York: Bloomsbury, 2015), 826.

278 "After its initial growth, Boonesborough gradually shriveled" Meredith Mason Brown, *Frontiersman: Daniel Boone and the Making of America* (Baton Rouge: Louisiana State University Press, 2008), 279.

278 "The 1810 Census counted sixty-eight people" Richard Ulack, Karl Raitz, and Gyula Pauer, eds. *Atlas of Kentucky* (Lexington: University Press of Kentucky, 1998), 61.

278 "The 1820 census did not even record Boonesborough" Nancy O'Malley, *Searching for Boonesborough,* Archeological Report 193 (Lexington: University of Kentucky, 1990).

278 ". . . it had almost disappeared as a village" Lewis and Richard Collins, *Collins' Historical Sketches of Kentucky,* vol. 2, *History of Kentucky* (Covington, KY: Collins and Co., 1874), (https://archive.org/details/collinshistorica02coll), 493.

Chapter 22

282 "Every traveller has a home of his own" Charles Dickens, "Speech: Commercial Travellers. London, December 30, 1854," in *Speeches: Literary and Social*. eBooks@Adelaide, The University of Adelaide Library, University of Adelaide, South Australia, https://ebooks.adelaide.edu.au/d/dickens/charles/d54sls/chapter14.html.

Further Reading

Adams, Noah. *Far Appalachia: Following the New River North*. New York: Delta Books, 2001.

Aron, Stephen. *How the West Was Lost: The Transformation of Kentucky from Daniel Boone to Henry Clay*. Baltimore: Johns Hopkins University Press, 1999.

Baker, Mark A. *Sons of a Trackless Forest: The Cumberland Long Hunters of the Eighteenth Century*. Franklin, TN: Baker's Trace, 1999.

Belue, Ted Franklin. *The Long Hunt: Death of the Buffalo East of the Mississippi*. Mechanicsburg, PA: Stackpole Books, 1996.

Berry, Wendell. *The Unsettling of America: Culture and Agriculture*. San Francisco: Sierra Club Books, 1996.

Biggers, Jeff. *The United States of Appalachia: How Southern Mountaineers Brought Independence, Culture, and Enlightenment to America*. Berkeley: Counterpoint Press, 2006.

Bodett, Tom. "The Great Wagon Road and The Wilderness Trail." *America's Historic Trails*. DVD. Chicago: Questar, 2002.

Boone, Nathan. *My Father, Daniel Boone: The Draper Interviews with Nathan Boone*. Edited by Neal O. Hammon. Lexington: University Press of Kentucky, 2012.

Brigham, Ann. *American Road Narratives: Reimagining Mobility in Literature and Film*. Charlottesville: University of Virginia Press, 2015.

Brown, Meredith Mason. *Frontiersman: Daniel Boone and the Making of America*. Baton Rouge: Louisiana State University Press, 2008.

Bryson, Bill. *A Walk in the Woods: Rediscovering America on the Appalachian Trail*. New York: Broadway Books, 1999.

Calloway, Brenda C. *America's First Western Frontier: East Tennessee*. Johnson City, TN: Overmountain Press, 1989.

Campbell, John C. *The Southern Highlander and His Homeland*. New York: Russell Sage Foundation, 1921.

Caruso, John Anthony. *The Appalachian Frontier: America's First Surge Westward*. Indianapolis: Bobbs-Merrill, 1959.

Catte, Elizabeth. *What You Are Getting Wrong About Appalachia*. Cleveland: Belt, 2018.

Caudill, Harry M. *Night Comes to the Cumberlands: A Biography of a Depressed Area*. Boston: Little, Brown, 1963.

Davis, Donald Edward. *Where There Are Mountains: An Environmental History of the Southern Appalachians*. Athens: University of Georgia Press, 2003.

Eller, Ronald D. *Miners, Millhands, and Mountaineers: Industrialization of the Appalachian South, 1880–1930*. Knoxville: University of Tennessee Press, 1982.

———. *Uneven Ground: Appalachia Since 1945*. Lexington: University Press of Kentucky, 2008.

Faragher, John Mack. *Daniel Boone: The Life and Legend of an American Pioneer*. New York: Henry Holt, 1993.

Filson, John. *The Discovery and Settlement of Kentucke*. 1786. Reprint, Ann Arbor: University Microfilms, 1966.

Fletcher, Colin, and Chip Rawlins. *The Complete Walker IV*. New York: Alfred A. Knopf, 2012.

Hammon, Neal O. "Boone's Trace Through Laurel County," *Filson Club Historical Quarterly* 42 (1968): 21–25.

Heat-Moon, William Least. *Blue Highways: A Journey into America*. Boston: Little Brown, 1982.

Hinderaker, Eric, and Peter C. Mancall. *At the Edge of Empire: The Backcountry in British North America*. Baltimore: Johns Hopkins University Press, 2003.

Horwitz, Tony. *Confederates in the Attic: Dispatches from the Unfinished Civil War*. New York: Vintage Books, 1998.

Houston, Peter. *A Sketch of the Life and Character of Daniel Boone*. Edited by Ted Franklin Belue. Mechanicsburg, PA: Stackpole Books, 1997.

Hurlbert, Archer Butler. *Boone's Wilderness Road*. Historical Highways of America 6. Cleveland: Arthur H. Clark, 1903.

Iyer, Pico. *The Global Soul: Jet Lag, Shopping Malls, and the Search for Home*. New York: Vintage, 2000.

Jones, Loyal. *Faith and Meaning in the Southern Uplands*. Urbana: University of Illinois Press, 1999.

Jones, Randell. *In the Footsteps of Daniel Boone*. Winston-Salem: John F. Blair, 2005.

Kincaid, Robert L. *The Wilderness Road*. Middlesboro, KY: Lincoln Memorial University, 2005.

Krakow, Jere L. *Location of the Wilderness Road at Cumberland Gap National Historical Park*. Washington, D.C.: National Park Service, United States Department of the Interior, August 1987.

Leopold, Aldo. *A Sand County Almanac and Sketches Here and There*. New York: Oxford University Press, 1989.

Manning, Maurice. *A Companion for Owls: Being the Commonplace Book of D. Boone, Long Hunter, Back Woodsman, &c*. Orlando, FL: Harcourt, 2004.

Morgan, Robert. *Boone: A Biography.* Chapel Hill: Algonquin, 2008.

Obermiller, Phillip J., Thomas E. Wagner, and E. Bruce Tucker, eds. *Appalachian Odyssey: Historical Perspectives on the Great Migration.* Westport, CT: Praeger, 2000.

Pudup, Mary Beth, Dwight B. Billings, and Altina L. Waller, eds. *Appalachia in the Making: The Mountain South in the Nineteenth Century.* Chapel Hill: University of North Carolina Press, 1995.

Pusey, William Allen. *The Wilderness Road to Kentucky: Its Location and Features.* New York: George H. Doran, 1921.

Roosevelt, Theodore. *The Winning of the West,* 4 vols. n.d. Project Gutenberg, 2004. http://www.gutenberg.org/cache/epub/11941/pg11941.html

Sears, Richard D. *A Utopian Experiment in Kentucky: Integration and Social Equality at Berea, 1866–1904.* Westport, CT: Greenwood Publishing Group, 1996.

Shattuck, Tom N. *The Cumberland Gap Area Guidebook,* 5th ed. Middlesboro, KY: Bell County Historical Society, 2005.

Sheridan, Mary, ed. *America: Readings in Themes and Eras.* Lanham, MD: University Press of America, 1992.

Speed, Thomas. *The Wilderness Road: A Description of the Routes of Travel by Which the Pioneers and Early Settlers First Came to Kentucky* (1886). New York: Lenox Hill, 1971.

Stewart, Rory. *The Places in Between.* Orlando, FL: Harcourt, 2006.

Turner, Frederick Jackson. *The Frontier in American History.* New York: Henry Holt, 1921.

Ulack, Richard, Karl Raitz, and Gyula Paper. *Atlas of Kentucky.* Lexington: University Press of Kentucky, 1998.

Vance, J. D. *Hillbilly Elegy: A Memoir of a Family and Culture in Crisis.* New York: Harper, 2016.

Williams, Elizabeth McCutchen, ed. *Appalachian Travels: The Diary of Olive Dame Campbell.* Lexington: University Press of Kentucky, 2012.

Woods, Mark. "An Appalachian Tale: Restoring Boone's Wilderness Road," *Cultural Resource Management* 5 (2002): 20–22.

Index of Places and Historical Figures

Page numbers in **boldface** refer to illustrations.